SRE
Made Simple

Master reliability through observability and automated infrastructure as code

Jayant Kumar

www.bpbonline.com

First Edition 2026

ISBN: 978-93-78549-076

LIMITS OF LIABILITY AND DISCLAIMER OF WARRANTY

The information contained in this book is true and correct to the best of author's and publisher's knowledge. The author has made every effort to ensure the accuracy of these publications, but the publisher cannot be held responsible for any loss or damage arising from any information in this book.

All trademarks referred to in the book are acknowledged as properties of their respective owners but BPB Publications cannot guarantee the accuracy of this information.

Distributors:

BPB PUBLICATIONS
20, Ansari Road, Darya Ganj
New Delhi-110002
Ph: 23254990/23254991

DECCAN AGENCIES
4-3-329, Bank Street,
Hyderabad-500195
Ph: 24756967/24756400

MICRO MEDIA
Shop No. 5, Mahendra Chambers,
150 DN Rd. Next to Capital Cinema,
V.T. (C.S.T.) Station, MUMBAI-400 001
Ph: 22078296/22078297

Published by Manish Jain for BPB Publications, 20 Ansari Road, Darya Ganj, New Delhi-110002 and Printed by him at Repro India Ltd., Rewari.

www.bpbonline.com

Dedicated to

My daughters:

Ashlesha

and

Banhishikha

About the Author

Jayant Kumar is a seasoned technology leader with over two decades of experience in architecting, building and operating large-scale, high traffic software systems. His career reflects a blend of deep technical expertise and executive leadership, spanning roles from hands-on software development and technical architecture to leading global **site reliability engineering** (**SRE**) organizations.

Jayant began his journey as a software engineer and evolved into an architect, where he played a pivotal role in architecting large-scale web systems. He contributed significantly to the evolution of leading job platforms such as Naukri.com and Shine.com where performance, scalability and reliability were business critical necessities.

Over time, his focus shifted to the world of SRE, where he led SRE and resilience engineering initiatives across global organizations, including JP Morgan Chase, DBS Bank and high-growth startups. In these roles, he was responsible for driving reliability at scale, building high-performing SRE teams, and embedding a culture of operational excellence within engineering organizations. His leadership experience includes senior roles such as vice president, director and chief technical officer at The Indian Express where he combined strategic vision with hands-on execution to deliver robust and scalable technology platforms.

In addition to his professional work, Jayant is also an author and thought leader. He previously authored two technical books on search technologies, sharing his deep insights into scalable systems and real-world engineering challenges. He has a bachelors degree in computer science and engineering and is also a TOGAF certified enterprise architect.

Currently Jayant is associated with an AI based startup as a co-founder and a CTO.

Through this book, Jayant aims to demystify SRE for engineers, architects, and leaders alike, thus bridging the gap between theory and real-world practice.

About the Reviewer

Saikrishna Koorapati is a software engineering leader with 19+ years of experience building distributed, cloud-native, and AI-driven systems at scale. He specializes in Java, modern backend architecture, frontend engineering, reliability, automation, and developer productivity. Over the course of his career, he has designed and delivered large-scale platforms focused on performance, resilience, observability, and operational excellence. His work has included AI-powered automation, OCR-based workflow systems, developer enablement platforms, and highly available microservices supporting large user bases. He has a strong interest in site reliability engineering, release engineering, observability, automation, and secure software delivery practices. Saikrishna is passionate about clean design, scalable architecture, and building systems that improve both customer experience and engineering efficiency. He also enjoys contributing to the technical community through reviewing and shaping high-quality engineering content that bridges real-world practice with practical learning.

Acknowledgement

I want to express my deepest gratitude to my family and friends for their unwavering patience, support, and encouragement throughout this book's writing, especially my wife Nidhi and my daughters Ashlesha and Banhishikha.

I am also deeply grateful to BPB Publications for their guidance and expertise in bringing this book to fruition. The reviewers, editors, and the publishing team gave their thoughtful feedback during the extensive journey of refining this work, which has helped to improve the quality of the book significantly.

I would also like to acknowledge the valuable contributions of my colleagues, co-workers, and teams over the years I worked. From my early days as an architect designing large-scale systems to leading site reliability engineering teams, every discussion, incident call, design debate, and postmortem has helped shape the perspectives captured in this book.

Finally, I would like to thank all the readers, whether you are an engineer, a leader, or someone who is curious about building reliable systems and has taken an interest in my book, for their support in making it a reality. Your encouragement has been invaluable, and I hope this book simplifies SRE for you.

Preface

Site reliability engineering (**SRE**) is a practice that improves the reliability of software systems. As enterprise software becomes increasingly complex with the addition of features and its usage increases with an increase in userbase, issues tend to crop up, leading to disruption, outage and even downtime, which can lead to loss of user trust and eventually reduction in revenue.

This book is designed to discuss the SRE practice, its adoption and the design patterns and tools that can help improve the reliability of software systems. This book dives into the mindset of a SRE engineer and how the team culture should evolve to support SRE. The readers will get insight into the metrics that need to be implemented, tuned and tracked for improving reliability as well as look at some of the sub-practices that need to be implemented as a part of the SRE practice.

This book also goes over the building blocks of SRE. Readers will dive deeper into the actions required in various situations for the implementation of SRE to cover different aspects of software engineering. Some of the tools to implement the sub-practices within SRE will also be introduced. Additionally, real-world examples will be included to help readers relate to the situation.

This book is intended for DevOps engineers, software engineers and site reliability engineers to help them understand and tweak their SRE practice to best suit their organization's goals. Architects can use this book to deduce which optimizations will benefit their systems the most. Team managers and senior leaders can leverage this book to build an SRE culture that promotes psychological safety and reliability engineering at its core. Additionally, this book is a handy guide for readers who are curious about the world of reliability engineering.

With this book, readers will gain the knowledge and skills to become a proficient reliability engineer and a leader. I hope you find this book informative and helpful.

Chapter 1: Introduction to Site Reliability Engineering – Goes into the origins or SRE and how it evolved as a discipline focused on reliability, scalability and automation. This chapter discusses the similarities and differences between SRE and DevOps and the importance of bringing SRE into the **software development lifecycle** (**SDLC**). This chapter also touches upon the core philosophies of SRE with the purpose of understanding SRE as a practice and a cultural change for the entire team.

Chapter 2: Understanding SRE Metrics – Presents the essential metrics that are used to define and measure reliability. This chapter also talks about identifying the right **service level indicators** (SLIs), setting meaningful **service level objectives** (SLOs) and aligning **service level agreement** (SLAs) with business needs. Error budgets are discussed as a metric used to balance reliability and feature delivery. This chapter provides a clear and actionable framework for using metrics not only to measure reliability but also to make data-based engineering and product decisions.

Chapter 3: Monitoring and Observability – Explores the constituents of observability namely metrics, logs and traces and how these work together to provide insights into system behavior. This chapter will discuss how to analyze metrics to identify unwanted system behavior, structure logs for efficient debugging and leverage distributed tracing to track requests across microservices. This chapter will also go into alerting strategies which focus on reducing false positives and best practices for building observability into systems. The purpose of this chapter is to help build a robust observability framework that not only detects issues early but also helps reduce **mean time to recover** (MTTR) and downtime.

Chapter 4: Incident Management – Goes in depth into incident management by covering topics like on-call rotations, on-call best practices, escalation paths and fatigue management while balancing responsiveness and sustainability. This chapter also discusses the process of **root cause analysis** (RCA) and blameless postmortems that encourages transparency and continuous improvement. The goal of this chapter is to help SREs turn incidents into opportunities of improvement, ensuring system reliability while also maintaining team morale and trust.

Chapter 5: Designing for Reliability – Focuses on building systems that are resilient, scalable and reliable by design. This chapter goes over few SRE design patterns, fault tolerance and redundancy designs that can be leveraged to ensure that software services remain available inspite of hardware and software failure. This chapter also cover exciting topics like chaos engineering, capacity planning and scalability designs. The purpose of this chapter is to equip engineers to architect systems that not only withstand failures but also adapt to changing demands, minimizing downtime while also optimizing efficiency.

Chapter 6: Release Engineering – Explores the principles and practices of modern release engineering for delivering software quickly, safely and reliably. This chapter goes over **continuous integration/continuous deployment** (CI/CD) pipelines that helps automate build, test and deployment of software. The chapter also discusses key deployment strategies like blue-green, canary and rolling updates that minimizes risk while reducing downtime. The chapter also covers rollback strategies and feature flags. The aim of this chapter is to help build a robus release engineering workflow that supports rapid deployment while maintaining system stability and user trust.

Chapter 7: Performance Optimization - Explains the importance of performance optimization for building scalable, responsive and cost-effective systems via key performance metrics like latency and throughput including how to measure and improve these metrics. This chapter also explores caching strategies, data optimization techniques and efficient resource (CPU, IO, memory and network) utilization. The purpose of this chapter is to provide a toolkit to diagnose performance issues so as to optimize and design systems that deliver speed and reliability while balancing cost.

Chapter 8: Automation, DevSecOps and AIOps – Explores the role of automation in SRE. The chapter goes over topics like **infrastructure as code** (**IaC**), automating CI/CD pipelines along with designing and building of auto-healing systems. It also goes over few tools that can be leveraged. The chapter explains how to measure the success of automation and then dives into DevSecOps and AIOps. The goal of this chapter is to help leverage automation for boosting efficiency, reliability and scalability while reducing human intervention and operational overhead.

Chapter 9: Security and SRE - Is dedicated SRE practices that can help in improving security and compliance for the organization. This chapter also looks at protocols for handling large-scale security incidents and highlights the importance of proactive security measures. The purpose of this chapter is to discuss how SRE can be used to safeguard systems, protect user data, maintain user trust while also ensuring alignment to evolving compliance needs.

Chapter 10: Team Dynamics – Explores the human side of SRE which focuses on team dynamics, collaboration and challenges in maintaining a healthy work life balance in high-pressure environments. The chapter discusses on-call best practices, fatigue management and strategies to mitigate burnout. This chapter also examines how to define and measure the KPI for SRE teams along with the career path for SREs. The goal of this chapter is to help leaders and practitioners create healthier and effective SRE teams by aligning technical goals with human needs.

Chapter 11: SRE in Small vs. Large Organizations – Discusses the nitigrities of adopting SRE in organizations of different sizes including how SRE culture varies across these organizations. This chapter also explores different models of embedding SRE within engineering teams like centralized and distributed approaches. It also covers effective strategies for communicating reliability metrics, risks and trade-offs to stakeholders and leaders. This chapter aims to provide insights for adopting SRE principles and practices within organizations of varying scale.

Chapter 12: Future of SRE – Discusses the evolving landscape of SRE in an AI-driven world. This chapter covers predictive incident detection and automated remediation using AIOps and observability tools. It also explores how machine learning and AI can augment human decision-making to reduce toil, enhance observability, augment RCA and reshape managing SRE at scale. The chapter also introduces future-ready SRE skills and discusses few AI tools that can be used in SRE.

Appendix A: Tools and Templates – Contains tools and templates that can be used during practical implementation of SRE. This chapter introduces tools for various aspects of SRE including tools for chaos engineering. It also shares templates for SLO, SLA and on-call runbook while sharing extensive checklist for incident response and RCA. The chapter also explains how to customize these templates based on your organizational needs.

Appendix B: Case Studies – Goes over real-world application of SRE across diverse industries like fintech and e-commerce. The chapter also dives into organization specific use cases and discusses the implementation of SRE in few organizations like Spotify, LinkedIn and DBS Bank. It also provides practical insights on how SRE principles were adopted to meet organizational and business needs.

Coloured Images

Please follow the link to download the *Coloured Images* of the book:

https://rebrand.ly/vqnv5lp

We have code bundles from our rich catalogue of books and videos available at https://github.com/bpbpublications. Check them out!

Errata

We take immense pride in our work at BPB Publications and follow best practices to ensure the accuracy of our content to provide an indulging reading experience to our subscribers. Our readers are our mirrors, and we use their inputs to reflect and improve upon human errors, if any, that may have occurred during the publishing processes involved. To let us maintain the quality and help us reach out to any readers who might be having difficulties due to any unforeseen errors, please write to us at:

errata@bpbonline.com

Your support, suggestions and feedback are highly appreciated by the BPB Publications' Family.

Piracy

If you come across any illegal copies of our works in any form on the internet, we would be grateful if you would provide us with the location address or website name. Please contact us at **business@bpbonline.com** with a link to the material.

If you are interested in becoming an author

If there is a topic that you have expertise in, and you are interested in either writing or contributing to a book, please visit **www.bpbonline.com**. We have worked with thousands of developers and tech professionals, just like you, to help them share their insights with the global tech community. You can make a general application, apply for a specific hot topic that we are recruiting an author for, or submit your own idea.

Reviews

Please leave a review. Once you have read and used this book, why not leave a review on the site that you purchased it from? Potential readers can then see and use your unbiased opinion to make purchase decisions. We at BPB can understand what you think about our products, and our authors can see your feedback on their book. Thank you!

For more information about BPB, please visit **www.bpbonline.com**.

Join our Discord space

Join our Discord workspace for latest updates, offers, tech happenings around the world, new releases, and sessions with the authors:

https://discord.bpbonline.com

Table of Contents

Chapter 1
Introduction to Site Reliability Engineering

Introduction

In this chapter, we will look at the origins of **site reliability engineering** (**SRE**) and how it evolved into a discipline focused on reliability, scalability, and automation. We will understand the need to bring SRE into the software development and deployment life cycle and how SRE relates to DevOps and where they differ in emphasis. We will break down how SRE compares or overlaps with DevOps, highlighting both shared goals and key differences in mindset and execution. The chapter will also touch upon the core principles of SRE, which include **service level agreement** (**SLA**), objective and indicator, embracing risk, eliminating toil, monitoring and observability, automation, release engineering, blameless postmortem, capacity planning and chaos engineering, which helps in measuring reliability, and prioritizing engineering solutions over manual toil. We will discuss in depth some of the core principles like embracing risk, measuring reliability (**service level indicators (SLIs)**/**service level objectives** (**SLO**)/ SLA), and automating toil and understand why they are important as a part of the SRE practice. The purpose of this chapter is to understand why SRE is a practice and a cultural change for the complete team and how it benefits the organization.

Structure

This chapter covers the following topics:

- Origins of site reliability engineering
- Similarities and differences between SRE and DevOps
- Core philosophies of SRE
- Embracing risk
- Measuring reliability
- Automating toil

Objectives

In the beginning of this chapter, we will look at the origins of SRE, how and why it was conceptualized at *Google*, and how it evolved and spread to other organizations. This will help us understand how SRE evolved as an engineering practice. We will understand the similarities and differences between SRE and DevOps and the scenarios in which either of them could be chosen. We will look at the core principles SRE focuses on and understand the importance of these principles. We will dive deeper and look at some of the principles like embracing risk, measuring reliability, and automating toil, and understand what these principles mean and how it changes the culture of developing, deploying, and maintaining software applications. By the end of this chapter, we will understand how SRE helps the team and the organization in delivering and maintaining quality while helping the business grow.

Origins of site reliability engineering

SRE, which will be further referred to as SRE, is a discipline that emerged from the necessity to maintain highly scalable and reliable systems in the face of rapid technological growth, including the addition of new features as needed by the users and the handling of a constantly increasing set of users accessing those features during peak hours. Unlike traditional IT operations, SRE applies software engineering principles to infrastructure and operational problems. We will explore the historical context, key innovators, and foundational ideas that shaped SRE into what it is today.

Pre-SRE landscape

During the early days of the internet (around the late 1990s), websites and services were typically hosted and maintained by system administrators. The system administrators were responsible for provisioning the hardware, installing software, upgrading the software as needed, and ensuring that the systems remain online. However, as web applications evolved and user expectations grew, the traditional methodology of hosting and maintaining a website struggled to keep pace with the scale and complexity of modern software systems.

During the old days, development and operations were often siloed, leading to friction between the two disciplines. Developers would write code and hand it over to operations to deploy and maintain, and when systems failed during real-world scenarios, both developers and system administrators would blame each other instead of sharing responsibility and getting the issue resolved. This model became increasingly unsustainable with the rise of large-scale distributed systems and later with the adoption of microservice architecture.

The following figure visually represents the historical separation of roles and the resulting blame culture between development and operations:

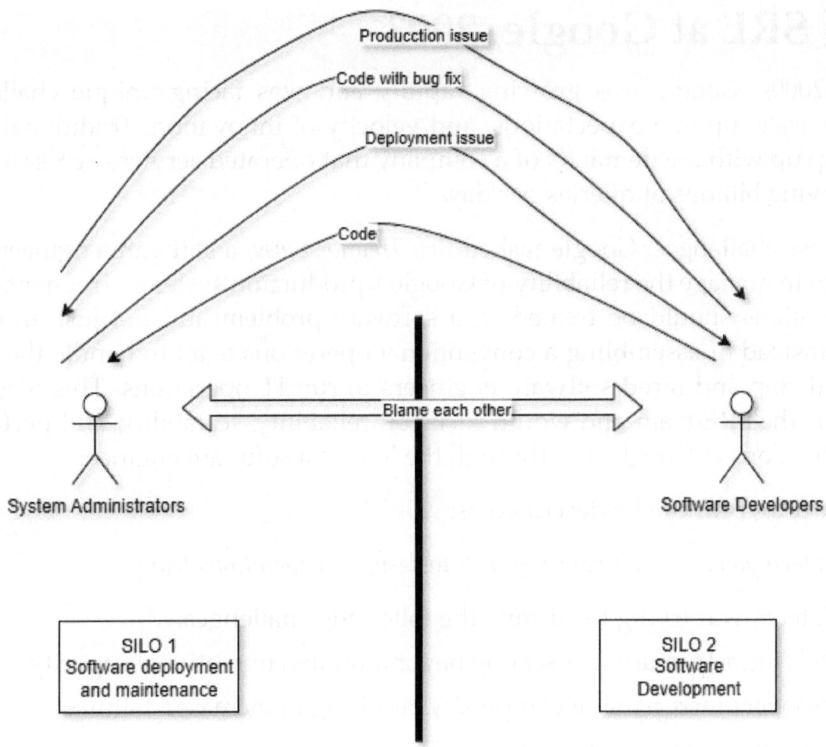

Figure 1.1: *Pre-SRE landscape*

In the pre-SRE landscape, system reliability was managed by two primary approaches:

- **System administration model**:
  - Incident response was always reactive. Teams responded to outages only after they had occurred.
  - Troubleshooting, configuration management, deployments, and redeployments were manual and labor-intensive.
- **Early DevOps movements**:
  - Some organizations recognized the inefficiencies of siloed teams and created DevOps teams. These teams had skillsets of both a developer and a system administrator.
  - The DevOps teams were able to use tools like Puppet (released in 2003) to automate certain tasks.

Even with these two approaches, there was still no structured approach to address reliability. These approaches struggled to keep up with the scaling needs of large-scale companies like Google, where having manual intervention turned out to be impractical.

Birth of SRE at Google, 2003

In the early 2000s, Google was growing rapidly and was facing unique challenges with infrastructure scale, uptime expectations, and velocity of innovation. Traditional operations could not keep up with the demands of a company that operated services across a global fleet of servers, serving billions of queries per day.

To address these challenges, Google tasked *Ben Treynor Sloss*, a software engineer at Google, to build a team to manage the reliability of Google's production systems. Treynor's key insight was that operations should be treated as a software problem and not just an operational problem. So, instead of assembling a conventional operations team to handle the challenges, he took a bold step and hired software engineers to run IT operations. This new team was later known as the SRE team and would focus on reliability, scalability, and performance of software applications at Google, but through the lens of a software engineer.

In Treynor's words, SRE can be described as:

What happens when you ask a software engineer to design an operations team.

Treynor's SRE team was trying to address the following challenges:

- Google's infrastructure was scaling beyond human operational capacity.
- Services were increasing in complexity, resulting in increased failures.
- Manual fixes were unsustainable.

Foundational principles of SRE

SRE approach differed from the traditional approaches as we saw previously, in the following ways:

- SRE used an engineering approach to solve operational problems. This resulted in the automation of several manual tasks such as deployments, monitoring, and incident response.
- Instead of aiming for 100% uptime, SREs introduced the concept of SLI, SLO, and an error budget. These concepts helped in creating a balance between reliability and innovation.
- Instead of following the previous model of passing blame from one silo to another, SREs introduced a concept of blameless postmortems, where incidents were reviewed to improve systems and processes, fostering a culture of learning rather than assigning fault.
- SREs aimed to reduce toil work that was manual, repetitive, and operational in nature. Automations were done to reduce toil, which freed uptime to focus on high-value engineering tasks.

Spread of SRE beyond Google

SRE remained internal to Google for a number of years. Google's SRE model proved highly effective and started attracting attention in the wider tech industry in the following ways:

- In 2014, Google SRE engineers began speaking publicly about SRE at conferences.
- In 2016, Google published the first book on SRE titled *Site Reliability Engineering (O'Reilly)*, making SRE principles accessible to the larger tech industry.
- From 2017 onward, a number of major tech companies like *Netflix, LinkedIn, Uber* have adopted SRE and customized it as per their needs.
- SRE concepts have now expanded beyond tech and into finance, healthcare, and government as well.

Ongoing evolution of SRE

As of today, SRE is no longer limited to large tech companies. Startups, cloud-native organizations, regulated enterprises, and various other organizations continue to adopt SRE practices to fit their scale and context.

The origins of SRE highlight a fundamental shift in how we should think about reliability in the following ways:

- Moving from reactive break-fix to proactive engineering.
- Moving from manual operations to automation-driven scalability.
- Moving from siloed teams to shared responsibility.

As systems grow more complex and user expectations continue to increase, the need for a disciplined, scalable, and software-centric approach to reliability becomes even more critical. The origins of SRE remind us that reliability is not just a function of infrastructure; it is grounded in practiced engineering excellence and culture.

Similarities and differences between SRE and DevOps

Both SRE and DevOps emerged to combat the inefficiencies of traditional IT operations. While they share common goals, which are improving software reliability, accelerating deployments, and fostering collaboration, their approach to these challenges differs in their principles and implementations. We will explore the key similarities and differences between SRE and DevOps.

Origins of SRE and DevOps

SRE was born out of necessity at Google to operate systems at a massive scale. In contrast, DevOps emerged as a cultural movement responding to the bottlenecks between software development and IT operations teams.

The following table compares the origin, initial purpose, and core belief of SRE and DevOps:

Aspect	SRE	DevOps
Origin	Coined by Google in the early 2000s	Emerged from the agile community in 2009
Initial purpose	Improve the reliability of large-scale systems	Improve collaboration between system administrators and software developers
Core belief	Operations is a software engineering problem and should be addressed accordingly	Improving culture and collaborations will lead to faster delivery of software

***Table 1.1**: Key differences in the origin and purpose of SRE and DevOps*

Key similarities between SRE and DevOps

Despite their differences, SRE and DevOps share the following core principles:

- **Collaboration**: Both SRE and DevOps are designed to break down silos between software development and IT operations teams. They encourage collaboration between the teams that build the software and those that deploy and maintain it.
- **Automation**: Both SRE and DevOps focus on automating *toil* or manual repetitive tasks. Both advocate for automated CI/CD pipelines, **infrastructure as code** (**IaC**), and self-healing systems.
- **Focus on reliability and performance**: Both emphasize system health through observability, proactive monitoring, alerting, and structured incident response. While SRE focuses on using SRE-related metrics like SLI, SLO, and error budget to generate dashboards and alerts, DevOps emphasizes logging and generating metrics for tracing and debugging.
- **Continuous improvement**: SRE and DevOps both have the core principle of continuous improvement built into their philosophy. SRE focuses on blameless postmortem as a practice to foster a culture of learning. Whereas DevOps encourages iterative improvements via feedback loops rather than one-time fixes.

Key differences between SRE and DevOps

While SRE and DevOps overlap in their philosophy and their goals, they still differ in their structure, methodology, implementation, and focus areas.

The following table gives the key differences between SRE and DevOps across different aspects:

Aspect	SRE	DevOps
Primary goal	Apply software engineering principles to operations.	Improve collaboration between software developers and IT operations.
Team structure	Dedicated SRE team with software engineering backgrounds.	Cross-functional teams with a DevOps skillset.
Measurement approach	Well-defined metrics like SLI, SLO, and SLA, and error budget.	Broader metrics deployment frequency, **mean time to recover (MTTR)**, lead time.
Reliability focus	Uses SRE metrics such as error budget to enforce reliability constraints.	Focused on speed, availability, and agility. Downtime lacks a proper definition.
Automation scope	Has a deeper focus on automation via automating toil, self-healing systems, and failure testing in addition to those that are there in DevOps.	Has a broad definition for automation, CI/CD, IaC, and deployment pipelines.
Incident management	Emphasizes blameless postmortems and robust incident handling playbooks.	Encourages shared responsibility between development and operations teams; however, it is less formalized.
Tools and practices	Strong on observability and production readiness tooling. E.g., Prometheus, chaos engineering, and canary releases. At the same time, acknowledging that the tools for DevOps are a basic need.	Strong on IaC and infrastructure automation. E.g., Jenkins, Docker, Kubernetes, and Terraform.

Table 1.2: *Key differences between SRE and DevOps*

In broader terms:

- DevOps can be used to establish the culture, organizational mindset, and delivery pipeline.
- SRE can be used to implement the operational engineering practices to ensure reliability, performance, and scalability on top of the practices already implemented by DevOps.

Analogy between SRE and DevOps

If DevOps is the why and how, SRE is the how well and how reliably.

Let us understand the purpose and practice of SRE vs. DevOps with an analogy of building and maintaining a high-performance car:

- **DevOps**: The pit crew and driver collaboration:
  - **Goal**: To make the car go faster
  - **Approach**:
    - The driver and pit crew collaborate closely.
    - They share tools, communicate constantly, and optimize for speed.
    - They use automated diagnostics to detect issues quickly.
    - The team iterates rapidly, tweaking the car between laps.
  - **Limitation**: Without strict rules, they might push the car too hard, risking breakdowns.
- **SRE**: The engineering team behind the car:
  - **Goal:** Ensure the car is reliable at high speeds using data-driven decisions.
  - **Approach**:
    - Define performance thresholds like the engine cannot exceed 95% of max RPM for more than 10% of the race.
    - Use telemetry to enforce these limits.
    - If reliability drops, upgrades to the car are halted until the performance is stable.
    - Automated repairs to minimize pit stops.
  - **Limitations:** Too much focus on reliability might slow down innovation and feature delivery.

SRE and DevOps can work together. In the previous analogy, the pit crew and driver (DevOps) can ensure that the car keeps running fast. Whereas the engineering team (SRE) can ensure that the car maintains its performance without exploding. Balancing speed and safety are the best approach in such scenarios.

Choosing the correct approach

While SRE and DevOps can co-exist, there are scenarios where organizations need to choose one of them due to bandwidth or budget constraints. Let us see some scenarios that will help us take the call:

- **Choose DevOps if**:
  - Team needs cultural transformation between development and operations teams.
  - Organization priority is speed and agility as compared to reliability.

- **Choose SRE if:**
  - o The organization operates at a large-scale and has critical systems (like financial services).
  - o Team needs quantifiable reliability controls (SLO, error budgets).

Many companies adopt DevOps culture first and then layer SRE discipline on top of it as they scale. The rise of cloud-native applications and microservices has further blurred the lines between DevOps and SRE. In the modern technical landscape, SRE and DevOps are blended together.

In many ways, SRE is an implementation of DevOps as it encourages a DevOps culture and mindset while balancing reliability, innovation and feature delivery.

Core principles of SRE

As we have seen in the previous section, SRE is a discipline that incorporates aspects of software engineering and applies them to infrastructure and operational problems. The goal is to build and maintain highly reliable, scalable, and efficient systems. SRE has evolved into a set of principles and practices that guide organizations in building and operating dependable systems at scale.

We will go over the core principles of SRE in this chapter, which serve as the foundation for adopting and evolving the discipline within organizations, as shown in the following figure:

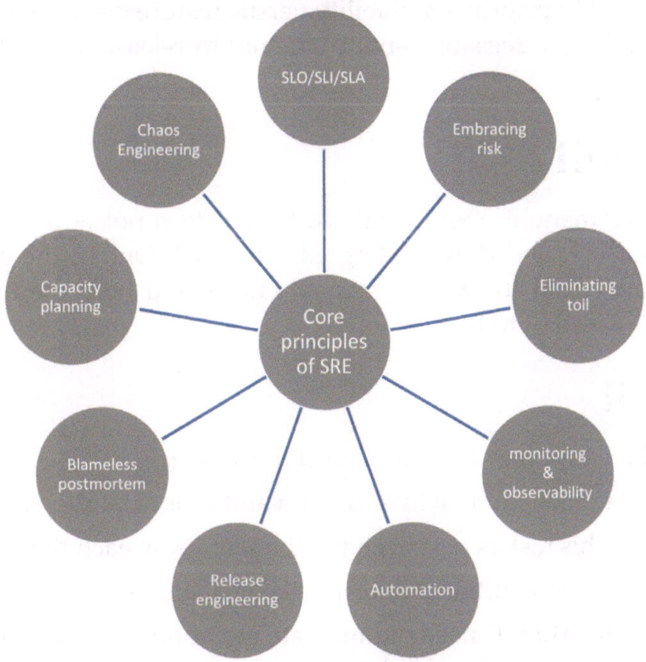

***Figure 1.2:** Core principles of SRE*

Service level indicators, objectives and agreements

At the heart of SRE is the concept of managing reliability via measurable terms, that is, SLI SLI, SLO, and SLA. These measurable terms not only clarify expectations but also align the associated teams and stakeholders on reliability, as follows:

- SLIs are quantifiable metrics that reflect a service's performance. (e.g., latency, throughput, error rate, availability).
- SLOs are internal targets for reliability based on SLIs (e.g., 99% of requests should have a latency of less than 100ms).
- SLAs are legal agreements with customers or users that are derived from SLOs, which are often stricter than SLAs to allow for margin.

Embracing risk

Systems can never be 100% available, and it is often unnecessary and expensive to strive for 100% availability. So, SRE accepts failure with a margin of error. This margin of error is measured via a term called the **error budget**.

An error budget quantifies the acceptable level of unreliability before user experience is harmed. It is derived from SLO (e.g., if a service has an SLO of 99.5% uptime, the remaining 0.5% can be allocated to error budget).

This error budget is used to prioritize reliability versus feature delivery. Using error budgets, teams can make data-driven decisions about whether to release a new feature or invest in improving reliability.

Eliminating toil

Toil refers to repetitive manual operational work that does not add long-term value (e.g., manual restarts, upscaling, and downscaling adjustments). One of the principles of SRE is to identify and eliminate toil to remove manual efforts and help the team focus more on engineering projects instead of toil.

Identifying toil

Toil can be identified if a task has the following characteristics:

- **It is manual**: Requires manual intervention and cannot be run autonomously.
- **It is repetitive**: This task is performed in the same way each time.
- **It is reactive**: Typically initiated in response to incidents, tickets, or alerts.
- **Lacks long-term value**: It needs immediate attention and does not contribute to the long-term value of the system evolution.

SRE principle for toil says:

If it has to be done more than twice, automate it.

The process is to identify and measure toil. Once identified, it is then recommended to automate such repetitive tasks. As a part of automation, it is also recommended to reduce manual intervention through self-healing systems. This also includes using automation tools for deployment and monitoring.

The purpose is to free up SRE time for engineering work, which improves systems in the long-term.

Monitoring and observability

Effective monitoring and observability are essential for detecting and diagnosing issues before they impact system users. We generally get confused between monitoring and observability. In broader terms, while monitoring helps to detect failures and anomalies, observability is a much broader term that focuses on understanding the internal state of systems from its external metrics.

Here is the difference between monitoring and observability:

- Monitoring is used to detect and alert on anomalies and failures. For example, it can be used to track down failure nodes that have high latency.
- Observability involves inferring the internal state of a system based on external outputs, often using logs, metrics, and traces.

Some key metrics to watch for are as follows:

- Traffic (e.g., hits per second or transactions per minute).
- Latency (e.g., 99% requests should be served within 100 ms).
- Errors (e.g., 5xx errors should be less than 1%).

Some of the key best practices are as follows:

- Defining meaningful SLIs and SLOs.
- Using dashboards, alerting systems, logging, and tracing.

Automation

Automation is not a feature; it is an essential requirement. Automation is needed in SRE to reduce manual effort, reduce human error, while also increasing efficiency and resiliency.

Some examples of automation are as follows:

- CI/CD pipelines for build and release.
- IaC for infrastructure provisioning.

- Automating alerts and escalation levels to elicit proper incident response.
- Upscaling and downscaling systems as needed.
- Self-healing systems like auto-restarting crashed services.

Release engineering and progressive rollouts

SRE promotes safe, incremental software releases to minimize risks. A few release strategies that help in the same way are as follows:

- **Canary releases**: Deploy changes to a small subset of users first.
- **Blue-green deployments**: Parallel deployment to another environment for testing before releasing to all users.
- **Rollback plans:** Can consist of automated rollbacks or quick rollback strategies.
- **Feature flags:** Used to enable/ disable a misbehaving feature without redeployment.

The goal of the previously mentioned strategies is to reduce the blast radius in case of an incident. This also helps in shortening the feedback loop and minimizing the impact of faulty releases on the end users.

Incident response and blameless postmortems

Incident response and blameless postmortems define the process of handling incidents and the process of conducting postmortems to understand the root cause without assigning fault. In SRE, failures are treated as learning opportunities.

The goals are as follows:

- Rapid detection and mitigation of an incident is critical.
- Postmortems should be blameless, focusing on identifying systemic weakness and not on assigning fault to individuals.
- Foster a culture of learning through **root cause analysis** (**RCA**) and its preventive action items.

Capacity planning, demand forecasting, and performance optimization

SREs should design systems to handle growth efficiently. The reliability of the system depends on predicting and preparing for growth.

Approaches for capacity planning and demand forecasting are as follows:

- Use historical data for predicting load.
- Capacity should be planned with buffers in place for unknown spikes.

- Automate horizontal or vertical scaling wherever possible.

Approaches for performance optimization are as follows:

- Load balancing and caching at various levels.
- Profiling and performance tuning (e.g., optimizing database queries).

Chaos engineering and disaster recovery

Within SRE, chaos engineering and disaster recovery are two complementary disciplines that aim to ensure that the system remains resilient and recoverable during planned or unplanned failures.

SREs should be prepared for failure, as it ensures resilience. Chaos engineering proactively tests system resilience by injecting failures (using tools like *Chaos Monkey*). This helps in identifying breakage areas and fixing them before moving to production.

Disaster recovery is another strategy used to ensure system availability in case of a data center outage or similar scenarios. It consists of backup strategies and failover mechanisms to bring up an alternate site in a different data center to ensure business continuity even in the case of a major outage.

We will dive deeper into chaos engineering and disaster recovery in *Chapter 5, Designing for Reliability*.

Culture of collaboration and ownership

Cross-functional collaboration and shared responsibility are two of the core principles of SRE. Unlike traditional IT operations teams that may work in silos, SRE teams operate in close partnership with the development, operations, product, and business teams, as a part of the culture that inculcates strong collaboration across different teams.

In SRE, ownership does not end at code handoff. Developers are encouraged to own their code in production. They are responsible for the impact of the features they ship, while SRE owns the operational health of the system. The reliability metrics (SLO, error budget) and on-call rotations, which can also include the developers, help reinforce the shared ownership beyond job titles.

This also supports transparent communication across teams during incidents and helps in collaboratively developing ideas to reduce them. Blameless postmortems provide the psychological safety needed to help with this shared ownership and collaboration. Engineers and SREs feel safe to speak up regarding potential risks rather than hiding them due to fear.

In the long-term, the culture of collaboration and ownership helps reduce incidents, helps predict system behavior, improves team morale, and hence helps improve reliability.

This cultural mindset of SRE helps organizations in moving quickly while maintaining reliability.

In conclusion, these core principles of SRE enable teams to deliver reliable services without impacting the speed of innovation. By adopting and practicing these SRE principles, organizations can achieve the right balance between reliability and agility.

Embracing risk

Site reliability engineers operate under a fundamental paradox. They are the guardians of uptime and defenders of the SLA. However, to build reliable systems, SREs must embrace risk instead of eliminating it. Risk is not the enemy of reliability if appropriately managed; it can fuel innovation and progress, and if mismanaged, it can lead to outages. Hence, SREs treat risk as a strategic resource to be managed and not avoided.

Risk is part of change

Modern systems are extremely complex, distributed, and constantly changing. Every change, be it a deployment, a configuration tweak, a toggle of a feature flag, a schema migration, or even scaling up or down, introduces risk into the system. These changes are needed to serve the constantly increasing number of users. In such situations, zero risk is neither possible nor desirable. The cost of building a zero risk system massively outweighs the benefits of the rewards that the users will get out of it.

SRE's role here is to manage risk and shift from a fear-based culture to a risk-aware culture. Regarding this, the following steps should be followed:

1. SREs need to quantify acceptable risk using the metrics SLO and error budget.
2. SREs need to build for resilience using techniques/practices like chaos engineering.
3. SREs need to build automated mitigation for quick recovery.

Risk reward trade-off

SREs constantly navigate the trade-off between risk and velocity. Avoiding risk reduces the velocity, whereas increasing velocity can cause instability in the systems. The example is as follows:

- If SREs setup strict SLO/SLA to reduce user impact, feature development will take a hit.
- Whereas if SREs plan for a less stringent SLO resulting in a larger error budget to allow faster iteration of changes, it may increase the outages.
- SREs need to consider the option of rollback vs. roll-forward after understanding the cost or impact of each option.

The concept of error budget provides a structured way to quantify, measure, and manage risk. This allows SREs to have a balance between stability and innovation without compromising the user experience.

Risk decision matrix

While making a risk-related decision, SREs need to consider the following questions:

- Does this risk affect user-facing SLO/SLA, and to what extent?
- Can the impact or blast radius be contained?
- Is the benefit to the users worth the cost of impact on the error budget?
- Do we have enough observability in place to learn from the outcomes of taking this risk?

Based on the previously mentioned questions, SREs can identify the benefit of taking the risk.

Here is a risk decision matrix that can be used to identify that high-probability, high-impact scenarios should be prioritized for engineering intervention, while low-impact, low-probability risks may be accepted within the error budget based on the type of risk. Refer to the following table:

Probability vs. impact	High-impact	Low-impact
High-probability	Auto-mitigate and re-engineer to build for reducing either probability or impact	Experiment with a smaller set of users
Low-probability	Monitor setup alerts and auto-mitigate	Accept the change and burn the error budget

Table 1.3: *Risk decision matrix*

Organization's approach to risk

The organization's culture towards risk-taking should incorporate psychological safety and blameless postmortems. If engineers fear blame or punishment for the risk they took, they will move towards safe choices, resulting in slowing down innovation.

Instead, the organization's approach should be blameless by design. The idea is to figure out what failed and why, and build processes around it to avoid such failures in the future.

As a part of the risk-aware culture, an organization can insist on having the following practices in place:

- Learnings from postmortems should be highlighted.
- Calculated risk-taking should be encouraged.
- Error budget should be transparent and communicated to the stakeholders.
- Regular retrospectives of risks taken and learnings that the team gained from them.

Chaos engineering and learning from risk

Chaos engineering helps teams embrace risk proactively by inducing failure in controlled environments to test assumptions, validate resilience, and improve response. Chaos engineering helps engineers discover scenarios that will result in system failure and engineer better systems that either do not fail in such scenarios or recover faster. We will go in depth into chaos engineering in a later chapter.

Stakeholder management

SREs must be proactive communicators. Embracing risk also means aligning multiple stakeholders across engineering, product, and business, as follows:

- Translate technical risk into business terms for their understanding.
- Communicate and escalate early instead of when things break.
- Provide clarity in ambiguity, especially during incidents.

Leading SRE is not about rank; it is more about clarity, confidence, and compassion under pressure.

Risk management is core SRE competency

Embracing risk as an SRE means accepting change, failure, and recovery as part of the process. SRE's mission is not to prevent all failures, but rather to make systems safe to operate in the face of uncertainty. Reliability is a moving target, and managing risk is how we maintain reliability. SREs are tasked to balance a world where reliability and innovation move forward together.

Measuring reliability

Reliability is the cornerstone of any successful digital service. In SRE, measuring reliability is a necessity as it provides quantifiable metrics to objectively assess system health, prioritize improvements, or make informed decisions regarding risk and innovation. Measuring reliability provides the foundation for the following things:

- Making informed engineering decisions.
- Aligning system availability and feature delivery with business priorities.
- Proactively identifying and mitigating risks.

Importance of reliability

Users expect services to be fast, available, and error-free. Poor reliability leads to frustration, churn, and reputation damage. It can eventually lead to lost revenue.

By measuring reliability, organizations can do the following things:

- Detect problems and fix them before users notice.
- Attract more users with better reliability. Improve brand reputation.
- Communicate effectively about system health and status, gaining user confidence.
- The team can justify the time spent in managing technical debt.
- Proper allocation of engineers to the most impactful areas.
- Showcase to engineering leaders how infrastructure choices and investment affect business outcomes.

Measuring reliability leads to data-based decision-making. Without proper metrics on reliability, teams rely on gut feeling or anecdotal evidence, leading to misaligned priorities. Let us look at the details:

- **Balance innovation and stability**: Teams constantly need to balance shipping new features against keeping systems stable. Without measuring reliability, this becomes an emotional or subjective decision. With proper metrics, the right level of reliability (instead of perfect reliability) can be adopted. By keeping an eye on the reliability metrics, SREs can be proactive rather than reactive. SREs can do the following things:
    - Catch reliability degradation early.
    - Prevent incidents by taking proactive measures instead of responding to them.
    - Reduce false alerts and firefighting.
- **Reduce cost and improve operational efficiency**: Measuring reliability and proactively preventing incidents leads to reduced downtimes and less firefighting. Error budget can be used to maintain a certain level of reliability that is within the organizational budget. Planning for the right level of availability can help in right-sizing the infrastructure. This will help in forecasting and planning for capacity as the user base grows.
- **Cultural benefits of measuring reliability**: Measurement becomes a common language that helps developers, operations, and engineering leaders co-own system health. The benefits of measuring reliability and using the same as a common language are as follows:
    - Set clear and agreed-upon targets that are visible to all stakeholders.
    - Product managers can understand the cost of pushing risky features.
    - Engineers are aware of when to slow down and focus on technical debt.
    - Allow structured and blameless learning from postmortems.
    - Reliability is a metric that can become a part of the management report.

Reliability is not a one-time goal but a continuous process. Measuring it ensures that the system improves over time while adapting to user needs and technological changes.

Automating toil

In SRE, toil refers to repetitive manual operational tasks that provide little long-term value, but consume significant engineering bandwidth. Examples of toil are as follows:

- Manual restarting of services.
- Repeatedly responding to similar alerts.
- Repeatedly performing routine configuration updates.
- Running routine database and logs cleanup manually.

Characteristics of toil

Toil is usually identified via:

- **Manual**: Executed manually and not programmatically.
- **Repetitive**: Executed often as needed.
- **Reactive**: It is triggered by issues or events.
- **Scales with service size**: As the user base increases, toil also increases.

Benefits of reducing toil

SREs aim to balance engineering work along with operations work. When toil takes up SRE bandwidth, engineers fail to allocate time towards innovation, improvement, and incident reduction.

The core principle of SRE with respect to toil is that SREs should spend no more than 50% of their time on toil. If the effort spent in manually executing toil exceeds 50% of the SREs' bandwidth, then it is important to identify and automate toil to reduce the overhead on engineering teams.

Automating toil helps with the following things:

- Eliminating manual grunt work.
- Reducing context switching, allowing engineers to focus on strategic projects.
- Improved operation efficiency:
  - Faster response to incidents.
  - Reduction of human error.
  - Consistent execution of operational tasks.
- Scaling without increasing headcount:
  - Using automation, teams can support growing infrastructure without growing proportionally.

- Global large-scale services can be managed by smaller SRE teams, improving reliability:
  - Prevents costly outages caused by human error.
  - Standardizes procedures and processes.
  - Can also help in automated recovery (self-healing).
  - Faster recovery and lower MTTR as automated systems can be programmed to detect and resolve incidents faster than humans.
- Improve team morale and retention:
  - Engineers hate mundane work; toil is demoralizing. Hence, reducing toil boosts team morale.
  - High toil leads to burnout and attrition.
  - Engineers get to spend time on meaningful engineering projects.
  - Reduce on-call fatigue by handling repeated alerts automatically.

Business and organizational benefits

Automating toil will lead to increased engineering bandwidth, which will eventually lead to faster time to market for the features. Less manual overhead will lead to the following things:

- Releases with higher frequency and improved stability.
- Automation of rollbacks and roll-forwards improves system stability.
- 24x7 global operations without 24x7 human presence.
- Rapid failover and automated disaster recovery.
- Compliance and auditability for event and execution logs.
- Reduce the cost of **network operations center** (**NOC**) teams as automation helps smaller teams handle more.
- Lower cost during upscaling or downscaling since it is automated and triggered without human intervention.
- Eventually leading to higher ROI on engineering effort.

Conclusion

In this chapter, we saw the pre-SRE landscape and understood the reason for the birth of SRE at Google. We also went over and understood the core principles of SRE and its benefits to the engineering, operations, product, and business teams while driving organizational growth. We went in depth on a few of the core principles of SRE, like embracing risk, measuring reliability, and automating toil. We understood the importance of these principles and their benefits. In the next chapter, we will look at SRE metrics and understand how they are implemented and used within SRE. We will also explore some tools that help in observability.

CHAPTER 2
Understanding SRE Metrics

Introduction

Metrics are the backbone of **site reliability engineering** (**SRE**) because they provide the data and insights needed to understand, measure, and improve system reliability. In this chapter, we will understand the essential metrics, **service level indicator** (**SLI**), **service level objectives** (**SLOs**), and **service level agreements** (**SLAs**) that are used to define and measure reliability. We will learn how to identify the right SLIs, set meaningful SLOs, and align SLAs with business needs while keeping a buffer to be able to meet the business agreements.

We will look at the four golden signals: latency, traffic, errors, and saturation, and their relevance in monitoring system health and diagnosing issues quickly. These signals help the team to detect problems early and prioritize fixes that have the most significant user impact.

We will also look at the concept of error budgets, which are used by the engineering team to balance reliability with feature delivery. Instead of pursuing unrealistic uptimes, error budgets give teams flexibility to innovate and release features while maintaining acceptable levels of reliability. This helps avoid over-engineering and fosters healthy collaboration between product and engineering teams.

This chapter will provide a clear and actionable framework for defining meaningful SLIs, setting realistic SLOs, negotiating business-aligned SLAs, and leveraging error budgets. Most importantly, we will understand the use of metrics not only to measure reliability but also, to make data-based engineering and product decisions.

Structure

The chapter covers the following topics:

- Role of metrics in SRE
- SLI, SLO, and SLA
- Four golden signals
- Error budgets

- Right metrics through SLI, SLO, and SLA
- Visualization and alerting on metrics
- Other critical SRE metrics

Objectives

By the end of this chapter, we will be able to understand the most important SRE metrics and their significance in building reliable systems. We will learn how to define SLOs that reflect user expectations and SLAs that align with business goals for different service types, while also gaining insights into using error budgets for making effective decisions regarding risk management by balancing reliability with innovation. We will also look at case studies and real-world examples to see how organizations apply these concepts in practice, learning from successes and failures. Eventually, this will help us in being able to implement effective monitoring and alerting strategies, enabling teams to proactively detect issues, reduce downtime, and maintain user trust.

Role of metrics in SRE

In SRE, metrics are the foundation of reliability, performance optimization, and data-driven decision-making. Metrics are not just numbers; they are the language of reliability. Unlike traditional IT operations monitoring, where uptime is often the sole focus, SRE uses a quantitative approach to balance system reliability, feature velocity, and user experience. Without clear, meaningful metrics, reliability becomes subjective instead of a clear, measurable objective.

Metrics help SRE teams in:

- Measuring system health by identifying bottlenecks and failures.
- Ensuring the system performance meets user expectations.
- Deciding when to optimize versus when to add new features.
- Improving incident response through faster detection, diagnosis, and resolution.
- Providing transparency between development and operations teams.

In the absence of proper metrics, the team would tend to operate blindly, reacting to outages instead of focusing on preventing them. Metrics act as a bridge between systems and human understanding. They help in transforming complexity into clarity and ambiguity into action.

Aligning monitoring with user expectations

In traditional IT systems, the monitoring teams focus on key metrics like **central processing unit** (**CPU**), memory, and disk usage with the sole purpose of keeping the lights on. There could be scenarios where, systems may appear healthy based on infrastructure metrics, yet still fail to meet user performance expectations. Hence, SRE reorients metrics tracking by prioritizing user-centric metrics that directly showcase performance and reliability.

For example, instead of just measuring the CPU load, SRE would also focus on measuring the request latency and tracking how fast the end users are getting a response.

This shift in the model ensures that the teams focus on what the end users actually experience instead of just internal system states.

Metrics for balancing reliability and innovation

SREs teams typically do not target 100% uptime because it is impractical and often very expensive, while also slowing down innovation. Instead, SREs use metrics to define an acceptable level of reliability and then manage risk using error budgets. We will go in depth on error budgets and how they help in balancing reliability and innovation later in this chapter.

However, without proper metrics, teams would either over-prioritize stability, leading to slower releases, or ignore reliability, causing frequent outages. Thus, metrics provide SREs with an objective data point to strike the right balance and align reliability with business goals. With the help of metrics, SREs can define the business impact of an outage and thus provide the business data points on whether to push for reliability or innovation.

Example: An e-commerce site achieved a checkout success rate of 98.5% during the festive sale, missing its SLO. A detailed analysis revealed increased errors during checkout due to elevated tail latency. Re-engineering this fix by introducing caching led to improved reliability during checkout, boosting sales and providing a direct benefit of improving reliability to the business.

Key properties of good metrics

Not all metrics are useful for SRE. Effective SRE metrics should have the following characteristics:

- **Actionable**: Drives decisions.
- **User-centric**: Reflects real user experience, for example, checkout success rate instead of server uptime.
- **Measurable and consistent**: Easy to collect, compare, and trend over time.
- **Tied to business goals**: Should align with business goals, for example, system uptime impact on revenue.

Let us look at an example of a good metric based on the above characteristics:

- **P95 API latency < 200ms**: This showcases the impact of latency on end users. If the latency increases and the metrics go below the 95th percentile, engineers need to focus on improving performance. This metric showcases the following characteristics of a good metric:

  - **Actionable**: When the latency exceeds 200ms for the 95th percentile, engineers have a clear signal to investigate performance bottlenecks, optimize queries, or scale infrastructure. It provides a direct trigger for corrective action.
  - **User-centric**: Latency directly affects how users perceive the system's responsiveness.
  - **Measurable and consistent**: This metric can be tracked continuously using monitoring tools and represented in dashboards, alerting systems and SLO reports. Also, using the 95th percentile avoids distortion caused by extreme outliers while still capturing the experience of the vast majority of users.
  - **Tied to business goals**: Fast response times translate into better user engagement, higher conversion rates, and improved retention. Better latency supports better revenue and improves customer trust.

The example of bad metrics is as follows:

- **Number of servers running**: This gives a high-level idea of the infrastructure cost; however, there are other metrics that can give a better idea of the same. Note that the number of servers running cannot be associated with user experience in any way.

Common pitfalls in using metrics

While metrics are powerful, they can cause confusion and can be misleading if not used properly. Let us look at some of the common mistakes made:

- **Too many metrics**: Will eventually lead to noise, false positives, alert fatigue, and decision paralysis.
- **Vanity metrics**: Metrics which does not reflect user experience are called **vanity metrics**. It would be a waste of resources and effort to track such metrics.
- **Lack of context**: Metrics that are raw numbers and are not compared against a baseline or previous data points lose their meaning.
- **Misaligned incentives**: Chasing metrics instead of focusing on their interpretation and the balance of reliability and innovation.

Successful SRE teams choose metrics with care, constantly refine the metrics, and align them with what truly matters: user experience and business continuity.

In an ever-changing landscape of modern systems, metrics provide a common language that SREs, developers, and business leaders use to discuss reliability. They tell us where we are, how far we have strayed, and what direction we need to take. When implemented thoughtfully and interpreted with care, metrics empower SRE teams to build, maintain, and evolve systems that are not only reliable but trustworthy.

Four golden signals

In SRE, monitoring and observability are critical to maintaining system health and performance. Modern distributed systems are complex, where services depend on other services and users interact across a diverse network while traffic patterns change unpredictably. In such scenarios, the four golden signals, latency, traffic, errors, and saturation, stand out as the most essential indicators of system behavior. The signals are as follows:

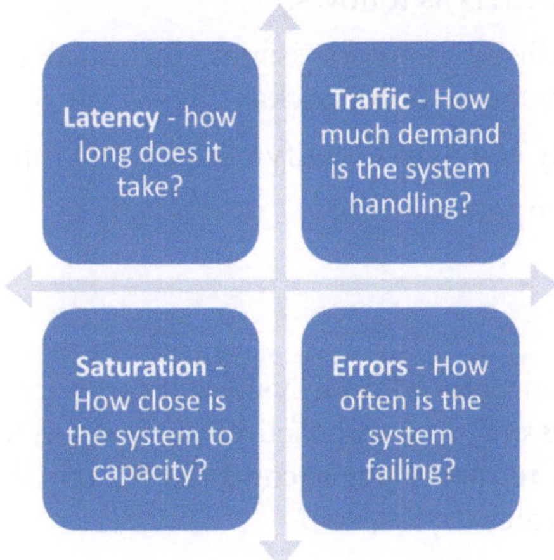

Figure 2.1*: Four signals and the questions they answer in operational practice*

These signals (as popularized by *Google SRE practices*) provide a comprehensive view of system performance, which helps teams detect and mitigate issues before they escalate. They offer a reliable framework to help engineers monitor what truly matters, the health and performance of the system as experienced by the user.

Latency

Latency measures the time taken for a system to process a request and return a response. It is a crucial indicator of user experience. Whether it is a search query, image upload, or API call, users expect fast responses. High latency can lead to sluggish performance and frustrated users. Measuring latency helps detect when the system slows down, even without a complete outage.

Types of latency are as follows:

- **Successful request latency**: Time taken for successful requests.
- **Failed request latency**: Time taken for failed requests.

Metrics for measuring latency are as follows:

- **Request latency**: Captured in milliseconds is the round-trip time or the time taken from the initiation of the request to the return of the response.

- **Percentiles (P50, P95, P99)**: It defines the percentile latency. High percentile latencies are crucial, as averages can hide tail latency. P99 latency can reveal rare but painful slowdowns. For example, if P99 latency jumps from 200ms to 1 second during peak hours, it needs to be flagged as performance degradation under load.
- **Segregated latency**: Separating successful and failed request latencies to isolate root causes.

The importance of latency in SRE is as follows:

- High latency can indicate network issues, technical debt, inefficient algorithms/ implementations, or resource bottlenecks.
- Monitoring tail latency can help identify outliers that may affect a subset of users.
- Latency can directly impact the SLO.

Traffic

Traffic is the measure of demand placed on a system. It can refer to the volume of requests or workload the system is processing, like transactions, messages, jobs processed, API calls, etc. It is generally represented as **requests per second** (**RPS**), **requests per minute** (**RPM**), user concurrency, or data transfer rates (bytes/sec).

Metrics for measuring traffic:

- RPS/RPM for web service.
- **Queries per second** (**QPS**)/**queries per minute** (**QPM**) for backend systems.
- **Transactions per second** (**TPS**)/**transactions per minute** (**TPM**) for APIs or transactional systems.
- Data throughput (MBs or GBs) for data-heavy applications.
- Concurrent sessions or users.

The importance of traffic in SRE is as follows:

- A sudden spike or drop in traffic can indicate outages or user-facing issues.
- Traffic metrics help in correlating spikes with performance issues.
- Helps in capacity planning and scaling decisions.

Example: If during peak hours the historical baseline is generally 5000 TPS in the system, however, the SRE sees that the number has dropped from 5000 to 500 TPS, it can indicate an issue in the transaction API, which will need further investigation. If the TPS goes up to 10000, then there would be a need to analyze and scale the system further.

Errors

Errors are the rate of failed requests or unexpected behavior in the system. These can range from 5xx errors, exceptions, business logic failures, or a failed job in the background queue, which should be tracked to understand the service availability.

Types of errors:

- **Client-side errors (4xx)**: Authentication failures, page not found, or bad requests.
- **Server-side errors (5xx)**: Internal server errors or timeouts.
- **Partial failures**: Empty or incomplete data indicating degraded responses.

Metrics for measuring errors:

- Error rate, which is a percentage of total requests.
- HTTP status codes, count of 4xx, 5xx as a ratio of 2xx and 3xx.
- Timeouts or retries.
- Exceptions and crashes.

The importance of errors in SRE is as follows:

- A rising error rate is a clear indicator that users are being impacted by some issue in the system.
- Errors are used to calculate the error budget allowed in the system.
- Errors usually cascade and impact other services dependent on the erroneous service.
- Monitoring error patterns helps in **root cause analysis** (**RCA**) in case of any incident.

Example: If during deployment there is a deviation from the historical trend of 5xx errors, it would indicate that the system is unavailable to the end users or that the new code being deployed is misbehaving and needs further testing.

Saturation

Saturation measures how full the system is or how close it is to its resource capacity limits. In most cases, saturation is the leading indicator of performance degradation or a forthcoming incident.

Metrics for measuring saturation:

- CPU utilization or load as a % of total.
- Memory utilization as a % of total.
- Disk **input/output** (**I/O**).
- Network bandwidth.
- Queue length or backlog size.
- Open connections, threads, or file descriptors.

The importance of saturation in SRE is as follows:

- High saturation leads to increasing latency and errors.
- Monitoring saturation can help in proactive scaling and throttling.
- Proactive alerts based on saturation can result in preventing incidents before they affect end users.

Example: If the database connection pool is reaching 100% utilization, the queries will start piling up, and API requests will start timing out, while the database itself is not down. In such scenarios, SRE needs to evaluate the database connection pool and determine if it can be increased based on the available system resources.

Correlating the four golden signals

Let us look at an example of a flash sale on an e-commerce website. We will see how the four golden signals can be used to interpret what is happening in the following table:

Signal	Metrics observed	SRE interpretation
Traffic	RPS has spiked from 1000 to 10000.	There is a traffic surge, which may be causing resource saturation.
Latency	P99 latency has increased from 200ms to 2000ms.	End users are experiencing slowness as requests are taking longer due to high demand on the system.
Errors	Error rate has gone up from 0.5% to 5%. Increase in 5xx errors as compared to the previous baseline.	Backend systems are likely overloaded and unable to process the current demand.
Saturation	CPU has spiked to 95% from the normal trend of 50%. Database connections are at peak, 990/1000.	The database is struggling to keep up with the transactions. The application servers are queueing requests, resulting in high latency.

Table 2.1*: Flash sale example for the four golden signals*

Together, these metrics paint a clear picture that the database systems are operating at full capacity and acting as a bottleneck as the connection pool is exhausted. This is resulting in increased latency and traffic piling up as users are waiting longer for a response from the system and eventually getting errors as requests are timing out.

The immediate fix for such an incident is to scale up the systems, horizontally scale up the application servers so that they are able to distribute the load, and vertically scale up the database systems (for scaling up database writes) or add more read replicas (for scaling up database read requests) so that the database can process more requests simultaneously.

The long-term fix would be to optimize the application business logic or database query that is causing the bottleneck and increasing response times.

The four golden signals provide a holistic view of system health, and by continuously monitoring these metrics, SRE teams can:

- Detect anomalies early.
- Improve incident response times.
- Make data-driven scaling decisions.
- Build data-driven autoscaling algorithms.

Implementing these signals in dashboards and alerting systems ensures that reliability remains a top priority, aligning with the core principle of SRE of balancing feature development with system stability.

SLI, SLO, and SLA

SRE is a discipline that incorporates aspects of software engineering and applies them to infrastructure and operational problems. At the heart of SRE, there are three fundamental concepts that help quantify and measure reliability:

- SLIs
- SLOs
- SLAs

In SRE, reliability is a feature and not an afterthought. These metrics help in measuring reliability in a quantifiable and actionable way. Together, they form the core framework for tracking reliability metrics, aligning technical performance with user experience and business goals.

Service level indicator

SLIs are the quantitative measures of the behavior of a service that directly reflect user experience. They are the raw metrics that SRE teams use to assess whether a service is meeting its reliability goals. SLIs are primarily derived from the four golden signals (latency, traffic, errors, and saturation), and their focus is on user-visible behaviors.

Characteristics of good SLIs are as follows:

- **User-centric**: Should measure what matters to end users.
- **Measurable**: Must be quantifiable with available instrumentation.
- **Actionable**: Should provide insights that can drive engineering decisions.
- **Correlated**: Should align with actual user experience.

Examples of SLIs are as follows:

- **Request success rate**: Percentage of time the server is operational and able to handle requests. It is calculated as:

*Request success rate = (Successful requests / total requests) * 100*

- **Latency**: The time taken to serve a request. It is measured as percentile values (P50, P90, P99), as follows:
    - o **P90—200ms**: Which means that 90% of the requests have a latency <= 200 milliseconds.
- **Throughput**: Number of requests the system can handle per unit of time. It is typically measured in RPS, as follows:
    - o For example, an API service can handle 1000 RPS during peak hours.
- **Error rate**: The percentage of requests that fail. It is calculated as:
    - o **Error rate**: *(Failed requests / total requests) * 100*
- **Saturation**: Measures the extent of utilization of resources constituting a service. This is measured as CPU utilization, memory utilization, queue lengths, or disk I/O utilization.
    - o For example, the CPU is at 60% load during peak hours.

Service level objective

SLOs are the internal goals for service reliability that teams use to make decisions about risk management and resource allocation. They represent the target values or ranges for SLIs that a service team aims to achieve. So, SLOs define the acceptable level of service performance over a specified time window.

SLO components are as follows:

- **SLI**: The metric being measured
- **Target**: The desired level of reliability
- **Time window**: The period over which the measurement is evaluated
- **Conditions**: Any specific circumstances or caveats

SLO characteristics are as follows:

- SLOs should be aspirational but achievable.
- They should be aligned with user needs and not just internal metrics.
- They should be used to prioritize reliability vs. feature development.

Setting appropriate SLOs is as follows:

- Start with what the user needs. SREs need to understand what reliability means for end users.
- Align with business requirements or organizational priorities.
- Balance cost and reliability. Higher reliability is often expensive as it needs more resources.

- Use error budgets to determine the level of unreliability that is tolerable.

Examples of SLOs are as follows:

- **Availability**: 99.9% of requests should be successful over a 30 day window.
- **Latency**: 95% of requests should be served within 200ms over a 24 hour window.

SLOs allow teams to balance reliability and innovation or feature delivery. As long as teams stay within the boundaries defined by SLO, they are reliable and can keep on pushing out new features. However, once they violate the SLO targets, they start burning the error budget and may need to focus more on reliability as compared to feature delivery.

Service level agreement

SLAs are formal contracts between service providers and customers that specify the guaranteed level of service, typically including consequences (such as financial penalties or service credits) if those guarantees are not met.

SLA characteristics are as follows:

- SLAs are legally binding and have contractual implications.
- SLAs are external-facing and are shared with the customers.
- SLAs are typically set below the SLO target to provide a buffer.

SLA components are as follows:

- **Service description**: Services that are covered.
- **Performance metrics**: The SLIs are guaranteed.
- **Measurement methods**: How the metrics are being calculated.
- **Remediation**: Implications of SLA violation.
- **Exclusions**: Cases where SLA does not apply.

Examples of SLA are as follows:

- Monthly uptime percentage of 99.95%.
- Credit of 10% of the monthly fee for each hour of downtime beyond 0.05%.
- Excludes outages due to unexpected natural disasters.

Generally, SREs do not set SLA; however, they need to be aware of them because any SLA violation can have serious business implications.

Difference between SLI, SLO, and SLA

Here is a table that shows the difference between SLI, SLO, and SLA:

	Insight	Audience	Purpose
SLA	The agreement between client and user	Meant for customers	Legal guarantee
SLO	The objective a service provider must achieve to meet the agreement	Meant for internal stakeholders	Define reliability goals
SLI	The real number on performance	Meant for engineers	Measure performance

Table 2.2: *SLI vs. SLO vs. SLA*

This hierarchy ensures that what you measure (SLIs) informs what you aim for (SLOs), which ultimately supports what you promise (SLAs).

Implementing SLIs

For implementing SLIs, start with the user experience and ask what failure looks like to the user. For this, SREs need to identify critical user journeys and determine which metrics best represent the end user experience. Next, they need to setup systems that are able to collect these metrics. And finally, setup dashboards for real-time monitoring of these metrics.

Best practice: SLIs must be automatically measured in real-time using logs, metrics, and traces.

Implementing SLOs

For implementing SLOs, start with baseline measurements. Look at historical data and set initial targets. In the absence of historical data, it is recommended to gather data from SLI for a small duration (say, a week) and then use that as a reference. Gather user feedback and communicate with business stakeholders, and refine the SLOs to align with both of them. Finally, implement error budgets to guide the development team on where to focus their efforts.

Some best practices are:

- Limit the number of SLOs as too many may dilute focus. Instead, have a few SLOs that are meaningful, high-impact objectives for each service.
- Tie SLO to alerting and dashboards. Alerts should reflect SLO violations, not every spike.
- Iterate and calibrate, as it is difficult to get the perfect SLO on the first try. Tweak SLO based on data, user impact, and business objectives.
- Communicate and ensure that all stakeholders are aware of SLOs, error budget, and its implications on reliability vs. feature delivery.

Implementing SLAs

For implementing SLAs, SREs need to discuss the SLOs with the business stakeholders and figure out which SLOs should be customer-facing. Once the SLOs are identified, SREs, along with the business stakeholders, need to add additional buffers to account for variability. Next, the business stakeholders need to define clear remediation policies and establish measurement and reporting procedures that can be communicated to end users or clients.

SLIs, SLOs, and SLAs are more than buzzwords; they are the quantitative backbone of SRE. By grounding decisions in measurable, actionable metrics, they bring clarity to complex systems, accountability to operations, and alignment across engineering and business.

Error budgets

An error budget is a critical concept in SRE that quantifies how much unreliability a service can tolerate over a specific time period before users are negatively impacted. It represents the balance between reliability and innovation, allowing teams to make informed decisions about releasing new features vs. maintaining stability.

In short, an error budget is the tool that allows SREs to find the balance.

Calculating error budget

Error budget is derived from SLO.

The basic formula for calculating the error budget is as follows:

Error budget = 100% - SLO

Example 1: Monthly availability:

- SLO is 99.9% availability over 30 days
- *Error budget = 100% - 99.9% (SLO) = 0.1%*
- *30 days = 30 days * 24 hours * 60 minutes = 43200 minutes*
- *Allowed unavailability minutes = 43200*0.1% = 43.2 minutes (in a month)*

Example 2: Request success rate:

- SLO is 99.9% successful requests in 30 days
- *Error budget = 100% - 99.9% (SLO) = 0.1%*
- *Total requests = 1million requests per month*
- *Failures allowed = 0.1% * 1,000,000 = 1,000 failed requests*

Importance of error budgets

Error budgets are a crucial part of the decision-making framework. They allow the engineering teams to:

- **Make trade-offs between speed and safety**: If the error budget is healthy, more aggressive changes can be deployed. If it is nearly exhausted, slow down and stabilize.
- **Enforce accountability**: Keeps reliability measurable and tied to agreed objectives.
- **Avoid over-engineering**: There is no need to aim for five nines if the business and users are happy with three nines.
- **Improve communication**: Provides a shared language for SRE and product teams.

Error budget implementation process

The implementation of the error budget is done by following the steps:

1. **Define SLO**: As discussed in the previous section, SLO must be:
   a. Measurable
   b. User-focused
   c. Time-bound
2. **Calculate error budget**: Calculate the error budget percentage using the formula:
   a. **Error budget**: *100% - SLO*
   b. Convert the error budget into a tangible number (for example, number of minutes of downtime allowed over the defined period)
3. **Monitor SLO consumption by setting up monitoring and alerting to track**:
   a. Current budget remaining
   b. Consumption rate
   c. Causes of error budget depletion
4. **Act-based on error budget health**:
   a. **70% remaining**: If the budget is healthy, the team can proceed with normal or accelerated release cadence.
   b. **25-70% remaining**: If the budget is at risk or depleting, the team needs to focus more on testing and reliability, and slow down the releases.
   c. **<25% remaining**: If the budget is exhausted, freeze non-critical changes, prioritize reliability fixes, and maybe rollback buggy features.

Implementation example of e-commerce checkout service

The steps to implement an example of an e-commerce checkout service are as follows:

1. **Define SLO**:
   a. **SLO**: 99.9% of checkout requests must complete successfully over a 30 day period.

2. **Translate to error budget:**
    a. **Error budget**: *100% - 99.9% = 0.1%.*
    b. **Expected requests/month**: 10 million checkout requests.
    c. **Error budget**: 0.1% of 10M = 10,000 failed checkouts allowed.
3. **Monitor**:
    a. Instrument API metrics to track success/failure counts.
    b. Dashboard should show:
        i. **Total error budget for the month**: 10,000 failures.
        ii. **Current usage**: Number of failures to date, for example, 2,500 failures after the first week.
4. **Act**:
    a. If failures spike to 7,500 by mid-month (fast burn), freeze non-critical deployments and investigate root causes, for example, payment gateway latency.

Multi-SLO error budget management

There can be a scenario where a particular system can have multiple error budgets. In such scenarios, all such error budgets should be derived from their SLOs and calculated accordingly, and displayed in the observability dashboard.

For example, if a system has both availability and latency SLOs and a corresponding error budget, the following steps show how the multi-SLO error budget is managed in this case:

- **Total requests per month**: 1 million
- **Total minutes per month**: 43200 minutes
- **Availability SLO**: 99.9% over a 1-month period
- **Latency SLO**: 95% of requests should be served within 250ms
- **Availability error budget**: 0.1% = 43.2 minutes of downtime
- **Latency error budget:** 5% = 50,000 requests served above > 250ms allowed

In this scenario, if either of the error budgets (latency or availability error budget) is at risk or depleting, appropriate actions need to be taken by the team, like slowing down or rolling back releases, focusing on reliability projects to maintain the SLO and avoid SLA violations.

Example scenario: Suppose the team releases a change in the CDN and, within the next 2 days, observes the following:

- Latency error budget is depleted to 20,000 from 50,000 requests served above 200ms.
- Availability budget is at 42 minutes.

This signals an issue with the recent release with respect to the CDN and needs immediate rollback to avoid error budget exhaustion, which will lead to SLA violation.

Action: Immediately roll back the release. Pause future releases as the latency error budget is at risk of depletion. Focus on reliability projects.

Common pitfalls

The common pitfalls are as follows:

- SLO should be properly aligned with the user expectations and historical performance. If the SLO is too strict, we will always blow away our error budget, whereas if the SLO is too loose, it becomes meaningless.
- Measurements should be accurate. Incorrect measurements will result in unexpected reliability for the users.
- It is important to act on the budget we are tracking. If we are just reporting the error budget without acting on it, it would be meaningless.
- Error budget is a tool for balancing and should not be considered as punishment for any team.

Summary

Error budgets provide a quantitative framework for balancing reliability and velocity. By implementing error budget tracking with clear policies and visualization, teams can:

- Make data-driven decisions about releases and reliability work.
- Prevent reliability regressions while still enabling innovation.
- Create shared accountability between development and operations teams.
- Focus engineering effort where it will have the most impact.

Teams should adapt error budgets to their specific needs while maintaining the core principle: error budgets represent the acceptable level of unreliability that enables both innovation and stability.

Right metrics through SLI, SLO, and SLA

Establishing effective SLIs, SLOs, and SLAs is both an art and a science. These metrics are meaningless without context. Defining them properly requires proper consideration of technical realities, user expectations, and business objectives. We must know what is acceptable to both our users and business.

In practice, many organizations either measure the wrong things or set unrealistic targets, leading to wasted effort, unnecessary firefighting, and customer dissatisfaction.

Understanding service and user

Different services have different definitions of *good enough*. Hence, for each service, we must ponder and figure out the meaning of reliability for each service and the user base it serves. Let us see some examples:

- **Payment gateway**: Reliability means that transactions never fail and are completed within seconds. Here, the success rate and latency threshold are important SLIs.
- **Search service**: Reliability means that results should appear within milliseconds. Here P95 / P99 latency become important SLIs.
- **Video streaming service**: Reliability means uninterrupted playback even when there is a bottleneck in bandwidth usage and quality drops. Here, start time, buffer ratio, and resolution adoption become important SLIs.

Hence, in order to understand the service better, it is recommended to decompose the service further. The steps for the same are as follows:

1. **Mapping user journey**:
    a. Document critical paths throughout the application
    b. Identify touchpoints where reliability matters most for the user
    c. Let us look at an example of an e-commerce site:

    Critical user journey: Product search | add to cart | checkout | payment | email/SMS notification

2. **Dependency analysis**:
    a. Catalog all internal and external dependencies
    b. Classify by impact level (critical, important, secondary)

Let us look at examples of some dependencies as follows:

- Database servers
- Payment processors
- Authentication services

The two previously mentioned steps will help us get a clear picture of what reliability looks like from the point of view of the users. While also highlighting the critical services that serve those user flows. In addition to this, it is also recommended to talk to product, support, and customer success teams to get qualitative feedback on user experience.

Identifying the right SLI

SLI should always be a direct measure of the user experience and not an internal health metric. For example, measuring request latency, error rate or availability from the user's perspective reflects how users actually interact with the service. On the other hand, internal metrics like memory usage or disk I/O do not directly capture the user's perspective. Let us look at the criteria for selecting SLIs based on the above understanding.

Criteria for selecting SLIs

The criteria for selecting SLIs are as follows:

- **User perceivable**: change in the metric should be visible to the user.
- **Quantifiable**: Should be possible to measure automatically and accurately.
- **Actionable**: In case of degradation, we could do something about it quickly.
- **Minimal set**: Start with 1-2 SLI per service to avoid metric overload.

We can use the following decision metrics to select the appropriate SLIs, as shown in the following table:

Service tier	Recommended SLIs	Measurement frequency	Collection method
User-facing	Availability, latency, error rate	Per-request	Endpoint monitoring
Middle-tier or service layer	Throughput, queue backlog, processing time	1 minute intervals	Monitoring service mesh
Data layer or database cluster	Read/Write latency, storage utilization, replication lag	5 second samples	Database event loggers or data exporters

Table 2.3: Decision metrics for selecting appropriate SLI

Once we have a potential list of SLIs, it is important to validate them against real user impact:

- **Customer feedback analysis**: In order to understand if the SLIs are impactful to the users, it is important to review existing support tickets for repeated reliability complaints or conduct user interviews to identify reliability pain points they have experienced.
- **Business metrics correlation**: Next, it is important to correlate the potential SLIs with business metrics like conversion rates, session duration, and bounce rates.
- **Competitive benchmarking**: Once we have narrowed down the potential list of SLIs, the next step is to compare them with industry benchmarks and see where we stand. This will help us in identifying the gap while setting up SLOs on those SLIs.

Examples of SLIs for a search service area are as follows:

- **SLI1**: P95 or 95th percentile latency for search.
- **SLI2**: Quality percentage of search queries returning correct results, where correctness is measured via a labeled evaluation set and periodic audits.
- **SLI3**: Percentage of successful requests (HTTP 200 response without errors).

Implementing SLIs

In order to implement the SLIs, we need to identify the collection points (refer to *Table* 2.3) for the metrics we finalized. We may need to access different logs, such as:

- Real user monitoring logs for user-side metrics.
- CDN logs for edge or http behavior metrics.
- Application performance logs for application-related metrics.
- Infrastructure logs like Prometheus exporters for infrastructure-related metrics.

Once we have the metrics in place, the next step is to collect them using a tool such as **Elasticsearch, Logstash, Kibana** (ELK), and use the data points for creating dashboards, which will eventually be used for alerting. The following figure shows a sample data pipeline used for collecting SLI metrics and creating dashboards:

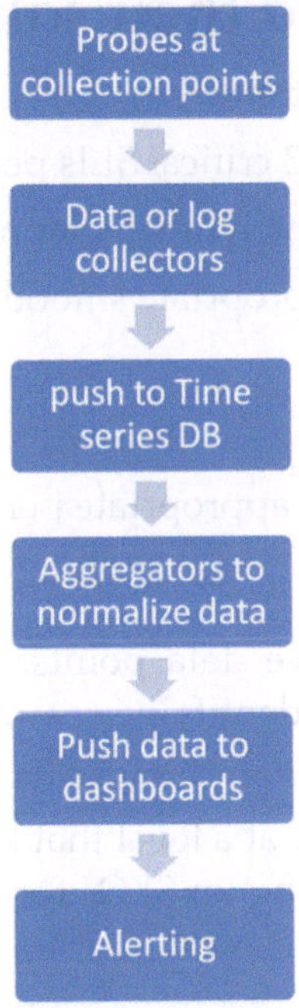

***Figure 2.2:** Data pipeline for implementing SLI*

Checklist for implementing SLIs

The checklist for implementing SLIs is as follows:

- **Standardize metric naming**: The purpose of standardizing metric names is to help anyone viewing the metric easily understand what the metric stands for. Each metric should have a proper name, for example, `http_requests_search_total`.

- **Establish baseline measurements**: Here, the purpose is to set baseline measurements that can be derived from historical data and use them as a reference for setting up SLOs.
- **Configure metric retention policies**: Storing metrics data can turn out to be expensive and may even slow down the SLI dashboard. Hence, it is important to have a metric retention policy in place (for example, 90 days of data). For historical data, metrics can be summarized or aggregated and pushed to another system for long-term retention, for example, 1 year of summarized data.
- **Implement dimensional tagging**: When the metrics are distributed across multiple services and regions, it is important to tag them appropriately for proper identification. For example, `http_search_request_total` can be tagged as *India* and the *U.S.* based on the region it is serving.

Common SLI pitfalls and their solutions

The pitfalls and their solutions are as follows:

- **Metric overload**: Start with 2-3 critical SLIs per service and then gradually expand.
- **Measurement gaps**: Implement synthetic monitoring for uncovered paths.
- **Noisy data**: Need to apply appropriate smoothing and outlier removal.

Implementing SLOs

Now that SLIs are in place, we can set appropriate performance targets or SLOs.

In order to setup SLOs, we need to:

- Look at historical performance data points. We can calculate percentiles over the trailing 30-90 days while also identifying seasonal patterns and peaks. SLOs should be a stretch but achievable.
- We need to maintain reliability at a level that keeps users happy. Here is a framework that can be referred to for setting up SLOs for different types of services, as shown in the following table:

Service type	Availability SLO	Latency SLO	Error budget
Mission-critical	99.99%	P99 < 500ms	4.3 min/month
Business essential	99.9%	P95 < 1s	43 min/month
Support	99%	P90 < 2s	7.2 hours/month

***Table 2.4**: Service type SLO framework illustration*

- Factor in the cost of reliability. Higher targets are achievable; however, they will need more investment in infrastructure and engineers while also reducing the feature delivery rate. We need to strike a balance.

- Align with business goals. It would be a waste of resources to invest in improving the reliability of a feature that is not critical. (Refer to *Table 2.4*).
- Error budget calculation for implementing SLO:
  `Error budget = (100% - SLO%) * time window`

Practical guidelines

The practical guidelines are as follows:

- SLOs should be documented in detail. The calculation methodology should be clearly defined, and the measurement scope and exclusions highlighted.
- Avoid alerting on every SLO violation. Instead, use rolling measurement windows to smooth out anomalies.
- Burn rate alerts should be highlighted.
- Avoid five nines (99.999%) availability unless absolutely mission-critical; it is expensive to implement and an overkill.
- Balance aspirational and realism to avoid engineer burnout.
- For implementing the dashboard, include:
  - Current SLO status
  - Error budget consumption
  - Historical trends

Top contributing factors

The example SLOs for the search service are as follows:

- **P99 latency**: 99.9% of search queries should be served within 300ms.
- **99.95% availability**: 99.95% of requests should be successful over a 30 day rolling window.

Defining SLAs

Now that SLOs are in place, we can take the next step of making public or contractual commitments to our users by defining SLAs, which are based on the SLOs we configured.

SLA should be less ambitious than internal SLOs to provide a buffer. In addition to this, there should be clear penalties defined within the SLA, like service credits or refunds if the SLA is breached. Also, there should be a clear methodology defined for measurement. We documented this while implementing SLO; however, we now need to make it understandable to the user on how these measurements are done and the calculations for SLA, so that both parties share the same measurement interpretation.

SLA definition checklist

The checklist to define SLAs is as follows:

- **Scope definition**:
  - List of services and features covered
  - Geographical coverage defined
- **Performance terms**:
  - Specify measurement methods
  - Define reporting standards
- **Remediation terms**:
  - Service credit calculations
  - Claim procedures
  - Dispute resolution
- **Exclusions**:
  - Maintenance windows
  - Force majeure

Sample SLA

Let us look at a sample SLA structure for the search API:

- 99.5% monthly uptime guarantee.

  `Monthly uptime percentage = (total minutes - downtime) / total minutes`
- Measured by external probes and tools across three global monitoring locations. Excludes scheduled maintenance windows.
- 10% monthly service credit if the SLA is violated. The maximum annual credit should not exceed 50% of annual fees.

Best practices for implementation of SLI, SLO, and SLA

Organizational alignment is critical for the proper implementation of SRE metrics, as follows:

- **Engineering collaboration**:
  - Development teams should be involved during SLO setting.
  - Map SLOs to sprint planning. So that the development teams can map their efforts for reliability in their sprints.
- **Business coordination**:
  - Align SLOs to revenue-impacting features so that the business can identify and participate in setting up proper SLOs.
  - Align SLA terms with legal and sales so that they can share the same with users and act accordingly when needed.

- **Customer communication:**
  - o Publish SLA performance reports, and keep customers informed of the performance metrics.
  - o Provide a status dashboard for enterprise customers, which they can refer to in case they are facing any issues. There can be scenarios where issues can be with the customer network. Such dashboards help customers in identifying their own issues and fixing them rather than reaching out to support and creating false alerts and noise.

Continuous improvement process

SLI, SLO, and SLAs need to be continuously audited to improve them further. These reliability metrics are living agreements that evolve with the system, user expectations, and business goals. As applications grow in scale and complexity, what was once considered as acceptable performance may no longer satisfy or align with user expectations. Let us look at a process that will help us continuously improve these metrics.

Quarterly reviews

The quarterly reviews are as follows:

- Analyze SLO performance trends and see if it needs to be tweaked based on historical performance and the number of alerts. If there is a decrease in the number of alerts and historical performance has improved, we need to make the SLO stricter.
- Review alert effectiveness and see if the alerts are proper and actionable. If there are too many false alerts, they need to be fixed.
- Assess error budget utilization and how much of the error budget has been utilized, and how much is remaining. This also needs input from the product and business teams. If there is an increase in the error budget, engineering teams can increase the frequency of feature delivery. However, if the error budget has been reduced, focus has to be on reliability engineering. And if business is aligned, the error budget can be tweaked (increased or decreased) to meet the business needs.

Annual refresh

The steps for the annual refreshing of SLI, SLO, and SLA are as follows:

1. Revalidate SLIs against user needs. Re-run the SLI identification process to include the features that have been rolled out during the year and revisit the existing SLIs to see if we need to remove some or add more SLIs.
2. Adjust SLO targets based on capability. Revisit the SLO implementation steps to see if the SLOs reflect the user and business needs, or if they need to be tweaked.

3. Update SLA terms as per market expectations and based on the improvement in reliability or business decisions.

Post-incident analysis

The post-incident analysis is as follows:

- Evaluate SLO coverage during incidents.
- Identify missing early warning signals. If an incident has happened and SRE was not able to foresee it, there was something missing that needs to be captured as an alert.
- Update monitoring to help SRE identify early symptoms and reduce incident detection time.

Summary

Implementing effective SLIs, SLOs, and SLAs requires methodical identification of meaningful metrics, careful implementation of measurement systems, and ongoing refinement based on operational experience. By following this structured approach, from service decomposition through continuous improvement, organizations can build a reliability framework that provides clear signals for engineering prioritization while meeting business requirements and customer expectations. Remember that these metrics should evolve alongside our services, requiring periodic reassessment as architectures change and user needs develop.

Other critical SRE metrics

While the SLI, SLO, and SLA form the foundations of SRE metrics, there are other critical metrics that offer the teams deeper visibility into specific aspects of system health, operational efficiency, and engineering productivity.

They help SREs in detecting early signs of degradation, optimizing resource usage, maintaining a sustainable pace of development and operations, and identifying long-term improvement opportunities.

Let us go over these critical metrics one-by-one.

Mean time to detection

Mean time to detection (MTTD) is the average time taken to identify an issue in the system from the moment it starts affecting users. It is a critical metric as faster detection leads to quicker resolution and reduced user impact:

```
MTTD = total detection time across incidents/number of incidents
```

A quick detection window minimizes potential damage. The sooner the issue is detected, the sooner mitigation and recovery can begin. The importance of MTTD is as follows:

- **Lower MTTD**: Monitoring and alerting systems are effective at catching issues quickly.
- **Higher MTTD**: There are possible gaps in observability, or alert configurations are ineffective.

Let us look at the illustrative ranges of industry benchmarks for MTTDs in the following table:

System type	Good MTTD	MTTD needs improvement
Critical systems (for example, payments, authentication)	Less than 5 minutes	Greater than 15 minutes
High-traffic web applications	Less than 10 minutes	Greater than 30 minutes
Internal tools	Less than 30 minutes	Greater than 1 hour

***Table 2.5**: Industry benchmarks for MTTD*

Examples of MTTD are as follows:

- If an incident starts throwing errors at 12:00 and the alert for the same is triggered at 12:04, then the MTTD is 4 minutes.
- If an incident starts at 10:00 am and the alert for the same is triggered at 10:09, then the MTTD in this case will be 9 minutes.

Mean time to recovery

Mean time to recovery (**MTTR**) is the average time taken to detect, diagnose, and resolve incidents.

```
MTTR = Total downtime from detection to recovery/number of incidents
```

The importance of MTTR is as follows:

- MTTR directly impacts user experience and business continuity.
- A system that recovers within minutes has less impact on the users and hence retains more user trust. MTTR can also act as a benchmark to compare incident responses across teams.

Components of MTTR are as follows:

- MTTR timeline generally starts after detection of the incident but is dependent on the criticality of the service as well.
- It comprises the **mean time to investigate** (**MTTI**) and **mean time to fix** (**MTTF**).
- In an ideal scenario, the total time from detection to recovery should be within one hour for critical incidents.

The following figure shows the components of MTTR:

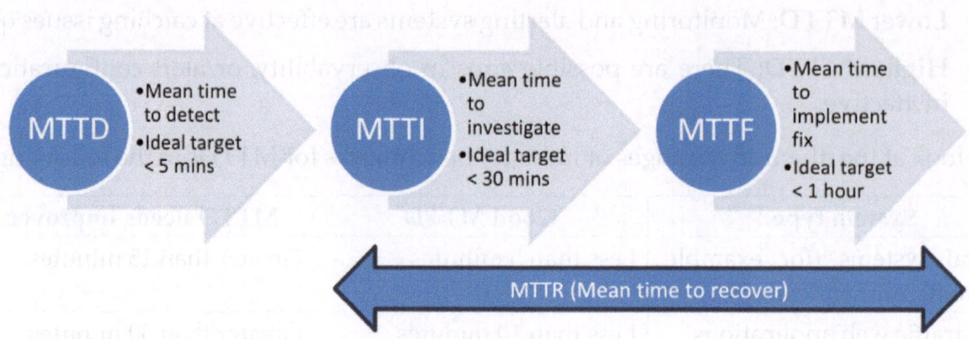

Figure 2.3: MTTR components

Best practices to improve MTTR are as follows:

- Automate detection of incidents.
- Run incident drills using tools like chaos engineering.
- Improve the efficiency of the incident response process by incorporating quality communication during incidents.
- The team should have a library of runbooks or automated fixes in place to speed up the recovery process.

Examples of MTTR are as follows:

- If an outage starts at 12:00 and is detected at 12:05 and resolved at 12:30, the MTTR is 25 minutes.
- If an outage starts at 10:05, is detected at 10:15, and is resolved at 10:30, the MTTR is 15 minutes.

Change failure rate

Change failure rate (CFR) is defined as the percentage of production changes that result in service degradation or require a rollback.

```
CFR = Failed Deployments / Total Deployments * 100%
```

The importance of CFR is as follows:

- CFR reflects the stability of deployment processes and the quality of testing before releases.
- A high CFR indicates insufficient testing, poor release discipline, unmanageable payload of release, or inadequate **continuous integration/continuous deployment** (CI/CD) practices.

Industry benchmark for CFR is as follows:

- **Excellent**: CFR < 5%
- **Acceptable**: CFR between 5 and 15%
- **Needs improvement**: CFR > 15%

Deployment frequency

Deployment frequency refers to how often code is deployed into production.

While more frequent deployments can accelerate innovation, they must be balanced with reliability safeguards. Tracking deployment frequency alongside CFR helps measure both velocity and stability.

Example: An organization that has multiple deployments per day and still maintains a CFR of less than 5% means they have high reliability due to robust CI/CD pipelines, canary or blue-green deployments, and have automated rollbacks in place.

System saturation metrics

Saturation measures how much of the system capacity is currently in use, such as the CPU, memory, disk I/O, and network throughput, before performance degrades.

The importance of saturation metrics is as follows:

- Consistent high saturation can lead to poor performance and increased latency.
- It is an important metric to use for autoscaling resources in case saturation is high.
- Whereas in the case of low saturation, we can avoid over-provisioning of resources and optimize costs.

Industry benchmark for saturation metrics is given in the following table:

Metric	Measures	Recommended warning threshold
CPU usage	Measures processor load	> 70% sustained utilization
Memory usage	Measures available RAM	> 80% utilization
Disk I/O	Measures read/write latency	> 90% capacity
Network bandwidth	Measures traffic congestion	> 80% of max capacity

***Table 2.6**: Industry benchmark for saturation metrics*

Toil ratio

Toil ratio is defined as the proportion of the team's operational work that is toil, repetitive, manual, automatable tasks, vs. engineering work that adds long-term value.

The importance of the toil ratio is as follows:

- A high toil ratio will lead to burnout and limit innovation.
- As an industry standard, engineering teams should strive to keep toil below 50% of total effort.

The best practices to improve the toil ratio are as follows:

- Track toil in sprint retrospectives.
- Prioritize automation during sprints.
- Set a toil budget (for example, cap toil to a fixed percentage like < 50% of engineering time) and actively invest in automation when toil exceeds the limit.

Error budget burn rate

Error budget burn rate is defined as the rate at which a service consumes its allocated error budget over a given period of time. It indicates how quickly a service is exhausting its allowance for failure or unreliability. The formula for error budget burn rate is as follows:

```
Burn rate = (observed error rate / SLO error budget) * (time window / SLO measurement period)
```

The importance of the error budget burn rate is as follows:

- Even if uptime is currently within SLO limits, a high burn rate indicates that reliability may soon fall below target, triggering a freeze on feature releases.
- For example, if the burn rate is 1x, then we are spending the budget at the expected pace. However, if the burn rate is 5x, then the error budget will deplete 5x faster, and we need to take preventive measures to avoid the same.

On-call metrics

The on-call metrics are the measurements used to evaluate the effectiveness, sustainability, and fairness of an organization's on-call practices. They help SRE and operations teams understand not just how incidents are being handled, but also how the on-call process impacts engineers.

The on-call metrics can include the following sub-metrics:

- **Alert frequency**: The number of alerts per engineer per week.
- **False positive rate**: We track the number of alerts that do not require any action.
- **Out of hours page rate**: Number of pages to engineers outside of working hours.

On-call metrics can be used to improve the quality of metrics over time, while also focusing on team health by reducing stress, increasing productivity, and avoiding burnout.

Incident metrics

Incident metrics can be derived from the historical information of all incidents to date. The following table depicts the measurement criteria of those metrics and recommended targets for them:

Metric	Measured as	Target
Incident volume	Total number of incidents per month	Track and improve the trend
Severity distribution	% of sev1, sev2 and sev3 incidents	Track and reduce high-severity incidents
Mean time between failure (MTBF)	Reliability duration between failures	Track and increase over time to improve reliability
Postmortem action completion	% of fixes implemented	Ideally, implement more than 90% of the identified fixes

***Table 2.7**: Incident metrics, their measurement, and recommended targets*

The importance of incident metrics is as follows:

- Incident metrics help in discovering recurring issues (which have a similar root cause).
- Tracking these metrics helps in measuring reliability improvements.
- Also, with proper tracking of postmortem action points, there is proper accountability and a reduction of the overall number of incidents (improving reliability).

Best practices for improving incident metrics are as follows:

- Classify incidents by root cause.
- Review trends quarterly to adjust reliability-related investments.
- Publicize improvements to build trust.

Visualizing and alerting on metrics

SRE is much more about clear visibility than it is about proactive action. In SRE practice, simply collecting data about SLI, SLO, SLA, and other critical metrics (including the four golden signals) is not enough; these metrics must be visualized in a way that is instantly understandable and should be paired with an effective alerting mechanism to enable timely intervention.

Without visualization, metrics remain raw numbers buried in logs or dashboards that no one consults until something goes wrong. Without alerting, issues are often detected too late, after customers are already impacted.

Properly visualized SLIs, SLOs, SLAs, and the four golden signals: latency, traffic, errors, saturation, and other critical metrics enable teams to:

- Detect issues before users do.
- Communicate system health clearly.
- Make data-driven reliability decisions.
- Optimize incident response.

Importance of visualizing SRE metrics

Raw logs and metrics are difficult to interpret quickly. Visualization transforms them into context-rich insights by using charts, graphs, heatmaps, or status indicators. Let us look at some of the key benefits of visualizing SRE metrics with examples of those benefits, as given in the following table:

Benefit	Example
Real-time system awareness	Graphana dashboard showing live error rates.
Historical trend analysis	SLO compliance over the last 3, 6, 9, and 12 months.
Cross-team alignment	Shared SLA dashboards for engineering and business teams.
Quick anomaly detection	Spike in latency visualized in Prometheus.

***Table 2.8**: Benefits of visualizing metrics with examples*

Let us go over some of the most common metrics that would add value if visualized correctly for most systems, as follows:

- **SLI/SLO**: For SLI/SLO, SREs can focus on visualizing the following metrics:
  - Current vs. target performance
  - Error budget remaining
  - Burnout trends
- **Four golden signals**: Visualizing the following metrics will be beneficial for most systems:
  - **Latency**: P50, P90 and P99 response times
  - **Traffic**: Requests/sec (or requests/min) and concurrent users
  - **Errors**: 4xx/5xx rates and failure percentage
  - **Saturation**: CPU, memory, disk, and network usage
- **Incident metrics**: The following incident metrics are generally visualized for most systems:
  - MTTR and MTTD trends
  - Alert volume over time

Role of alerting in SRE

Alerting is the mechanism that converts observable metric deviations into time-actionable notifications. Effective alerting ensures that incidents are detected early, ideally before customers report them. Let us look at some of the principles of alerting that add value to the alerts being generated, as follows:

- **Relevance**: alerts should only be triggered when immediate action is required.
- **Signal-to-noise ratio**: Minimize false positives to prevent alert fatigue. Best practice is the focus on burn rate (SLO or error budget) rather than instantaneous breaches to avoid noisy alerts for transient blips.
- **Actionability**: Every alert should clearly state the issue and possible next steps or runbook to execute to mitigate the alert. If no human action is required, it should not be an alert.
- **Prioritization**: Critical alerts, which may impact the SLA, should be handled first, while informational alerts can be routed to logs or chat/notification channels.

Integrating visualizing and alerting

Visualizing and alerting are two sides of the same coin. Visualizations provide context for alerts, helping engineers quickly understand the situation. Alerting ensures that deviations shown in visualizations are acted upon immediately. Let us look at an example workflow:

- Alert is triggered for SLO burn rate that has exceeded 2x the normal threshold.
- When the engineer checks the dashboard, he is able to see that there is a sharp rise in latency and errors.
- The engineer rolls back the recent deployment to mitigate the issue immediately.
- Later during the postmortem, engineers can look at the trend graphs to identify what caused the bottleneck.

Tools for visualizing and alerting are as follows:

- Prometheus and Grafana can be used for metric collection, querying, and visualization.
- Dynatrace, New Relic, or a similar **application performance monitoring** (**APM**) tool can be used for full-stack monitoring with integrated alerting.
- Google Cloud Monitoring or AWS CloudWatch can be used for cloud-native observability.
- Pagerduty or Opsgenie can be used for incident management and on-call routing.

Best practice is to link these tools so that alerts are linked directly to the relevant dashboards, allowing rapid diagnosis.

Common pitfalls to avoid are as follows:

- **Alert fatigue**: Over-alerting can lead to alert fatigue and ignored notifications. The solution to over-alerting is to implement alert snoozing and deduplication of alerts. However, the team needs to be careful not to get into under-alerting, where critical incidents can be missed entirely.

- **Dashboard overload**: Too many dashboards can cause confusion and delays while mitigating an incident or finding the root cause of the incident. The recommended solution in this case is to follow the one service = one dashboard rule.
- **False positives**: Repeated alerts or alerts sent immediately during an instantaneous spike can lead to false positives and alert fatigue. The solution in such a scenario is to have a sustained breach of a certain duration (five minutes, for example) before alerting.
- **Static thresholds**: Rigid thresholds may miss anomalies and create noise. The recommendation is to use dynamic thresholds wherever possible.
- **No visualization context**: Alerts that are not accompanied by a visualization link will slow down diagnosis. Always add the relevant visualization link to the alert.

Summary

In SRE, visibility drives reliability. Metrics like SLIs, SLOs, SLAs, four golden signals, and other critical metrics are the backbone of observability, but without effective visualization, they are just numbers, and without actionable alerting, they cannot prevent outages.

Effective alerting and visualization can help in faster detection (lower MTTD), quicker resolution (lower MTTR), better incident communication, error budget management, and continuous improvement, which will eventually help the team and the organization in gaining customer trust and improving the business.

Conclusion

In this chapter, we understood the role of metrics in the SRE practice and how they serve as the foundation for building and maintaining reliable systems. We understood the four golden signals (latency, traffic, errors, and saturation) and then saw the key SRE metrics (SLI, SLO, SLA, and error budget) and understood their importance in balancing competing priorities of reliability with innovation. These metrics not only quantify user experience but also guide engineering decisions and business commitments. We also went over some other critical SRE metrics (like MTTD, MTTR, CFR, etc.), which help in further enhancing the understanding of system reliability to the business and customers. In the end, we understood the importance of visualizing and alerting on these metrics to ensure teams can act quickly, reduce downtime and maintain user trust.

In the next chapter, we will explore observability and monitoring and understand how to use them. We will also look at some tools that help in observability and monitoring.

CHAPTER 3
Monitoring and Observability

Introduction

Effective monitoring and observability are critical for maintaining reliable systems. This chapter explores the constituents of observability, namely, metrics, logs, and traces. We will look at how these three constituents work together to provide insights into system behavior. We will learn how to analyze metrics to detect anomalies and **service level objective** (**SLO**) risk, structure logs for efficient debugging, and leverage distributed tracing to track requests across microservices. This chapter will also go into alerting strategies, emphasizing actionable alerts and reducing false positives through proper threshold tuning and anomaly detection. We will look at best practices for building observability into systems from the ground up, including instrumentation, correlation of telemetry data and choosing the right tools. In effect, this chapter will help us understand how to build a robust observability framework that not only detects issues early but also provides enough data points to help resolve these issues faster, thus reducing **mean time to recover** (**MTTR**) and minimizing downtime.

Structure

The chapter covers the following topics:

- Overview of monitoring and observability
- Understanding metrics, logs and traces
- Implementing effective alerts
- Building observability into systems
- Observability tools like Prometheus, Grafana, Dynatrace
- Alert triage flowchart

Objectives

By the end of this chapter, we will understand how to implement monitoring and observability in our systems and how to tune them to produce actionable alerts. We will also touch upon some tools and look at the alert triage flowchart. This will help implement effective monitoring and observability in production systems.

Overview of monitoring and observability

Monitoring and observability are often used interchangeably; however, they represent different concepts. Traditional monitoring practices have helped engineers detect when something is wrong. However, in today's technical landscape, where environments are highly distributed, monitoring alone is no longer sufficient.

This is where observability comes in. While monitoring focuses on tracking predefined conditions, observability provides the ability to explore system behavior and answer new, unforeseen questions. Together, they form the foundation of resilient, scalable, and reliable system operations.

Monitoring

Monitoring is what we do when we already know what questions we want to ask. It is about watching known failure modes and predefined metrics. Monitoring is defined as the act of collecting, aggregating, and analyzing data to understand the known unknowns of a system. It is largely about measurement and alerting.

Monitoring is based on predefined metrics. That is, metrics are chosen beforehand, such as CPU usage, latency, and error rate. Alerts are triggered when these metrics cross a predefined threshold. In such scenarios, monitoring often tells us something is wrong only after it happens. It is not proactive.

Observability

Observability is what we use to explore and understand a system when we do not already know what questions to ask. Observability is defined as the ability to understand the internal state of a system based on its outputs. Unlike monitoring, which looks for specific signals, observability enables engineers to ask *open-ended questions*.

Observability is exploratory in nature. It enables the team to answer unanticipated questions about system behavior. It is driven by signals built on its three pillars: metrics, logs and traces. Unlike monitoring, observability is proactive in nature. It enables debugging, root cause analysis and performance optimization. Observability helps in understanding complex distributed interactions.

Observability over monitoring

Observability does not replace monitoring; it subsumes it. If monitoring is having a dashboard of dials, observability is having a complete, searchable telemetry data set and the tools to explore it.

Let us understand this with an example of a system built using the microservices architecture.

A user reports that the app is running really slowly when he is checking the order history, as follows:

- Monitoring approach might be to check the predefined dashboard, such as CPU, memory, and database latency. If CPU is fine, memory usage is normal, and database latency is also normal, then the issue might be incorrectly dismissed due to a lack of supporting evidence.
- Whereas using the observability approach, the SRE would use its three pillars (metrics, logs and traces) to conduct an in depth analysis of the orders service. We will go in depth into these three pillars later in this chapter; however, for the sake of understanding this example, let us look at what happens in this scenario:
    - **Metrics**: We see a slight overall latency increase in the orders service.
    - **Traces**: We query traces for all requests for the `GetOrderHistory` endpoint for the last 5-10 minutes. And we may see every slow trace is stuck at another service (say `UserPreferences` service).
    - **Logs**: Now that we have identified the service (`UserPreferences` in this case). We can query the logs of the affected service and see the actual error or warning in the logs. It could be a cache miss, leading to query execution at the database level, which is slow and hence causing the issue.

We did not have a monitoring setup for the `UserPreferences` service in this scenario. However, using observability, we were still able to debug the issue and identify the root cause.

Let us look at the differences between monitoring and observability across different aspects for better understanding:

Aspect	Monitoring	Observability
Purpose	Detect problems	Understand problems
Nature	Reactive	Proactive
Scope	Expected failures	Unexpected behavior
Data used	Predefined metrics, logs	Metrics, logs and traces combined
Core question	Is the system broken?	Why is the system broken?
Complexity fit	Works well for simple systems	Essential for complex, distributed systems.

***Table 3.1**: Monitoring and observability key differences*

Monitoring and observability are complementary. Monitoring is the first line of defense that detects degradation. Observability is the second line of defense that enables fast diagnosis and resolution.

Understanding metrics, logs and traces

Observability is built on the foundation of data (also called the **three pillars**). These three complementary telemetry signals, when combined, give a complete picture of a system's health. The three fundamental sources of observability data are:

- Metrics or numerical indicators of system behavior over time.
- Logs or records of discrete events in the system.
- Traces, or end-to-end records of requests as they move across distributed systems.

Together, these are also referred to as the three pillars of observability, which play a critical role in detecting, diagnosing and resolving issues.

Metrics

Metrics are numerical measurements that represent the status of a system at a specific point in time or aggregated over time. They are captured or scraped at regular intervals and stored as time-series data (a stream of timestamped values). They are lightweight, fast to query and ideal for dashboards and alerting.

Analogy of a car's dashboard

The speedometer, tachometer and fuel gauges in our cars are all metrics. They give us continuous numerical readouts of our car's vital signs.

Characteristics of metrics are as follows:

- **Structure of metrics**: Metrics generally have a name, a value, a timestamp, and an optional label.
- **Metrics have low volume**: A single metric data point is just a few bytes, even at high frequency.
- **Metrics are incredibly cheap to store and process**: It makes them efficient for long-term trend analysis and real-time alerting.
- **Metrics can tell us that something is wrong:** There is a lack of context, as they can rarely tell us why.

Types of metrics are as follows:

- **Counters**: Values that only increase (e.g., no of HTTP requests received).
- **Gauges**: Values that can go up and down (e.g., CPU or memory utilization).

- **Histograms**: Distribution of values over time (e.g., request latencies).
- **Summaries**: Client-side calculated quantiles over a time window (e.g., request latency quantiles).

Instead of getting lost in numerous metrics, it is important to focus on the metrics that are related to the four golden signals:

- Latency, for example, `http_request_duration_seconds` (histogram)
- Traffic, for example, `http_requests_total`
- Errors, for example, `http_request_total{status=~"5.."}`
- Saturation, for example, `node_cpu_seconds_total`

Metrics can be used to track performance, plan capacity and forecast when to scale resources and also for SLO measurement. Let us look at an example and tools that help us in the same:

- **Example**: On an e-commerce website, checkout latency is the metric being tracked. And the 99th percentile checkout latency is 250ms. If this increases to 2000ms, monitoring tools can alert the SRE immediately.
- **Tools**: Prometheus is the most essential tool. It can scrape metrics from our services, store them efficiently, and allow us to query them using Grafana to create dashboards and alerts. Other tools are CloudWatch, Datadog and New Relic.

Logs

Logs are immutable, timestamped records of discrete events that happened within a service or application. They capture granular details of what happened within a system. Unlike metrics, which are numerical, logs are typically textual or structured data.

Analogy of a ship's logbook or journal

On a ship, the captain records every significant event in the ship's logbook. Example *12:05: Departed port. 12:47: Spotted iceberg. 13:15: Changed course to avoid iceberg*. Each entry is a standalone fact with a timestamp and description.

Characteristics of logs are as follows:

- **Structure of logs**: They are often emitted as unstructured text, but best practice is to emit structured logs, for example, JSON.
- **Logs are high in volume**: A busy application can generate gigabytes of logs in an hour.
- **Logs provide rich and detailed context**: They are the best source for the *who, what* and *where* of a specific event.
- **Logs are expensive**: To store, and building infrastructure to index and search them at scale can be difficult.

Types of logs are as follows:

- **System logs**: That log events at the **operating system** (**OS**) level (e.g., system errors or kernel logs).
- **Application logs**: Which logs messages from the application code (e.g., exceptions or errors).
- **Audit logs**: Which logs security and compliance related data (e.g., user access and activity logs).
- **Access logs**: Records of HTTP requests and **application programming interface** (**API**) calls (e.g., web server logs).

Best practice for logging

Instead of logging every piece of information, focus on logging those events that can be used for debugging or auditing:

- Errors and warnings (with full-stack traces).
- Key business events (like user login, order placed).
- State changes (log cache flush or loading of configuration).
- Always include relevant identifiers (like `user_id`, `request_id` or `order_id`) to help connect logs.

Logs are used for debugging and tracing step-by-step what went wrong. It is also used for detecting unauthorized access or malicious activity. Logs also act as data for compliance, as they store records for regulatory audits. See the following example and related tools for logging:

- **Example**: A log entry for an e-commerce application can capture:

  ```
  2025-08-21T16:45:15Z ERROR user_id=12345 payment failed order_id=98765 trace_id=2025082116451512345
  ```

  In this example, if we search for the `trace_id` or `order_id` in the payment gateway logs, we can get the reason on why the payment failed.

- **Tools**: **Elasticsearch, Logstash, Kibana** (**ELK**) stack or Grafana Loki as some of the tools that are used to store and search logs. Splunk is another tool that is widely used for storing and searching logs.

Traces

A trace (or distributed trace) represents the end-to-end journey of a single user request as it flows through multiple services in a distributed system. They show how much time was spent in each segment of the path, helping to identify bottlenecks.

Each trace is made up of spans. A span refers to a single operation within a trace. Each span has a start time, duration and metadata. Together, all spans form the complete timeline of the request.

Analogy of package tracking number

When we order a package, we get a single tracking number (tracking number which is the **`trace_id`**). We can use it to see the entire journey of the package - *Left warehouse, Arrived at hub, Out for delivery*. Here, each step is a span. The tracking number connects all these discrete events into a single, coherent narrative.

Characteristics of traces are as follows:

- **Structure of trace**: Trace is a hierarchy of spans, all linked by the shared **`trace_id`**.
- **Traces are medium in volume**: It is too expensive to trace 100% of the requests. Hence, we sample them (e.g., trace 1 request in 1000 or trace all requests that are slow).
- **Traces connect the dots**: Traces show you how work propagates through our system, making them unparalleled for identifying performance bottlenecks and understanding dependency failures.
- **Traces integration**: Traces require us to modify our system and code to generate and propagate the **`trace_id`** across multiple services.

Best practice for tracking:

- Ideally, it is recommended to trace the entire lifecycle of any user request, especially those that are slow or failing.
- It is recommended to generate a **`trace_id`** with the user request and propagate the same across multiple API or microservice calls so that the **`trace_id`** is able to create the complete path of the user request.

Traces are primarily used for performance analysis and dependency mapping. It can be used to identify where latency was introduced and visualize the complete path of service-to-service calls. During root cause analysis of an incident, traces can be used to find which component caused the error. See the following example and tool for tracing:

- **Example**: Suppose we are tracing the request form a user accessing an on-demand video service. The trace of the *play movie* request in this scenario shows the following:
    - **API gateway**: 10ms
    - **Authentication service**: 20ms
    - **Catalog service**: 50ms
    - **Recommendation engine**: 500ms

  In this situation, we can see that there is an unexpected latency in the recommendation engine causing the slowness to the user.
- **Tools**: Jaeger or Zipkin are dedicated tracing systems that visualize the flow of requests, making bottlenecks instantly visible.

Metrics, logs and traces working together

The real power of observability is unleashed when we use these three pillars together. Let us look at a real-world example of an online food delivery app:

- **Metrics**: Alert is raised when order placement latency exceeds 2 seconds.
- **Logs**: Show repeated database connection errors from the order service.
- **Traces**: In this scenario, traces can reveal that the database interaction has a bottleneck in the payment service, which is causing the increased latency.

Without one of these signals, the investigation would be incomplete:

- Metrics alone would only show the latency spike.
- Logs alone might show database errors, but without understanding their impact on users.
- Traces alone would highlight slowness but not reveal the specific SQL errors.

By combining all three, SRE can quickly resolve incidents and improve reliability.

Best practices

Let us look at some of the best practices of implementing metrics, logs and traces:

- **Architect early**: It is important to build metrics, logs, and traces into our system design, not as an afterthought.
- **Use structured logs**: Like JSON or key-value logs which are easier to parse and analyze.
- **Adopt a common standard:** E.g., OpenTelemetry helps unify data collection across all three signals.
- **Correlate signals**: Ensure metrics, logs, and traces can be tied together using unique request IDs.
- **Avoid noise**: It is important to collect the right amount of data. Storing too much data will be expensive and cause storage and analysis overhead.

Implementing effective alerts

In modern operations, alerts on monitored systems are the actionable signals that bring attention to critical issues. However, a bad alerting strategy can lead to the burnout of an on-call engineer. A 3 am alert that turns out to be a trivial, non-urgent issue is highly disruptive for the on-call engineer. This would eventually lead to alert fatigue. Alert fatigue is defined as a condition where people start to ignore alert pages because they assume that it is just another false alarm or something unimportant. This can be incredibly dangerous.

Effective alerting is not about catching every possible thing that could go wrong. It ensures that engineers are notified only when human intervention is required and that the on-call engineer has the right context to take action quickly.

We will look at a simple, actionable framework for writing alerts that are worthy of waking someone up.

Golden rule of alerting

The single most important rule of alerting is to alert on symptoms and not on causes. Let us understand this with an example:

- **Alert on a cause**: Page if CPU > 90% for 5 minutes.

  High CPU is a cause; however, it may not be impacting users at all. Our service might be efficiently processing a large queue resulting in the CPU spike. However, the end users may not be impacted. So, by alerting for this cause, we are paging the on-call engineer to investigate an internal system state and not to fix a user problem.

- **Alert on a symptom**: Page if 99th percentile latency for the payment service is > 2 seconds for 5 minutes.

  High latency is a symptom that the users are experiencing a problem and are directly impacted. In this situation, the alert is not related to the internal system states (high CPU, high memory usage or slow database). Since this alert indicates that users are impacted it requires immediate human intervention.

  Ideally, an alert should be triggered only when it is based on the four golden signals discussed in the previous chapters, which represent user symptoms.

Effective alerting principles

Effective alerting principles are critical because they ensure that alerts drive timely and meaningful action while reducing noise and fatigue. Well-designed alerts help teams quickly identify real issues, understand their impact, and respond efficiently, reducing downtime and customer impact. Clear thresholds, actionable context, and alignment with business objectives ensure alerts reflect what truly matters. Let us look at some of the principles and implementation strategies that will make our alerts highly effective.

Alerts should be designed to be actionable

Alerts should require human intervention. If an alert does not require human intervention, it should not exist.

Example: **`alert: Disk usage > 95% and automatic volume expansion failed.`**

Here, if an alert is triggered only for disk usage exceeding a threshold, it may not need human intervention. However, if the alert states that after exceeding the threshold, auto-scale did not happen, it needs human intervention, which is actionable.

Alerts should be tied to SLO

When alerts are tied to the **service level indicator** (SLI) and SLO, they are aligned with the user experience. Hence, they suggest user experience rather than infrastructural noise.

Example: `alert: 99th percentile latency > 1 Second for 5 minutes`

In this example, the alert is triggered because the users have been experiencing a latency which is impacting the SLO. The alert would need an engineer to dig into the system and figure out the cause for the increase in latency so that the SLO and hence the SLA is not breached.

Minimize noise while alerting

Alerts need to be tuned so that it is not triggered for every spike. Alerts should only be triggered when there is sustained breach for a certain duration. Historical data should be considered while tweaking the alerts to reduce unwanted noise.

Prioritize alerts based on severity

All alerts should not be treated equally. It is better to classify them into different priorities (e.g., P1, P2, P3), as shown in the following table:

Alert priority	Severity level	Example	Trigger via	Expected response time
P1	Critical	Home page is down for everyone	PagerDuty, Opsgenie, SMS, call	Immediate
P2	High	Disk space on logs > 90%	Jira, email	Hours
P3	Medium	Some requests are failing due to malformed input	Dashboard, emails	Days
P4	Low	A certain less used report is throwing multiple errors while being generated	Dashboard, emails	Weeks

Table 3.2: Alert priorities with examples and response times

Here are some strategies that can be followed to implement severity while alerting:

- Configure our alerting tool (like Grafana) to have different notification channels for each severity level.
- Our alert rules should have severity labels.
- Finally, we need to route our alerts based on these labels to the correct alert channel.

This will ensure that only P1 or critical alerts are paged to the on-call engineers.

Alerts should contain the context and next actionable

When an on-call engineer receives an alert, he should be equipped by the alert to answer the following questions:

- What is broken?
- Why does it matter or the impact?
- What should I do next?

To provide answers to these questions, the alert should have the following structure:

- **Summary**: A quick one-liner stating what is wrong. This can be paged as an SMS message so the on-call engineer knows that there is a user impacting problem.
- **Description**: The description can have more details on what is happening and the related impact. This can be shared as an email message.
- **Dashboard URL**: A direct link to the relevant dashboard of the failing service should be shared with the alert. This will help navigate the on-call engineer to the relevant dashboard saving precious minutes.
- **Runbook URL**: A runbook is a pre-written guide for diagnosing and fixing this specific alert. The runbook will act as a guide helping the on-call engineer figure out how to verify the alert and indicate which steps should be taken to triage the issue. It will also recommend guidelines to escalate the issue depending on the impact and the time to resolution.

Following this, the alert will have enough information so that the on-call engineer can provide a quick resolution of the issue.

Avoid alert duplication

Another important principle is to avoid duplicate alerts. The idea is to consolidate multiple alerts into a single notification if they are related.

E.g., if a service has 10 instances, instead of sending 10 alerts for each instance, consolidate the 10 alerts into a single alert at the service level.

Proper alert routing

Instead of sending all alerts to everyone, route alerts to the right team and service owners. This minimizes response delays and confusion during incidents while reducing alerting noise and avoiding alert fatigue. When alerts are accurately routed based on service ownership, severity, and expertise, teams can respond more effectively and resolve issues faster. Poor routing can often lead to unnecessary escalations, missed alerts, or prolonged outages, as responders may lack the context or authority to act. Thus, proper alert routing improves operational efficiency, accountability, and overall system reliability.

Implement automation and self-healing

If an issue can be remediated without human intervention, it is recommended to write a script (for example) to implement automation. So, when the alert is triggered, the script is invoked and the issue resolves automatically.

Example: Restart HTTP server if latency > 500ms for 5 minutes.

The idea here is to have the most common resolution automatically executed instead of having the engineer execute it manually. However, even after execution, if the resolution does not work and the monitoring system sees the same issue again, the alert needs to be redirected to the on-call engineer for proper resolution.

Test and audit alerts regularly

In order to see if the alerts are effective, we can simulate failures and ensure that the alerts are triggered at the right time. As a part of alert audit, it is recommended to review the historical incidents and threshold breaches and refine the threshold to reduce noise and make the alert even more effective.

Types of alerts

Types of alerts are as follows:

- **Threshold based alerts**: These alerts are triggered when a metric crosses a set value.

  Example: CPU > 90% for 5 minutes.

- **Rate of change alerts**: These alerts are triggered when metrics change abnormally fast.

  Example: Error rate increased by 40% in last 5 minutes.

- **Anomaly detection alerts**: These alerts are triggered based on statistical models that detect unusual patterns.

  Example: Request traffic is 50% below the average baseline during peak hours.

- **Composite alerts**: Combining multiple alerts can give us a composite alert that will have better context. Composite alerts reduce noise but at the risk of partial failures, so they need to be designed carefully.

  Example: Latency > 500ms and error rate > 5% for the last 5 minutes.

Alert hygiene checklist

Here is a checklist that can be used to ensure effective alerting:

- Is it a symptom?
- Is it actionable?
- Does it specify the impact?
- Does it remove unwanted noise?
- Is it routed correctly?
- Does it have a runbook?

Effective alerting is not about creating more alerts. It is about creating the right alerts. When executed well, effective alerting will transform monitoring from a noisy warning system to a reliable early detection and response mechanism. It is important to review the alerts regularly. If an alert fires when it should not have, we need to fix it. If an alert is not actionable, we need to delete it. This continuous refinement will ultimately improve the system's reliability and user trust.

Building observability into systems

In modern systems that are complex and distributed, observability should be designed in from the start, not added later. Instead of bolting on monitoring later, observability needs to be engineered into the system from the start. Observability becomes a first-class concern and an integral part of the **software development lifecycle** (**SDLC**). This section provides a practical guide to achieving this.

Shift left observability

The core principle of building observability into systems is to shift left, that is, to integrate observability practices early in the design and development phases and not just in production.

Reactive monitoring is no longer enough. In modern systems, problems can emerge in ways the teams did not anticipate. Without observability, blind spots emerge and the team can run into unexpected failure modes that can be impossible to debug. Engineers can spend hours searching logs or correlating metrics if observability fails, which will lead to slow resolution of issues. This will eventually affect the end users who would experience extended outages as root causes are difficult to find.

By embedding observability into the systems, engineers and architects ensure that when problems occur, the system is capable of explaining itself.

Designing for observability

While metrics, logs and traces are the three pillars of observability, building them effectively into the system requires a standardized approach. Designing for observability ensures that systems are built with transparency, diagnosability, and reliability from the outset. By embedding metrics, logs, and traces directly into system architecture, teams gain deep visibility into system behavior and performance. This proactive approach enables faster root cause analysis, reduces MTTR, and minimizes operational blind spots. Observability-driven design also supports scalability and resilience, allowing systems to adapt to changing workloads and complexities. Ultimately, designing for observability supports informed decision-making, improves system reliability, developer productivity and overall user experience.

Prioritize instrumentation

Instrumentation logic that generates metrics, logs and traces should be built into the system from the start and not as an afterthought. Best practices for instrumentation are:

- Adopting frameworks like OpenTelemetry for standardizing instrumentation.
- Exposing internal state quantitatively as metrics (like queue depth, retry count, throughput, error count).
- Capture meaningful events in logs (not just errors).

Structured logging

Plain text logs may be easier for humans to read; however, they are hard for machines to parse, making it difficult to search. Instead, follow the following best practices for building structured logging into the system:

- Use structured formats (like JSON).
- Include fields that help provide context and tracing like **`timestamp`**, **`service_name`**, **`request_id`**, **`user_id`**, **`severity_level`**.
- Ensure a consistent schema of logs across all systems.
- Tools like the log4j2 library for Java, Winston library for Node.js, and structlog library for Python emit structured JSON, which can be easily indexed via Elasticsearch and used for searching logs efficiently.

Distributed tracing by default

Every request must carry a unique **`trace_id`** that is passed across services. This enables correlation between different services. Without proper propagation of the **`trace_id`** across all services, APIs, queues and microservices, the trace will break and debugging will become difficult.

To achieve this, we need to instrument services to accept and forward standard headers (like **`traceparent`**). Most frameworks like Spring and Express handle this automatically.

Standard dashboards

Dashboards should not be just reactive tools for the operations team, but should share data for visibility across platforms for all teams (engineering, SRE, product).

Dashboards should also provide service owners with self-service observability.

Implementation strategies and best practices

Implementation strategies and best practices are as follows:

- **Define SLOs**: A SLO is a formal quantitative goal for a service's reliability. Without SLOs, we lack a clear prioritization for what matters most to users. The following is the process for identifying and quantifying SLOs:
    1. Identify key user journeys such as actions which are most critical for the user.
    2. Define SLIs or the metrics that measure the journey (e.g., latency of the `/payment` endpoint).
    3. Set SLOs for the defined SLIs (e.g., 99% of the `/payment` requests should complete in 250ms).

When SLOs are properly defined, they provide a precise business alerting threshold and tell us when to alert, eliminating noise and focusing on what truly matters to the users:

- **Standardize and automate instrumentation**: The way to standardize instrumentation is to create shared libraries by developing client libraries that wrap standard libraries like OpenTelemetry or Prometheus clients. These shared libraries should handle:
    - Common ETags (like `service.name`, `service.version` or `env`).
    - Automatic tracing context propagation.
    - Standard metric collection (like `http_server_request` duration).
    - Structured logging configuration.

  The way to automate instrumentation is to use code annotations and templates. For example, in Java, we can use annotations like `@Timed` and `@Counted` so that every new service comes pre-wired with observability.

- **Design for production**: Here are some of the design practices that will help during debugging with observability:
    - **Health endpoints**: Every service must have a `/health` endpoint that reports its status (like up or down) and can check downstream dependencies (like database or cache). This is crucial for load balancers and orchestration tools like Kubernetes.
    - **Feature flags**: Build in the ability to toggle features on/off without a deploy. Feature flags enable controlled rollout and help measure feature impact through telemetry.
    - **Debug endpoints**: Each service should have debug endpoints (internal-only) that can be used to dump internal state (like cache content or thread dump) for deep debugging.

- **Correlate**: The true power of observability is unlocked only when the three pillars (metrics, logs and traces) are able to correlate well. Ensure that every log entry or metric sample can be linked back to a specific trace.
- **Feedback loops**: After every incident, it is important to have a check on how observability helped in debugging the incident as a part of the root cause analysis process. If there is a gap in observability, we need to add the missing metrics, logs, and traces to help us debug issues quickly. Such gaps should be taken up as technical debt and prioritized.

Checklist for a new service

Here is the checklist for building observability into a microservice before deploying it into production:

Area	Checklist item
Logging	• Logs are emitted as structured JSON • Includes `trace_id`, `service_name` and other context • Log levels are used appropriately (DEBUG, INFO, ERROR)
Metrics	• `/metrics` endpoint is exposed • Key business and operational metrics are well-defined • http request duration and error metrics are collected
Tracing	• `trace_id` propagates and creates trace context • spans are created for key operations (e.g., database queries)
Health	• `/health` endpoint reports service status and downstream health
Documentation	Service SLO and key dashboards are documented and easily accessible

Table 3.3: Checklist for creating a new service with observability

Use case

Let us look at a use case to understand how built-in observability helps solve an issue.

Scenario: A social media app's newsfeed service begins experiencing intermittent latency spikes. Alerts are firing, but the cause is unclear.

Steps to identify and resolve using observability are:

1. **Alert**: On-call engineer gets a page, `Newsfeed P99 latency > 2 seconds for 5 minutes`. The alert includes links to the dashboards and the sample `trace_id`.
2. **Dashboard**: The engineer clicks the link to the pre-built Grafana dashboard for the newsfeed service. He sees a correlation: latency spikes coincide with a massive spike in cache miss rate (`redis.cache_misses`) and a rise in database CPU.

3. **Trace**: The engineer clicks on a high-latency trace from the sample. The trace visualization shows that the `getUserFeed` call is spending over 1.9 seconds in the `cache.get` span.
4. **Logs**: The engineer queries the logging system for a particular `trace_id` of the slow trace. The application log shows: `"message": "Cache key generation collision for key: feed_user_*", "level": "WARN"`. The engineer can get the code block of the file where this is happening from the logs.
5. **Root cause**: On checking the recent deployment and looking at the diff of the code for that particular file (identified via logs), the engineer can see that the recent deployment introduced a bug where a wildcard (*) was incorrectly added to a cache key, causing a cascade of cache misses for all users and overloading the database.
6. **Fix**: Once the bug is identified, the deployment is rolled back and the issue is fixed.

The entire triage process took less than 10 minutes because the signals were built-in, correlated, and easily accessible.

Building observability is not about adding more tools; it is about cultivating an engineering culture that values transparency and data-driven debugging. By investing in these practices early, we can build systems that are not only more observable but also more resilient and easier to maintain throughout their lifecycle.

Observability tools like Prometheus, Grafana and Dynatrace

Choosing the right tool for the right job is essential. Modern systems generate massive amounts of data, and organizations need powerful platforms to capture, analyze, and visualize it in real-time. This ecosystem often leans towards a combination of open-source powerhouse tools like Prometheus and Grafana, complemented by commercial, AI-powered solutions like Dynatrace for deep application insights. We will go over a practical guide on these tools in this section.

Prometheus for metrics collection and alerting

Prometheus is an open-source pull-based metrics collection and alerting toolkit. It is designed for reliability, scraping metrics from configured targets at given intervals, storing them efficiently, and allowing us to query them.

Key features are as follows:

- Prometheus is a pull-based metric collection tool that scrapes targets via HTTP endpoints (usually `/metrics`).

- The metrics are stored with labels in a time-series database for efficient querying.
- Prometheus has a powerful query language called PromQL for analyzing metrics.
- Prometheus integrates with Alertmanager, which routes alerts to Slack, email, or PagerDuty, etc.

Instrumentation is as follows:

- Each service exposes metrics in a standard format. Client libraries are integrated into the application code to expose internal metrics.
- For third-party systems like a database (e.g., *MySQL Exporter*) or hardware (e.g., *Node Exporter*), we run an exporter (like sidecar deployment pattern) that translates system metrics into Prometheus-readable format.
- Prometheus scrapes metrics at defined intervals and stores them as time-series data with dimensions or labels.
    - We define a **`prometheus.yml`** (configuration file) that specifies:
        - **Scrape_interval**: How often to scrape targets.
        - **Scrape_configs**: Source of our metrics (list of endpoints).
- PromQL is later used to query for dashboards and alerts.
- We define alerting in a separate file. When a PromQL expression evaluates to true, it triggers an alert and sends it to the alert manager. The alert manager then handles deduplication of alerts, silencing, and routing of alerts to the correct channels, like Slack or PagerDuty.

Strengths and limitations

Prometheus is strong at metrics and alerting. It is open-source and widely integrated with Kubernetes.

However, it lacks long-term storage and needs external storage solutions. Also, logs and traces must be handled by an external system as Prometheus lacks the capability to handle them.

Grafana for visualization and dashboards

Grafana is an open-source platform for analytics and monitoring visualization that plays a critical role in the modern observability stack. It connects seamlessly to multiple data sources (like Prometheus, Elasticsearch, Loki, etc.) and allows us to create dashboards composed of rich panels including graphs, gauges, tables, heatmaps and logs. With features like templating, alerting, and **role-based access control** (**RBAC**), teams can tailor dashboards to specific services and audiences. By transforming raw metrics into meaningful insights, Grafana helps teams monitor system health, analyze trends, and respond to incidents more effectively.

Key features are as follows:

- Grafana is a data source agnostic. It can connect to any data source, such as Prometheus, Elasticsearch, InfluxDB, or more.
- Grafana supports custom dashboards via drag-and-drop visualizations.
- Grafana can also trigger alerts based on visualized metrics.
- Grafana has dynamic dashboard templates that easily adapt to different services or clusters.

Instrumentation is as follows:

1. The first step is to point Grafana to our Prometheus server's URL. It can also connect to Loki (for logs), Tempo (for traces), Elasticsearch, databases, and even Dynatrace.
2. Dashboards are built using a set of panels. Each panel is a visualization that queries a data source. We can use the same PromQL queries (developed in Prometheus) to power our graphs.
3. For building effective dashboards, we need to follow the following rules:
    a. Each dashboard should answer a single specific question.
    b. Dashboards should follow the top-to-bottom design.
        i. **Top**: Should be high-level business SLOs like **`checkout_success_rate`**.
        ii. **Middle**: Can be key application metrics like **`request_rate`**, **`error_rate`** or **`latency`**.
        iii. **Bottom**: Should consist of the underlying infrastructure metrics like CPU, memory and network catering to the above services.
    c. We should use drop-down filters like service, pod, or environment (as variables) to make our dashboards dynamic and reusable.
4. Grafana can also evaluate alert rules itself by querying the data sources (like Prometheus) on a defined interval. We can define the alert rules directly in the **user interface** (**UI**), specifying the condition, evaluation interval, and where to send notifications. However, it is recommended to use a single tool for alerting (either Prometheus or Grafana). Using multiple tools can lead to unregulated alerts, causing false positives.

Strengths and limitations

Grafana is able to provide flexible and beautiful visualizations. It can connect to multiple observability tools and provide visualizations in a single view.

On the other hand, Grafana lacks native metric collection and relies on other tools (like Prometheus) for the same. It also needs a thoughtful dashboard design to avoid clutter.

Dynatrace for AI-powered full-stack observability

Dynatrace is a commercial Software Intelligence Platform that uses AI (*Davis AI* engine) to provide automatic and intelligent observability. It is known for its automated discovery, code-level tracing, dependency mapping and deep observability.

Key features are as follows:

- Dynatrace uses its proprietary agent called **OneAgent** to auto-discover applications, services, processes, and dependencies.
- Dynatrace uses its Davis AI engine to detect anomalies, correlate root causes, and reduce false positives.
- Dynatrace provides full-stack coverage, from infrastructure to applications, containers, logs, traces, and user experience as well.
- Dynatrace provides code-level visibility whereby tracing requests can lead down to individual method calls.
- Dynatrace has the capability to connect technical health with business outcomes.
- We need to install its proprietary agent (called **OneAgent**) on our hosts (**virtual machine** (**VM**), Kubernetes nodes, etc.). The OneAgent automatically discovers all processes, containers, and applications running on each host on which it is installed. Also, it automatically instruments them without requiring code changes, collecting metrics, logs, and full distributed traces.
- Dynatrace automatically builds a real-time dependency map called **Smartscape**, which shows how every service, process, and host connects. This is invaluable for impact analysis.
- The Davis AI engine automatically baselines normal behavior for every metric it collects. It can then correlate anomalies across the entire stack to find the root cause of the problem.
- Dynatrace provides deep code insights, whereby it provides code-level details for each transaction, showing which specific database query or method call within the application is the bottleneck.
- Dynatrace is a unified platform. While Prometheus and Grafana need to be configured to work together, Dynatrace provides a single platform for infrastructure monitoring, application performance monitoring, synthetic, and real user monitoring, along with automated root cause and intelligent alerting (also known as **AIOps**).

Strengths and limitations

Dynatrace is an all-in-one observability tool with AI-powered analysis. It requires minimal manual configuration as compared to other open-source tools.

Dynatrace is a commercial tool, and hence its licensing cost can be high. Also, it can be less flexible than most open-source tools.

Alert triage flowchart

Let us look at a detailed alert triage flowchart:

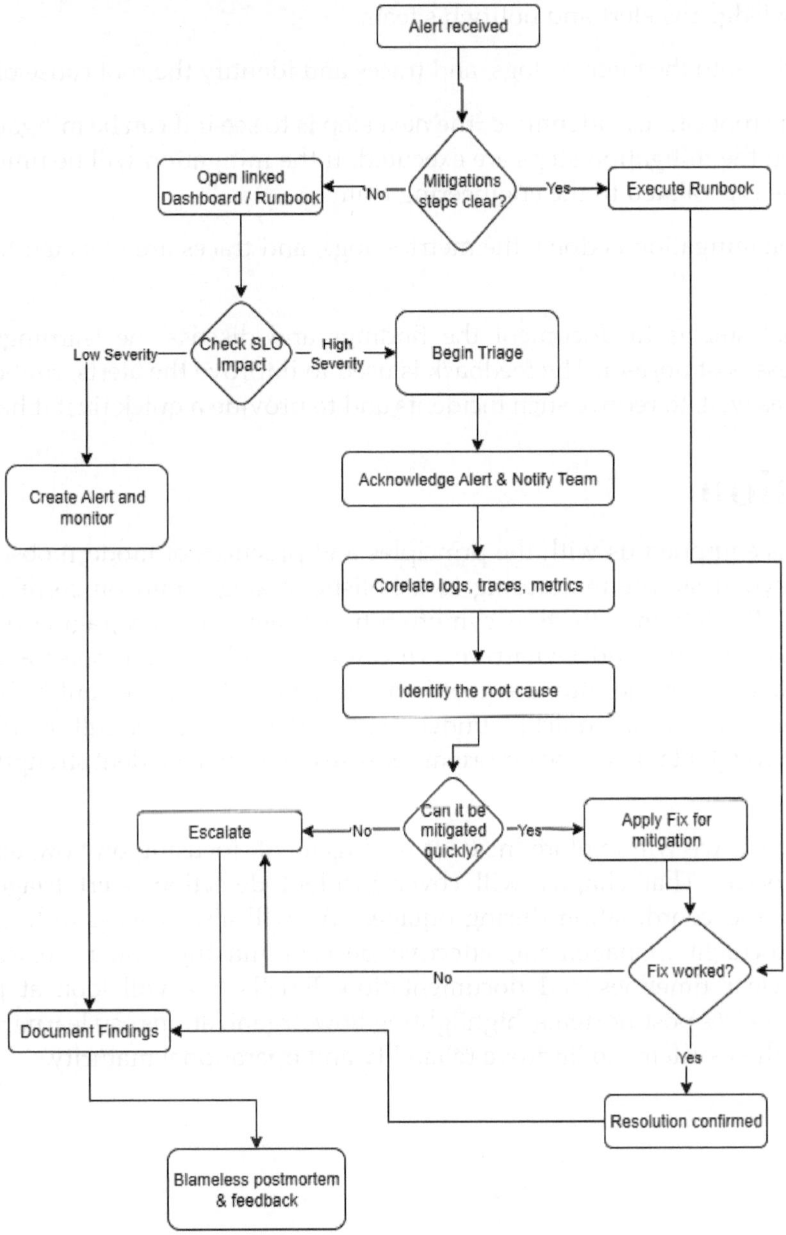

***Figure 3.1:** Alert triage flowchart*

Once the on-call engineer receives the alert, the engineer checks if the alert is understandable and if the mitigation steps are clear. If the mitigation steps are clear, they are executed, and the on-call engineer opens the linked dashboard in the alert. Via the dashboard, the on-call engineer can figure out the impact of the alert on the SLO. If the impact is low, the on-call engineer would create a ticket and monitor it. However, if the impact on the SLO is high, he needs to begin triaging the incident. He would follow the following steps to triage the incident:

1. Acknowledge the alert and notify his team.
2. Dive deep into the metrics, logs, and traces and identify the root cause of the issue.
3. Once the root cause is identified, the next step is to see if it can be mitigated quickly. If yes, then the mitigation steps are executed. If the mitigation will be time-consuming, the issue is escalated to the engineering team.
4. Once the mitigation is done, the metrics, logs, and traces are revisited to confirm the same.
5. The final step is to document the findings and discuss the learnings during the blameless postmortem. The feedback is used to improve the alerts, runbooks, and the system as well, to reduce such incidents and to provide a quick fix if it happens again.

Conclusion

This chapter has equipped us with the principles and practices of modern observability. We have moved beyond simple monitoring to a holistic strategy built on correlating metrics, logs, and traces. By defining effective, symptom-based alerts and leveraging powerful tools like Prometheus, Grafana, and Dynatrace, we can drastically reduce noise and mean time to resolution. Remember, the ultimate goal is not to eliminate failures but to build resilient systems where incidents are quickly understood and resolved. A culture of continuous improvement through blameless postmortems ensures that each incident strengthens systems and processes.

In the next chapter, we will explore incident management, focusing on how teams respond when failures occur. That chapter will cover incident detection, alert triage, escalation, communication and coordination during outages. We will also discuss different roles that participate in incident management, effective decision-making under pressure, and the importance of clear timelines and documentation. Finally, we will look at post-incident reviews and blameless postmortems, highlighting how organizations can learn from incidents and strengthen their systems to improve reliability and operational maturity.

CHAPTER 4
Incident Management

Introduction

The purpose of incident management is not only to effectively respond to incidents in order to reduce downtime, but also to incorporate learnings into the development and operations process to reduce similar incidents in the future. This chapter explores the full spectrum of incident management practices, covering on-call rotations, ensuring teams are prepared to respond promptly and efficiently to any incidents in any environment. We will explore the full spectrum of incident management best practices, including establishing reliable on-call rotations and escalation paths to manage fatigue and ensuring sustainable responsiveness across teams. We will go over the process of **root cause analysis** (**RCA**), emphasizing how to identify and address underlying issues rather than surface-level symptoms. Additionally, the chapter covers the postmortem process, focusing on transparent documentation, extracting actionable insights, and preventing recurrence while following a blameless culture that encourages transparency, accountability, and continuous improvement. By the end of this chapter, we will understand how structured incident response, thoughtful analysis, and a culture of learning can transform operational challenges into opportunities for long-term reliability, improved system design, and stronger team morale and trust.

Structure

The chapter covers the following topics:

- Incident management lifecycle
- Roles and responsibilities
- Metrics and continuous improvement
- On-call practices
- Root cause analysis
- Postmortem and blameless culture

Objectives

Incident management is a critical discipline for maintaining the reliability and availability of any system. It encompasses the processes, tools, and culture required to effectively detect, respond to, resolve, and learn from unexpected disruptions in service. A mature incident management practice minimizes downtime, mitigates impact on users and the business, and transforms failures into opportunities for strengthening the system. This chapter will explore the core components of a robust incident management program, from the initial alert to fostering a culture of continuous improvement.

Incident management lifecycle

The incident management lifecycle describes the journey of an incident from detection to resolution and eventual closure. Each stage has a distinct purpose, ensuring clarity and efficiency in the overall response. The process ensures a consistent and effective response and facilitates learning afterward. Refer to the following figure:

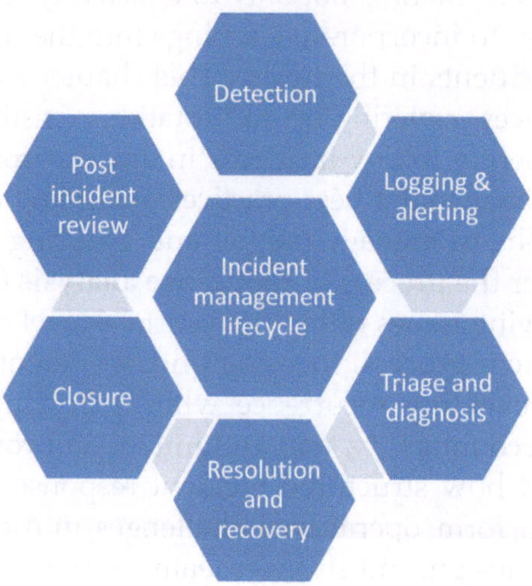

Figure 4.1: *Incident management lifecycle*

Incident detection and reporting

The incident management lifecycle begins when an incident is detected. This can happen through different channels, such as:

- **Automated monitoring**: Alerts from observability and monitoring tools can help in detecting an incident that is user impacting.
- **On-call monitoring**: An on-call engineer can also discover an incident during routine checks or investigations.

- **Reporting by user**: External reports from users via support tickets, social media, or other feedback mechanisms can also help in identifying an incident.

A clear and accessible observability and monitoring system will ensure the timely detection of an incident.

Logging and alerting

Once detected, the incident must be formally logged while also capturing all relevant information regarding the incident, such as:

- Time of detection
- Source of detection
- Symptom and impact of the incident

This incident log is often a dedicated channel or incident tracker and becomes the central source of truth for all incidents. Based on the severity of the incident and the on-call schedule, key personnel are alerted regarding the incident. The incident responders must acknowledge the incident to start the response clock. We have seen earlier that the acknowledgment time is typically tracked as **mean time to acknowledge** (MTTA).

Triage and diagnosis

The incident responders work on understanding the scope and severity of the incident. They work on triaging the incident by identifying its impact. They would determine the severity of the incident (*S1*, *S2*, or *S3*) based on the number of users being affected and whether a core business function is broken or it is a superficial issue.

After triaging the incident, the incident responders work on the diagnosis of the incident by gathering data from observability tools (logs, metrics, and traces). The diagnosis leads to the identification of contributing factors and the potential root cause of the incident. The goal here is to form a hypothesis. Strong collaboration is required across the teams to confirm the scope and root cause of the incident.

Resolution and recovery

Once the diagnosis is clear, the team works on restoring the service as quickly and safely as possible. This involves two steps:

1. **Mitigation**: The first task of the incident responders is to identify if implementing a short-term fix can help in mitigating the issue temporarily (like rolling back a deployment or restarting a service). If possible, steps to mitigate the incident are taken.
2. **Resolution**: It is the second step, which is to apply a permanent, long-term fix that addresses the root cause of the incident. This mostly happens after the incident is formally closed.

Closure

Once the mitigation steps are implemented and the immediate impact is reduced, the incident responders enter the closure state, where they monitor the observability tools, such as dashboards, logs, and alerting systems, for a pre-defined stabilization window (e.g., 30 mins of stable metrics), to confirm whether the service is stable and no residual issues remain. Once stability is confirmed, they report that the mitigation is successful and move the incident to a *closed* state, updating the incident record with the following datapoints:

- Time of resolution, which is the exact time stamp when the system was fully restored by removing the impact on users.
- Final impact assessment, which is the quantitative and qualitative evaluation of the business impact, including affected customers, duration, and severity.
- Actions taken to resolve the issue, which is a step-by-step summary of mitigation and recovery procedures, configuration changes, and patches applied.

These documents ensure that a proper record is maintained, which can be used to improve the system further.

Post-incident review

Once the incident is closed, the focus moves from short-term mitigation to long-term learning and improvement. This is when the teams conduct a post-incident review, which is a structured and collaborative session aimed at understanding the deeper causes, evaluating the response process, and driving systemic enhancements. The engineering team and incident responders collaboratively conduct a blameless postmortem, analyzing both technical and process-related aspects of the incidents to identify long-term improvement areas to the system, which can be picked up in the coming sprints based on the priority and effort needed.

On-call practices

The on-call rotation is the frontline defense of a system's reliability. It is the mechanism through which theoretical incident response plans are tested in reality. However, a poorly managed on-call schedule is a fast track to engineer burnout, high turnover, and a decline in system health as exhausted engineers cut corners. The ultimate goal of on-call is not just to respond to incidents, but to do so in a way that is effective, predictable, and sustainable for the humans involved.

Pre-requisites for a healthy on-call

At its core, on-call is about preparedness and ownership. Preparedness means that engineers are ready to respond to incidents at any time, and ownership means that the teams that build the systems are also responsible for their reliability by creating a feedback loop between designs and operations. On-call is not a firefighting practice. It is a deliberate resilience practice.

Let us look at some of the foundational elements that make on-call inherently sustainable:

- **Alert hygiene**: Every alert that an on-call engineer receives must be:
    - Actionable or should require a human to perform an action. It should not be only informational.
    - Relevant so that the alert indicates a problem impacting a user-facing service or critical dependency.
    - Unique or not a duplicate of another alert, so it represents a different issue.
    - Prioritized so that it has a clear severity level (*S1*, *S2*, etc.) based on the user impact that reflects the required response time.

  Eventually, every alert must prompt an action to fix the problem. If there is no fix needed, then it is better to stop the alert.

- **Comprehensive runbooks and documentation**: An on-call engineer should not be doing fresh debugging when paged. Instead, the engineer should refer to an already available runbook (or playbook) for diagnosing and mitigating common failures. The runbook should have clear steps and generic commands to triage and diagnose problems, and also include standard mitigation procedures. The goal here is to convert complex diagnostic processes into a repeatable, reliable checklist, reducing the **mean time to resolve** (MTTR) of the incident.

- **Effective tooling and access**: On-call engineers must have secure, reliable, and quick access to all necessary systems from anywhere. This includes access to VPN, mobile-friendly alerting and communication apps (like Opsgenie), observability tools for centralized logging, metrics, and tracing dashboards (like Grafana), and deployment and orchestration tools (like Kubernetes). This will help the on-call engineer to take appropriate actions to mitigate the issue without reaching out to different teams for access, and hence reduce the MTTR.

On-call best practices

Let us look at some of the best practices for an effective on-call process:

- **Clear and fair rotations**: The on-call schedules must be designed to ensure balanced rotations across the team and prevent concentration of responsibility on a few individuals. The on-call schedules must be predictable and equitable. Modern on-call tools (e.g., Pagerduty, Opsgenie) can be used to allow flexible rotation schedules like weekly, daily, or a follow-the-sun model.

  Best practice: Teams must publish on-call calendars well in advance and ensure that each engineer has adequate off-call recovery time.

- **Structured escalation paths**: A clear escalation policy ensures that unacknowledged alerts do not go unnoticed, while also protecting the primary on-call from unnecessary interruptions.

  A typical escalation path might have multiple layers, as follows:

  - Primary on-call is the first responder and has a strict SLA to acknowledge an alert.
  - Secondary on-call is the backup for the primary. If the primary on-call does not acknowledge within the defined time frame, the alert should automatically escalate to the secondary. This covers scenarios where the primary is temporarily unavailable (like while driving).
  - **Team lead/manager**: If the secondary on-call fails to acknowledge, the alert would escalate to the manager. This also acts as a safety net for critical failures that allows management to have visibility into recurring rotation problems.
  - A wide broadcast is needed for catastrophic, company-wide incidents (like total site downtime). In such scenarios, it may be necessary to page a wider group or all engineers simultaneously to marshal resources quickly.

  Best practice: The escalation path should be defined and automated within the alerting tool. The goal is to ensure that incidents get attention and the response to a missed page should be a blameless investigation into why it was missed (e.g., tooling failure, personal emergency, etc.).

Managing fatigue and burnout

The human side of on-call is the most critical factor needed for long-term success. An on-call rotation that ignores the human factor is bound to fail. It is important to address fatigue and burnout for on-call engineers, and the following are some of the best practices that can be implemented to handle the same:

- **Limits on frequency of on-call**: An engineer should not be on-call for long stretches of time. Common practice is to have on-call for 1 week, followed by 3 weeks of off-call. On-call schedules should be published well in advance, and rotations should be shared equally across all members of the team who are eligible for on-call. Teams can also implement the follow-the-sun model, whereby a globally distributed team should hand over the on-call responsibility to a team in a different time zone at the end of their workday. This eliminates the need for an engineer to be on-call during nighttime.
- **Secondary coverage for high incident volume**: A system that has a high number of incidents should implement the primary-secondary coverage model. This ensures that no single engineer bears the entire load of being on-call. Also, such a high volume of incidents signals deeper system reliability issues that need to be addressed as soon as possible.

- **Compensation and recovery**: On-call work should be compensated fairly. For significant off-hours work related to an incident, the engineer should be encouraged to take an equivalent amount of time off during his workday. This process officially acknowledges the personal sacrifice of off-hours work done by the engineer and prevents fatigue by mandatory rest. Companies can also offer additional on-call pay that would provide tangible compensation for the added stress and disruption of personal time.
- **Psychological safety**: Engineers must feel safe to escalate when overwhelmed with alerts. Similarly, if a page is missed, effort should be put into investigating the system (or process) and not blaming the individual. Such a blameless culture creates a psychological safety for engineers and encourages them to raise concerns about alert fatigue, poor handoff, or systemic issues.

Continuous improvement

The on-call process should be treated like a product that requires regular retrospectives and refinement and should evolve based on operational feedback, incident patterns and human experience. That is the only way to balance long-term sustainability with always-on responsiveness that is needed for on-call personnel. Let us look at some of the measures that should be taken to keep on improving the on-call process:

- **Regular retrospectives**: Teams should hold brief meetings at the end of each rotation to discuss what alerts were good and what were noisy and useless. They should also focus on what documentation is missing or outdated and whether there is any tooling issue. Retrospectives should include alert review, documentation health check, and tooling effectiveness.
- **Tune alerts and update runbooks**: Use the feedback from the above retrospective discussion to tune alerts by de-prioritizing noisy alerts and update runbooks so that gaps in documentation revealed by actual incidents are handled.
- **Track health metrics**: A great way to improve on-call is to track the health of the on-call process itself. Tracking the following metrics related to on-call can help keep a tab on the health of the on-call system:
    - The number of pages during an on-call shift should be trending down.
    - MTTA and MTTR should be trending down as runbooks and tooling are improved.
    - There should be regular surveys on on-call stress and satisfaction from the on-call engineers to keep a tab on their stress levels.

A sustainable on-call practice is the hallmark of a mature engineering organization. It recognizes that system reliability is inextricably linked to human well-being. The goal is to build a system so reliable and well-instrumented that pages are rare, and when they do occur, the process of resolution is well-supported, efficient, and minimally disruptive. On-call is a team responsibility. By investing in on-call best practices like fair scheduling, actionable alerts, strong escalation paths, clear playbooks, and, most importantly, fatigue management and health of the on-call engineers, we can build a culture of reliability that can thrive in the long run.

Roles and responsibilities

Incident management is not only about technical skills. It is also about leadership, communication, and decision-making under pressure. When an incident occurs, time is critical as customers are impacted and the organization may be losing money and trust. In these moments, adopting a set of roles, inspired by the **incident command system** (**ICS**) used by emergency responders, can provide the necessary structure to manage the chaos effectively. This model ensures that each critical function is covered by a dedicated individual, preventing overload and creating a single source of truth.

It is also critical to remember that these are roles, and in smaller organizations or smaller incidents, a single person may fill multiple roles. Whereas in a large organization or during severe incidents, each role should be assigned to a separate individual to distribute the cognitive load.

The four primary roles are: **incident commander** (**IC**), **communications lead** (**CL**), **operations lead** (**OL**), and scribe.

Incident commander

The IC is the single leader and coordinator for the entire incident response. Their primary responsibility is to manage the process and not necessarily the technical fix.

Responsibilities of IC are as follows:

- Owns the incident by taking responsibility for the resolution process.
- Declare and assign the severity level of the incident.
- Takes command and coordinates across teams by determining the priority of actions and delegating the tasks to the OC and other engineers.
- Protects the responders by shielding them from distractions, interruptions, and external pressure, allowing them to focus solely on the diagnosis and mitigation.
- Ensures adherence to the incident management lifecycle process and usage of the communication channels correctly.
- Make decisions quickly during imperfect or incomplete consensus. In case of a disagreement, the IC is the final decision-maker on the path to mitigation.
- Track progress and determine when the incident is resolved.

Best practices of IC are as follows:

- The first engineer to join the incident channel should take the IC role initially. The role can be handed over to another senior individual if the incident escalates or if a more suitable leader becomes available.
- Only one IC should exist per incident to avoid conflicts.
- IC should focus on delegating tasks instead of attempting hands-on troubleshooting.

Operations lead

The OC is the primary technical investigator and problem solver. These are the engineers or specialists with deep knowledge of the impacted systems. They investigate, diagnose, and resolve the technical issue.

Responsibilities of OL are as follows:

- Performs deep dive technical analysis using logs, metrics, and traces to diagnose the root cause.
- Propose and test mitigation strategies. Recommend temporary fixes or workarounds.
- Execute the mitigation steps, whether it is a fix, a rollback, a config change, a restart, a failover, or anything else.
- Continuously report their findings and updates to the IC and scribe on their progress, hypothesis, and what they need to investigate next.
- Request resources from the IC if specific skills and expertise are needed.

Best practices are as follows:

- The SMEs should focus on solving technical issues without being distracted by external communications.
- The SMEs should also avoid writing lengthy updates on the incident chat. They can verbally brief the Scribe, who can handle the communication better.

An engineer who has deep expertise in the failing service is best suited to be the OL. Complex incidents can have multiple operational leads.

Communications lead

The CL is responsible for all internal and external communication. They are the single source of truth for the incident's status, ensuring consistent and timely information reaches all stakeholders without distracting the technical team.

Responsibilities of CL are as follows:

- Prepare regular status updates for stakeholders, both internal and external.

- Communicate estimated time to resolution to all stakeholders and known impacts.
- Ensure consistency in messaging at every level to avoid confusion.
- Shield technical responders from unnecessary interruptions by handling inquiries in a separate channel and preventing the stakeholders from interrupting the main incident response channel.
- Handle public communication by drafting the external status page or customer communication with the help of marketing or customer support, and provide regular updates to the same.

Best practices are as follows:

- CL should use templated updates for speed and clarity.
- CL should share only confirmed facts and avoid any speculation.
- Updates should be provided at regular cadence (for example, every 30 minutes).

Scribe or incident recorder

The scribe ensures that a complete timeline of the incident is captured. In most of the scenarios, the CL can also act as a scribe by recording the timelines while communicating updates to the stakeholders.

Responsibilities of a scribe are as follows:

- Maintain the incident timeline by documenting every action, hypothesis, and discovery in the incident thread or tool in real-time.
- Track *who* performed *what* action and *when*.
- Capture all communications, decisions, and escalation steps with their respective timelines.
- All this information should be readily available as input for the incident postmortem.

Best practices are as follows:

- The scribe should focus on documentation and not provide their expertise on the incident mitigation.
- Documentation and logs should be centralized in an incident management tool or a central documentation for reference.
- The scribe role is the first to be delegated. The IC can start off as a scribe, but should explicitly handoff this role as soon as possible.

Stakeholders and management

Stakeholders are individuals who need to be informed about the incident's progress but are not directly involved in the resolution. Their role is only to observe and support.

Responsibilities of stakeholders and management are as follows:

- Stakeholders should stay informed on the progress of the incident mitigation by monitoring the dedicated stakeholder communication channel and status page for updates.
- Stakeholders need to provide context on the impact of the incident that can help the IC in making the right decisions.
- Stakeholders should support the incident resolution process by pulling resources, managing business expectations, and shielding the team from external pressure.

Best practices are as follows:

- The role should be only focused on resourcing and not on technical troubleshooting.
- Stakeholders should be invited to a separate stakeholder channel and should be discouraged from joining the primary incident response channel.
- Stakeholders should avoid injecting speculative root cause guesses into the incident channel to reduce noise risk.

Stakeholders are generally executives, product managers, customer support leads, and marketing managers.

RACI matrix for incident roles

The following is a **Responsible, Accountable, Consulted, Informed** (**RACI**) matrix for incident roles for ready reference:

Task/Role	IC	OL	CL	Scribe	Stakeholders
Incident declaration	A	C	I	I	I
Technical diagnosis	C	R	I	I	I
Mitigation actions	A	R	I	I	I
Stakeholder updates	I	I	R	I	C
Timeline documentation	I	C	I	R	I
Resolution confirmation	A	C	I	I	I

Table 4.1: *RACI matrix for incident management roles*

Example scenario

Let us look at an example scenario of how roles collaborate and handle the responsibility of managing an incident:

- Alert fires. On-call engineer joins the call.
- On-call engineer takes up the IC role and opens the primary incident response channel.

- Another engineer joins the call and takes up the OL role. The OL opens up the observability tools (logs, metrics, and traces) to initiate debugging the issue.
- A third engineer joins the call and takes up the scribe/CL role. The CL opens up another channel for communication with stakeholders, the incident-stakeholder.
- IC asks the CL to post the initial status on the incident response. While also asking for updates from the OL.
- OL mentions that the storage service is returning authentication errors and that the credentials have expired.
- Scribe documents the updates identified issue with storage service credentials, and shares updates on the incident-stakeholder channel.
- IC then asks the OL to focus on rotating or renewing the credentials.
- IC also asks the CL to update the incident-stakeholder channel and ask the product manager about the impact of the issue.
- CL gets the impact from the product manager via the incident-stakeholder channel, updates the documentation, and informs the same to the IC.
- Meanwhile, OL rotates the credentials and informs CL that the issue is mitigated and that he will be monitoring the system for some time.
- CL posts the updates to the *incident-stakeholder channel incident mitigated: credentials rotated. Monitoring for 15 minutes before closing the call.*
- IC and OL monitor the system for 15 minutes. At the end of 15 minutes, IC informs CL that they are closing the call, and CL documents the same.

This structured approach via well-defined roles ensures a calm, efficient, and documented response, turning a potentially chaotic process into a coordinated, efficient, and repeatable process.

Root cause analysis

Mitigating an incident is only the first step. The true goal of incident management is to ensure that similar incidents do not happen again. RCA is a structured method for identifying the underlying causes of the problem to avoid similar incidents in the future.

The RCA process seeks to understand the sequence of events and the set of contributing factors that aligned in order for the failure to occur. The output of the RCA process is a set of actionable items to improve the system further.

RCA process

The following figure shows the steps involved in the RCA process:

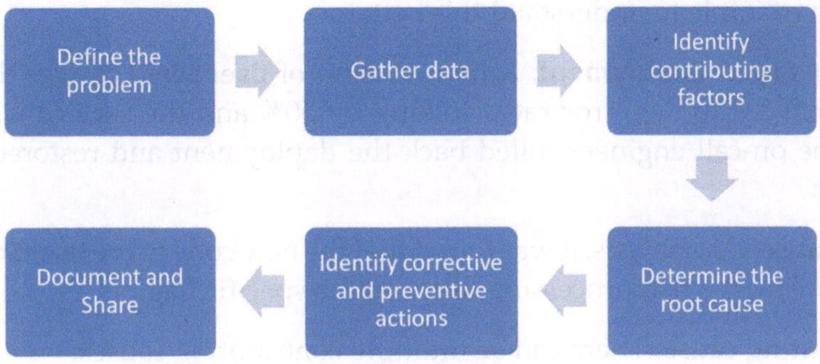

***Figure 4.2:** RCA process flow*

Let us understand each step in the RCA process:

1. **Defining problem**: Before seeking out the causes of the problem, the first step is to define the problem. Clearly state what happened, when it happened, and what the impact was. To define the precise problem statement, we need to first assemble the RCA team, which includes the operations lead, the scribe, and other engineers who worked on the incident. The next step is to reconstruct the timeline of the incident from the logs. The purpose of this step is to have a precise problem statement to keep the RCA team focused.

2. **Gather data**: Using the incident timeline, chat logs, and monitoring data, collaboratively build a detailed minute-by-minute chronology of the incident. Next, interview the incident responders for their observations and collect customer impact data like error rates, downtime, and financial loss. The scribe's incident notes act as a backbone of this step. The goal here is to get as much detail as possible regarding the incident.

3. **Identify contributing factors**: Now that we have all the sub-events that led to the incident, we can drill down and *ask how this event happened?* To identify the contributing factors for each sub-event. This is where techniques like *5 Whys* can be very helpful to drill down from the surface-level symptom to find the system or process flaw. The contributing factors can be system failures (hardware or software bugs), human actions (misconfigurations), process gaps (missing reviews), or external dependencies (cloud provider outage).

Determining root cause

Using the contributing factors, the team needs to group them into three categories (or layers):

- **Direct cause**: The immediate technical event that led to the incident.
- **Contributing cause**: The factors that enabled the direct cause to happen.
- **Root cause**: The underlying systemic, organizational, or process failure that led to the contributing cause to happen.

Let us look at an example to understand this better:

- **Incident failed deployment**: A new version of `UserService` was deployed at 10:00 am, which led to the error rates spiking by 50% and the service went into a restart loop. The on-call engineer rolled back the deployment and restored the systems by 10:20 am.
- **Direct cause**: On analysis, it was found that the new code in the `UserService` contained an infinite loop when processing users with a specific flag.
- **Contributing cause**: There can be multiple contributing causes:
    - The automated test suite did not include any users with that specific flag.
    - The code review did not identify the infinite loop logic, as it was more focused on the coding style instead of performance issues.
    - The staging environment data set was small, and it also did not have any users with that specific flag.
- **Root cause**: The root cause in this case is that the definition of done for a feature does not require extensive testing for edge cases and performance under realistic conditions. The team prioritizes speed of development over stability. This is a systemic, cultural, and process issue that needs to be addressed to avoid similar incidents in the future.

Identify corrective and preventive actions

For each identified contributing and root cause, we need to define one or more action items. Each action item must be:

- Actionable or should be a concrete task instead of a vague goal.
- Assigned to a specific person or a team.
- Time-bound or have a clear date for completion.

The corrective actions are generally aligned towards fixing the contributing factors, which are immediate fixes to prevent recurrence of the incident. Whereas the preventive actions are targeted towards fixing the root cause, which can be long-term systemic improvements.

Document and share

Document the RCA in a structured template and share it widely. The document should be visible to the affected team, the leadership, and the whole organization to prevent similar repeated issues.

The assigned action items must be tracked to completion. The facilitator or manager should follow up with the respective teams to ensure that they are done.

RCA template

An RCA template provides a well-defined structure for the postmortem analysis. Here is an RCA template that can be used for any organization. Once the RCA template is decided, it is important that all the fields of the template are completed (even with N/A if irrelevant) to encourage completeness.

RCA template:

```
Incident postmortem: [Incident title and incident number]
Date of incident: [incident date]
Created by: [Postmortem facilitator]
Severity level: [Sev1, Sev2, Sev3, etc]
Incident commander: [IC name]
Technical responders: [Names of technical responders for the incident]
Status: [Draft / In Review / Finalized]
Executive summary
Incident summary: [ 2-3 lines describing the incident in simple language]
Impact: [Incident duration, affected users, business impact]
Root cause: [A single line regarding the primary systemic issue]
Preventive actions: [List of action items to prevent recurrence of similar
incidents]
Impact assessment
Start time (UTC): []
End time (UTC): []
Total duration: []
Affected services: [Service A, Service B, Database D]
User impact: []
Business impact: []
SLA breach: Yes/No
Timeline (UTC)
A detailed chronology from the first signal to resolution
```

Time (UTC)	Event description	Actor/System
10:00 am	`UserService` error rates spiked 50% …	Monitoring

Table 4.2: Chronology of events

- RCA:
  - **Direct cause:** []
  - **Contributing causes:** []
  - **Root cause(s):** []

- **Action items**:
  - Corrective action 1: owner, due date
  - Corrective action 2: owner, due date
  - Preventive action 1: owner, due date
  - Preventive action 2: owner, due date
- **Lessons learned**:
  - What went well
  - What could be improved
- **Follow up**:
  - Next review date
  - Open action items tracking details (e.g., Jira tickets)
- **Appendix**:
  - **Key metrics graphs**: [links to graphs showing the failures during the incident]
  - **Relevant logs**: [links to log entries that helped in the diagnosis]
  - **Incident chat log**: [link to the full incident communication channel]

Best practices for RCA

Let us look at some of the best practices to improve the impact of the RCA process:

- RCA should be blameless, which focuses on systems and processes, not individual error.
- RCA should be data-driven to avoid speculation and rely on evidence.
- Collaboration across multiple teams, like engineering, operations, and business, generates a better perspective.
- Action items should be prioritized to address the most impactful root causes first (e.g., use ICE or RICE prioritization models to consider both impact and effort).
- Follow up on action items to ensure that they are completed. RCA with incomplete action items is wasted effort.

Metrics and continuous improvement

A mature incident management practice is a cycle of constant refinement, and metrics provide the objective data-driven foundation for this improvement. This section covers the key metrics to track and how to use them to fuel a process of continuous refinement.

Key incident management metrics

Let us look at the key incident management metrics, which are broken down into reliability metrics, response process metrics, and operational health metrics:

- **Reliability metrics**: The reliability metrics define the customer experience and the quality of our service. These include the **service level indicator** (**SLI**), **service level objective** (**SLO**), and **service level agreement** (**SLA**). SLO burn or breach typically triggers a formal incident declaration depending on policy.
- **Response process metrics**: These metrics measure the effectiveness of our incident management lifecycle. The response process metrics consist of the MTTA, **mean time to resolution** (**MTTR**), **mean time between failure** (**MTBF**), and incident volume. Here, MTTR is a key lagging metric and should be paired with detection quality and mitigation safety metrics. A decreasing MTTR indicates an improving process, better tooling, and more effective runbooks.
- **Operational health metrics**: These metrics measure the sustainability of our on-call practices and are crucial for preventing burnout. The operational health metrics consist of pages per on-call shift, alert acknowledgment rate, action item completion rate, and on-call satisfaction score. Let us understand these metrics one at a time:
    - **Pages per on-call shift**: The number of alerts that wake up an on-call engineer. This is a direct measure of the alert noise, and the target should be to reduce it.
    - **Alert acknowledgment rate**: The percentage of alerts acknowledged within the target SLA. A low alert acknowledgment rate may indicate alert fatigue or tooling problems and should be looked into.
    - **Action item completion rate**: The percentage of RCA action items completed on time. This measures the effectiveness of our postmortem and learning process.
    - **On-call satisfaction score**: A regular anonymous survey asking engineers to rate their stress level and satisfaction with the on-call rotation. This is the leading indicator of burnout.

Continuous improvement process

The previously mentioned metrics need a process to make them effective. The continuous improvement process is cyclic in nature and is broken down into four steps: plan, do, check, and act. Let us look at these steps in detail:

1. **Plan**: This step focuses on analyzing and strategizing the data available in the metrics. The team needs to hold periodic (monthly or quarterly) meetings to review the trends in MTTR, incident volume, and operational health metrics. The idea is to identify patterns to determine whether most incidents are related to a specific service. Whether there is a specific type of activity causing the majority of the incidents and whether the MTTR is increasing. Based on this analysis, the team needs to set clear goals for the next quarter. An example of such a goal is: Reduce Sev1 incident volume by 20% by focusing on the top error-producing service.
2. **Do**: This step focuses on implementing changes, which can include completion of action items from RCAs that directly address specific failures. In addition to this, the

team should launch broader engineering initiatives to meet the quarterly goals set in the previous step.

3. **Check**: This step focuses on measuring the impact of the changes implemented in the previous step. While also keeping a tab on the key metrics by comparing the current performance to the baseline derived from the plan step.
4. **Act**: At the end of the quarter, we need to figure out if we met our goals or not. If we have met our goals, we standardize the process as a successful practice. Document it and make it the new default across all teams. In case we are unsuccessful in meeting our goals, we begin the cycle again. We analyze why the change did not work and feed the learnings back into the plan step. This closed-loop process ensures that every incident and every data point feed directly into making the system more reliable and the on-call experience more sustainable. It transforms incident management from a reactive firefighting exercise into a proactive engineering discipline.

Postmortem and blameless culture

Restoring a service during an incident is a short-lived victory. True strategic victory is learning from the incident to ensure that it never happens again. This learning is captured in the postmortem or post-incident review, and the environment that makes this learning possible is the blameless culture, which encourages honesty.

Let us cover these topics to understand why these elements are necessary for a high-performing, resilient engineering organization.

Postmortem

A postmortem is a formal document and process that analyzes an incident from trigger to resolution, with the sole purpose of extracting learnings and driving improvements. It can also be said that a postmortem is a diagnostic tool for the system.

The goal of a postmortem is to document the incident and how it occurred with the purpose of identifying the root cause and contributing factors. This helps in capturing the lessons learned and identifying the opportunities for improvement with the aim of driving corrective and preventive actions to reduce recurrence.

Need for postmortem

Postmortems are needed as they serve not only the technical but also the organizational purpose of improvement, as follows:

- The primary goal of a postmortem is to prevent recurrence of the same incident from happening again by identifying actionable steps to prevent it.

- It helps improve the processes by exposing weaknesses not only in the technical architecture but also in the incident response, communication, and tooling.
- It helps in institutional learning by capturing tacit knowledge gained during the incident and sharing it across the entire organization, thus making every team smarter.
- It builds trust and demonstrates accountability as it is a transparent process that shows stakeholders and customers that the team takes reliability seriously and is committed to continuous improvement.
- It promotes cultural maturity by reinforcing that reliability is a shared responsibility and not an individual burden.

Postmortem meeting

The postmortem meeting should be scheduled within 1-3 business days of the incident. The atmosphere must be collaborative and blameless, with a focus on why and not on who.

The IC, technical responders, and other related engineers, along with the scribe, should be invited to the meeting. The meeting is generally driven by the IC or designated facilitator. The goal is to collaboratively reconstruct the timeline and understand the contributing factors.

The output of the meeting is the RCA document we have seen earlier, which lists the root cause, contributing factors, and the actionable items.

Blameless culture

A blameless culture is an organizational commitment to understanding that people do not cause failures. Rather, the system, processes, and conditions do. When an incident occurs, we assume that everyone involved was acting to the best of their ability, given the information they had, the time pressure they were under, and the tools and processes they were using. The goal is to find out *how* the failure happened, not *who* made it happen.

A blameless culture is essential to:

- **Encourage transparency**: In a blameless culture, engineers can admit their mistakes without the fear of punishment. This helps in finding the true cause and the process corrections that need to be implemented to prevent such occurrences in the future.
- **Uncovers root causes**: In a blameless culture, teams analyze *why* the mistake was possible and not *who* caused it. This helps in digging deeper to uncover the true root cause.
- **Fosters psychological safety**: Which is a state where individuals feel safe to take risks, admit mistakes, and ask questions without fear of being humiliated or punished. The focus shifts to systemic resilience rather than individual perfection.

Blamelessness is not:

- A lack of accountability. People are still held accountable for their work. In case of a failure, the individual is held accountable for helping the team understand the failure and implement the fix.
- Ignoring repeated negligence. If an individual consistently fails to follow established, well-documented procedures, that is a performance issue managed by leadership, not an incident investigation issue. These cases are typically less common than systemic failures.

Fostering a blameless culture

Building this culture requires intentional, continuous effort from leadership and the entire team. Here are a few actions that will help foster a blameless culture:

- **Leadership commitment**: Executives and managers must consistently model blameless behavior. If leadership punishes mistakes, the culture of fear spreads quickly. Instead, they must praise transparency and reward engineers for bringing tough issues to light, even if they caused an incident.
- **Postmortem standardization**: Using a consistent template and workflow for all postmortems helps build trust and repeatability. Postmortems should be shared across teams as part of transparency.
- **Blameless language**: Instead of using words like *fault, blame,* use words like *our* and *we,* and focus on the system.
- **Example**:
  - **Incorrect usage**: *Why did you deploy the buggy code?*
  - **Blameless wordings**: *How did our deployment process allow this bug to reach production?*
- **Focus on action items instead of individuals**: The entire output of a postmortem should be a set of action items that improve the system. The moment the discussion shifts to personal performance, the facilitator must steer it back to process and technology.
- **Celebrate learnings along with success**: The idea is to recognize and reward teams that conduct thorough postmortems and implement strong fixes. Learnings should be shared widely, as an incident that is learned from is more valuable than one that did not go wrong and no improvements were made.

When blameless postmortems are done correctly, they create a powerful and self-reinforcing cycle of improvement. During incidents, the team responds without fear while focusing on restoration. The team conducts an open and honest analysis focusing on systemic causes. The postmortem creates concrete tasks to improve the system. Action items are completed, making the system more resilient, alerts more precise, or runbooks more effective. The team sees that honesty leads to improvement, thus strengthening psychological safety for the next incident.

With postmortems and a blameless mindset, organizations can turn incidents from costly interruptions into powerful catalysts for growth, maturity, and reliability.

Conclusion

This chapter helps us understand that effective incident management goes far beyond the act of fixing broken systems or resolving immediate issues. It is a holistic discipline that combines technology, process, and culture to build resilient systems and empowered teams. True incident management is an ongoing effort to ensure that every outage, degradation, or disruption contributes to long-term system strength and operational maturity.

By establishing a structured incident lifecycle, fair on-call practices, clear roles, an effective RCA process, meaningful metrics, and a blameless postmortem culture, organizations can transform incidents from chaotic disruptions into opportunities for growth and reliability. Clearly defined roles and responsibilities promote accountability and coordination during high-pressure situations, while an effective RCA process enables teams to identify and address the underlying issues rather than superficial symptoms. The ultimate goal is not only to restore the service quickly but also to continuously improve the resilience and reliability of the systems that are built and the processes that are followed.

While incident management focuses on responding effectively when systems fail, the next chapter on designing for reliability shifts the perspective towards proactive resilience. It explores the architectural and operational strategies that minimize the likelihood and impact of failures before they occur.

Chapter 5
Designing for Reliability

Introduction

Reliability is the foundation of user trust. If our product is not reliable, no number of features or innovations will matter. Users expect systems to be available, consistent, and fast. When those expectations are not met, they will abandon our product for alternatives that offer better stability. In today's competitive landscape, reliability is a core requirement that determines whether users stay engaged or walk away.

Designing for reliability means making resilience, scalability, and recovery a part of the architecture from the very beginning, rather than adding them as an accessory later on. It requires anticipating failures, understanding how systems behave under stress, and ensuring that services can continue to operate even when components break. **Site reliability engineering** (**SRE**) embraces this principle by treating reliability as a core feature that shapes how systems are designed, built, tested, and evolved over time.

This chapter moves us from reacting to failures to proactively designing systems that are inherently reliable, stable, and scalable. We will explore proven SRE design patterns, resilience patterns, strategies for fault tolerance and redundancy, techniques for testing reliability through chaos engineering, and the importance of capacity planning to meet future demand. We will also look at recovery-focused practices that reduce downtime and help systems bounce back quickly after disruptions.

This chapter will equip us with the mindset, tools, and patterns needed to architect systems that not only withstand failures but also adapt gracefully to changing demands, minimizing downtime while optimizing resource efficiency and building user trust.

Structure

The chapter covers the following topics:

- Reliability as a feature
- SRE design patterns
- Fault tolerance and redundancy
- Scalability and load management

- Reliability testing using chaos engineering
- Capacity planning and scalability
- Designing for recovery

Objectives

This chapter will focus on how to build systems that are resilient, scalable, and reliable by design. We will see some SRE design patterns that will help the team anticipate and mitigate failures to minimize impact on end users. We will also look at how fault tolerance and redundancy can be leveraged to ensure software services remain available despite hardware or software failures. The chapter will also introduce a practice called chaos engineering, which is used to proactively identify weaknesses in the system during high-stress situations and use the findings to improve resilience further. The chapter will also cover capacity planning (forecasting/provisioning) and scalability (architecture and elasticity), helping teams predict user growth and design systems that are able to scale as the user base increases without performance degradation. This chapter will help us understand how to architect systems that not only withstand failures but also adapt to changing demands, minimizing downtime while also optimizing efficiency.

Reliability as a feature

When engineering and product teams think about features, they usually think about things like a new search function, a faster checkout process, or a sleek user interface. However, all of this would not matter if the system were unreliable. If an app crashes during payment or a website starts throwing errors during traffic surges or order shows an inconsistent state even when payment has been successful, users will not tolerate it, which means that reliability is a feature that underpins every other capability of our system.

The core principle of SRE is that reliability is the most fundamental feature. If your service is down, slow, or losing data, no other feature matters.

Importance of reliability

Reliability is not a technical nicety; it is a business imperative. It is a product-level commitment that our systems are predictable, dependable, and trustworthy for users by design. The following are the reasons that help us understand the importance of reliability:

- **User trust and retention**: Modern users expect services to be always-on. Even a small outage can cause frustration, erode trust, and push customers to competitors. Users will abandon such slow and unreliable services and move to competitors. Once their trust is lost, it is incredibly difficult to regain it.

- **Revenue impact**: In the modern ecosystem, the application is the business. Downtime directly translates to lost revenue. For example, a few hours of downtime during a peak sales period may even wipe out an entire quarter of profit.

- **Development velocity**: A focus on reliability also enables faster development and innovation as it helps keep the error budgets healthy. A stable and reliable foundation allows development teams to iterate and deploy new features faster and more confidently.

Quantifying reliability

To manage reliability, it is important to first measure it. This is where the **service level indicator** (**SLI**), **service level objective** (**SLO**) and error budget, which were discussed in the previous chapters, come into the picture.

Engineering teams use SLIs to identify metrics that directly measure user-visible reliability. Also, SLOs set targets for the acceptable level of reliability for users. Whereas the error budget is the amount of unreliability that is available to the engineering teams to spend over a period. If the error budget is intact, developers are free to launch new features. However, if the error budget is exhausted, the team's focus needs to shift to stability and repair. This concept makes reliability a shared and data-driven responsibility. These measures turn reliability from an abstract idea to actionable goals that engineering teams can track and prioritize.

Integrating reliability into design phase

Reliability considerations must be integrated into the **software development lifecycle** (**SDLC**) as early as possible. This concept is also called the **shift left approach**, whereby reliability becomes a part of the design and development phase and not just in production. The following are the phases where reliability must be considered during the SDLC:

- **Design phase**: We need to incorporate resilience, redundancy and graceful degradation into the architecture diagrams. Teams must conduct architecture review meetings where SREs or senior engineers must probe regarding how the failure of different components of a service are being handled. Reliability requirements should be well-defined in this phase, including SLOs, error budget policy, and launch criteria.
- **Development phase**: Software engineers must write code keeping observability, error handling and retries in mind. These concepts must also be discussed during code review meetings.
- **Testing phase**: During the testing of the application, engineers must not only focus on the correctness of the feature functionalities but also on fault tolerance and failure handling using tools that help in chaos engineering.
- **Deployment phase**: **Operational readiness reviews** (**ORRs**) should be conducted before launch, which includes checks on runbooks, dashboards, paging and rollback plans. To minimize the blast radius of bad releases, the teams need to use canary releases, rollbacks, or automation as much as possible.
- **Operation phase**: Once the system is deployed and operational, the teams must monitor the SLI and enforce SLO to ensure that the system meets the reliability targets.

Thus, by making reliability a core requirement throughout the lifecycle of an application development, the system will evolve with reliability as its core.

Embedding reliability into team culture

Treating reliability as a feature is not just a technical discussion. It is a cultural change for the team as the team must internalize that reliability is:

- A design principle that plans for failures and not for perfection.
- A shared responsibility between product managers, developers, and SRE, and all must care for it.
- A continuous commitment whereby, as system and user demands change, reliability needs to evolve and change.

By embedding this mindset, organizations can create an environment where reliability is seen as value creation and not just cost reduction.

SRE design patterns

In software engineering, design patterns are reusable solutions to recurring common challenges. The SRE extends this idea of design patterns to reliability challenges, thus providing SRE design patterns that make systems more resilient, scalable, and manageable. Many of these patterns originate from distributed systems and microservices resilience, while SRE operationalizes them. These design patterns are building blocks that can be used to construct a service that can withstand the inherent unreliability of networks, hardware, and other components. Implementing these patterns requires adopting a mindset of defensive programming and assuming that anything that can go wrong will go wrong.

Let us look at some of the key SRE design patterns that form the architectural backbone of a resilient service, including how they work and when to apply them.

Graceful degradation

Graceful degradation solves the problem whereby the failure of a non-critical dependency breaks a critical user journey. Using graceful degradation, the system can operate at a reduced level of functionality even when components fail. Graceful degradation should maintain correctness and avoid inconsistent states. This allows the core functionality to continue even when non-critical parts of the system fail.

Implementation

For implementing graceful degradation, we need to identify must-have and nice-to-have features, and when we encounter an issue, we can use feature flags to turn off the lower-priority features in production dynamically. This can also be clubbed with the circuit breaker pattern (which we will see later) to automatically disable the erroneous feature.

Some examples are:

- In a music app during peak loads, the lyrics or album art loading is impacted. This can be disabled while the core feature of music playback can continue functioning uninterrupted.
- In an e-commerce website, the product recommendation service is misbehaving. This can be turned off using a feature flag or automatically by the circuit breaker, so that instead of showing a broken page, the product detail page is loaded without the section displaying the product recommendations. A message such as *personalized product recommendations will be back shortly* is shown instead, and the core functionality of add to cart continues to work uninterrupted.

Benefits: Users prefer partial service instead of total downtime. Hence, this design pattern helps in maintaining user trust by keeping the core functionality working during partial outages.

Circuit breaker

When a remote service becomes slow or unresponsive, continuous retries to it can create a retry storm, which not only overwhelms the failing service but can also cause the failures to cascade backward, impacting other services. The circuit breaker pattern prevents a client from repeatedly trying to execute an operation that is likely to fail. Circuit breakers usually track failure rate over a rolling window and incorporate timeouts and fallback mechanisms.

Implementation

To implement a circuit breaker, we need to define the thresholds for failure, like timeouts or error rates. Once this is defined, we can use client-side libraries (like resilience4j for Java) to define different states:

- Closed for normal operation
- Open to stop traffic
- Half-open to test recovery

These states help in managing traffic to the failing service and help in its recovery.

Let us look at an example of a payment service that is calling a user's details **application programming interface** (API) (via the `/api/users` endpoint) for address display. In this example, the `/api/users` endpoint starts timing out, and based on the threshold for failure, the circuit breaker cycles through the following states as per its functionality:

- **Closed state**: Initially, the requests are flowing normally.
- **Open state**: After five failures in 10 seconds (which is the configured threshold), the circuit breaks for the next 60 seconds, and all calls from the payment service to `/api/`

users endpoint immediately fail fast and return a predefined fallback response (like **{"status":"service temporarily unavailable"}** without even making the API call.

- **Half-open state**: After 60 seconds, a test request is allowed to hit the **/api/users** endpoint. If it succeeds, the circuit is closed, and the user details API is expected to function normally. If the test request fails, the timer resets, and the circuit continues to be in the open state for the next 60 seconds.

Benefit: Circuit breaker pattern allows struggling dependencies to fail fast (using graceful degradation or a meaningful fallback path), thus preventing them from causing cascading failures and dragging down the entire system.

Bulkhead

A failure in one component can cascade and consume all shared resources (like CPU, memory, or threads), causing a total system failure. The bulkhead design pattern isolates elements of a service into pools, so if one component fails, the bulkhead helps in containing the failure.

Implementation

The implementation of the bulkhead design pattern needs the architecture to partition the workloads, queues, or database shards. Once partitioned, dedicated resources are allocated to each component by using separate thread pools, connection pools, or even entirely separate microservices.

Let us look at the examples:

- In an e-commerce site, the payment processing microservice and product review microservice are isolated by deploying on separate services with independent resource limits and autoscaling policies. So, a bug causing an infinite loop in the product review microservice does not prevent customers from completing payment purchases. The failure of the product review microservice is contained.
- A hotel booking system isolates requests per region, so an outage in the Europe region does not affect the US site.

Benefit: The bulkhead pattern is effective in reducing the blast radius of a failure. Thus, the impact of a failure is contained and limited.

Retries with exponential backoff

Transient failures (like a network glitch) are common. So, failing on the first error results in a poor user experience. So, instead of failing, retry the failed operation with controlled delays and randomness, which also prevents hammering the system.

Implementation

The implementation of the retry design pattern is done by configuring it in the http clients (like Apache HttpClient or Retrofit) or in the service mesh proxies. The configuration should combine retries with timeouts while also capping the maximum number of retries to avoid infinite loops.

Examples: A mobile app fails to post a comment via the comment service API, which can be due to network issues. Here is how the pattern will function:

- Attempt 1 fails, wait for 1s +/- 0.2s (jitter) = 0.8s
- Attempt 2 fails, wait for 2s +/- 0.4s (jitter) = 1.6s
- Attempt 3 fails, wait for 4s +/- 0.8s (jitter) = 3.2s
- Attempt 4 succeeds

This pattern gives time for the network to recover and prevents synchronized retries from multiple client requests.

Benefit: This design pattern handles transient faults automatically and prevents a retry storm, which can make outages worse.

Rate limiting and load shedding

Rate limiting and load shedding are self-defense mechanisms to prevent a service from being overwhelmed by too many requests. Rate limiting controls the number of requests a client or system can make within a time window. Whereas load shedding proactively drops low-priority traffic when the system is under extreme load.

Implementation

Both rate limiting and load shedding are configurable via API gateways (like *Kong* or *AWS API Gateway*) or service meshes. Rate limiting uses token bucket or leaky bucket algorithms and should respond with an informative error message (like 429: too many requests). For implementing load shedding, it is important to identify mission-critical and secondary workloads. They are implemented using priority queues by rejecting low-priority requests when thresholds are exceeded.

Let us look at some examples:

- Let us look at a rate-limiting example where a public API enforces a limit of 1000 requests per hour per API key. If a misconfigured client script makes 10 **requests per second** (**RPS**), it will be throttled with HTTP header **`HTTP/1.1 429 Too Many Requests`** responses after the first 100 requests, thus protecting the backend.
- Let us look at an example of load shedding of a news website during a major election. In this scenario, the traffic grows to 10x of the normal traffic, and the system is configured to do load shedding by:

- Serving a simplified cached version of the homepage.
- Temporarily disabling the expensive and personalized comments feed.
- Prioritizing GET requests for reading articles over the POST requests for posting comments as for a news site, displaying the article is more important than recording user comments.

Thus, ensuring that the core reading experience is available.

Benefits: Both these design patterns protect the service stability by enforcing capacity limits. The rate limiting prevents intentional or accidental abuse of the downstream services and protects them from overload. Whereas the load shedding keeps critical operations alive even during overload.

Sidecar pattern

Most of the earlier design patterns need to be implemented in each service's code, which can lead to inconsistency and complexity. The sidecar pattern simplifies this implementation by deploying a helper sidecar proxy alongside our application container, which provides the reliability features while minimizing changes to the core code.

Implementation

Sidecars can be deployed as containers in the same pod within Kubernetes. These sidecars are used to offload reliability concerns (like retries, metrics, and configuration reloads).
Some examples are:

- A logging sidecar can be used to stream logs from each container to a centralized logging system.
- A team writes a checkout service, but instead of coding the retry logic, they inject a sidecar proxy using service mesh (like Istio) that handles the timeout and retry logic for all calls to the checkout service. The configuration for this is managed by the SRE team, allowing for tweaks without changing the core code in the checkout service.

Benefits: The sidecar pattern separates cross-cutting concerns like logging, monitoring, or retries from the main application logic. This decouples the application logic from operational resilience, thus providing consistency and centralized control.

Immutable infrastructure

Traditionally, servers are managed over time through incremental updates, configuration changes, and patches. This can lead to configuration drift, where each server becomes a unique snowflake. This leads to debugging issues as no two servers are identical, and a fix applied to one server might not work on another. This inconsistency is a major source of outages.

The immutable infrastructure is a practice of replacing components rather than modifying them. A server (or container) is deployed from a single, versioned image and is never changed after deployment. If we need to update, patch, or reconfigure, we build a new image from a known baseline, deploy it, and terminate the old instance.

Implementation

This pattern is enabled by using **infrastructure as code** (**IaC**) tools like Terraform or AWS CloudFormation and image-based deployments using Docker containers or **virtual machine** (**VM**) images (like **Amazon Machine Image** (**AMI**) or **Google Compute Engine** (**GCE**) image). The idea is to deploy clean, versioned builds instead of patching live systems.

Let us look at the examples:

- Let us look at an example of patching a vulnerability on 100+ nginx servers. Here, instead of SSHing into the 100+ servers and running the `apt-get update nginx` command, we can do the following:
    - Update our Dockerfile or Packer template to use the new nginx base image.
    - Build the new image and tag it as a new version (say v1.1.0).
    - Deploy the new image, which automatically spins up new instances and terminates the old instances (like by using Kubernetes rolling updates).
- Let us look at another example of a configuration change. Here, to change a feature flag, we need to change the configuration on live servers. Instead, we update the configuration in our IaC template or configuration management repository, which then triggers a **continuous integration/continuous deployment** (**CI/CD**) pipeline that builds a new immutable artifact and deploys it.

Benefit: The immutable infrastructure pattern eliminates configuration drift while ensuring consistency across environments (development, staging, and production). It also simplifies rollbacks (by deploying just the previous image) and makes deployments predictable and auditable. This is a foundational pattern that makes all the other patterns more reliable.

Fault tolerance and redundancy

The universal truth about distributed systems is that everything fails, all the time. Hard drives can crash, memory modules can get corrupted, network switches can freeze, power supplies can die, software can have bugs, and data centers can lose connectivity. It is impossible to avoid these failures. Instead, a reliable system must have the ability to anticipate, withstand, and recover from these failures, preferably automatically. This is where fault tolerance and redundancy come in. Fault tolerance is the ability of a system to continue to function in the presence of component failures. At the same time, redundancy is the provision of backup capacity in the form of hardware, software, or processes that ensure that the system remains available even when parts of it go down.

This section explores the principles and practices of building systems that are not only aware of their potential points of failure but are explicitly architected to survive them.

Fault tolerance

Fault tolerance accepts that systems will never be perfect and instead designs for resilience in the face of faults. It also means that fault tolerance is designed for imperfection, where systems fail, but they do so gracefully.

Fallacies of distributed computing

The eight fallacies of distributed computing, as articulated by *Peter Deutsch* and others at *Sun Microsystems*, are a set of incorrect assumptions that developers new to distributed systems often make. Designing for reliability means actively rejecting these fallacies, which are:

- Network is reliable, but it is not, as packets get dropped.
- Latency is zero, which is not, as every hop adds delay.
- Bandwidth is infinite, which is incorrect, as networks get saturated.
- Network is secure, which is not, as we can be under constant attack.
- Topology changes as nodes join, leave, or are replaced.
- There is one administrator, which is incorrect as multiple teams manage different parts.
- Transport cost is zero, as serialization and deserialization of data use CPU.
- Network is homogeneous, which is not, as we have to deal with different protocols and hardware.

A fault-tolerant design rejects these fallacies and is developed by configuring for timeouts, retries, and authentication. We must assume that one or more of these fallacies will impact our systems and plan for what our system must do when that happens. This defensive mindset is the first step towards resilience.

Key principles of fault tolerance

Let us look at some of the key principles for designing fault-tolerant systems:

- Failure is expected, as seen in the previous section, and we must always design keeping that in mind.
- Redundancy enables survival, which means that a single failure should not take down the entire system.
- Degradation is better than collapse, so a system should provide partial service if all functionalities are unavailable.

- Detection and recovery matter, so a system must detect quickly and recover automatically to minimize downtime.

Examples of fault tolerance

Let us look at some examples to understand how fault-tolerant systems function:

- A database cluster remains available even if one node fails, as other functioning nodes hold replicas of data from the failed node.
- A load balancer routes traffic around unhealthy servers, thus preventing any user-visible downtime.
- An airline booking system can degrade gracefully to allow only ticket purchases if there is a partial outage that disables ancillary services like seat selection.

Redundancy

Redundancy is the practice of duplicating or having spare capacity for critical components in a system to increase its reliability. The goal is to eliminate a **single point of failure** (**SPOF**) by having extra components that take over when something fails.

Let us look at the different strategies for redundancy that apply to different layers of the stack of a system.

Hardware redundancy

Hardware redundancy is the most basic form of redundancy, which is handled at the infrastructure level. This typically involves having extra hardware components that take over if any of the existing hardware components fail. Let us look at the details:

- **Disk**: Teams generally use **Redundant Array of Independent Disk** (**RAID**) configurations for disks (like RAID 1 for mirroring and RAID 5 for parity). If one disk fails in a RAID setup, data can be rebuilt from the others without any downtime. Though RAID protects against disk failures, it does not protect against corruption, deletion, or ransomware; backups are still required.
- **Power**: Servers generally have redundant **power supply units** (**PSUs**) whereby each PSU is connected to a separate power circuit, which is then connected to **uninterruptible power supplies** (**UPSs**). Data centers themselves have multiple power grid connections and massive diesel generators to provide power to servers in any scenario.
- **Network**: Servers have multiple **network interface cards** (**NICs**) connected to different network switches. Data centers have multiple, diverse fiber paths for internet connectivity.

Example: Any major cloud service provider has the above redundancies built into their system, and when we provision a VM, the underlying redundant power, disk, and network are invisible to us but available to us as a service.

Application redundancy

For most software services, redundancy is built by running multiple identical instances behind a load balancer. The load balancer distributes the incoming user requests across a pool of healthy instances and also performs regular health checks on each instance. If an instance crashes or becomes unresponsive and its health check fails, the load balancer is able to detect it and stops sending traffic to it.

Example: In the case of *Netflix*, they have a massive user-facing API over a globally distributed fleet of application servers. If an entire server or even a rack of servers fails in their AWS environment, their elastic load balancers stop routing traffic to them, without any user-visible impact.

Data redundancy

Data is often the most critical and hardest to replace asset. The key strategy for data redundancy is to replicate it. Here are two ways the replication works and is a key architectural decision during the design of the system:

- Synchronous replication is mainly used for high availability. Here, data is written to multiple nodes simultaneously before the write is acknowledged back to the client API. This ensures strong consistency of data but adds latency in the system. Amazon Aurora is a real-world example of a quorum-based model where data is written to six replicas across three availability zones. A write must be durable on four out of six replicas to be acknowledged. This allows it to tolerate the loss of an entire availability zone and one additional node without data loss or downtime.
- Asynchronous replication is mainly used for disaster recovery. In this scenario, data is written to the primary node and replicated to the secondary node with a slight delay. This allows for better performance at the cost of a small amount of data loss. MySQL asynchronous replication is a real-world example of this. For a read-heavy application, all writes go to the primary database in the main data center. The data is asynchronously streamed and replicated to a MySQL replica in a secondary data center/region. If the primary data center fails, the application can be failed over to the replica on the secondary data center, where the most recent few writes may be missing.

Geographical redundancy

This is the ultimate form of redundancy where our entire service is deployed across multiple, geographically dispersed data centers, which helps to withstand natural disasters or regional outages. Here are two strategies used for implementing geographical redundancies:

- An active-active setup where multiple systems across all geographical locations handle live production traffic simultaneously. If one geographical location fails, traffic is redistributed to the remaining ones. *Spotify* is an ideal example of an active-active setup as they run a multi-region setup on *Google Cloud*. User data is sharded and replicated across all regions. A user in Europe will be served from the E.U. region, whereas another user in the U.S. will be served from the U.S. region. If one region has an outage, the global load balancer stops directing traffic there, and users in the affected area are often routed to the nearest healthy region. This provides incredible resilience and low latency.
- An active-passive setup is an architecture where one system (active) handles the traffic while another (passive) stays idle but ready. And when the active system fails, the passive system takes over. Traditional financial institutions like *JPMorgan Chase* maintain a hot disaster recovery site for their core transactional systems. Data is synchronously or asynchronously replicated to the disaster recovery site. And in the event of a primary site failure, if the team decides to run from disaster recovery, a detailed runbook is executed to bring the disaster recovery site online and redirect traffic. This process might take minutes to hours, but it is designed to protect against total data center loss.

Choosing a redundancy strategy

Selecting the right strategy involves balancing consistency, availability, performance, and cost. The CAP theorem tells us we cannot have perfect consistency, availability, and partition tolerance simultaneously and that we must make trade-offs. CAP trade-offs become unavoidable when a network partition occurs.

Refer to the CAP theorem Venn diagram:

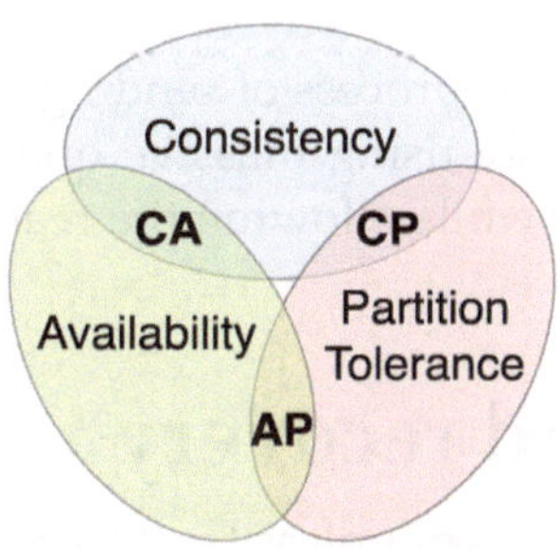

Figure 5.1: *CAP theorem*

Here is a table that can help in deciding which redundancy strategy to use in which scenario:

Strategy	Consistency	Availability	Performance	Cost	Use case
Active-active application tier	Not applicable as it is stateless	Extremely high	High	High	Web servers, APIs, image processing
Synchronous data replication	Strong	High	Lower (high latency)	Very high	Financial transactions, user data
Asynchronous data replication	Eventual consistency	High	Higher (low latency)	High	User activity streams, social data posts
Active-passive (hot)	Strong	High	Medium	High	Critical stateful services or core databases
Active-passive (warm)	Low	Medium (slow failover)	Medium	Medium	Disaster recovery for less critical systems

Table 5.1: Redundancy strategy choosing scenarios

Here is a real-world example of choosing the strategy for redundancy for Twitter's tweet delivery:

- **Scenario**: When a tweet is made, it needs to be written to a database and then delivered to millions of followers' timelines.
    - Choosing between consistency and availability. Strong consistency is needed for writing the tweet in the database, as it is critical data. However, for the visibility of the tweet in the timelines of the followers, availability is more important than consistency. It is acceptable if there is a slight delay before all followers see the tweet.
    - The strategy here is a mix. The tweet is written and synchronously replicated to a primary database. The process of sending the tweet to the followers' timelines is done asynchronously using massive queues and workers. This ensures the core write is durable while allowing the read path to scale globally and remain highly available.

Failure detection and recovery

Building redundancy itself is insufficient unless fault tolerance is used to automatically detect and recover from the failure. Here are a few ways in which fault tolerance can be used to detect and recover from failures:

- Health checks by regularly verifying whether all system components are responsive.
- Failover is automated, so the switch to redundant components can happen without human intervention.

- Monitoring and alerts to provide visibility on which redundancies are active and usable.
- Postmortems after a failure to identify where redundancies or fault tolerance are missing.

Summary

Fault tolerance and redundancy are the foundations of resilient system design. They transform inevitable failures from catastrophic outages into manageable events. By layering redundancy at hardware, software, network, and geographic levels, and by combining it with automation and fault isolation, SRE teams ensure services remain available even under adverse conditions. Balancing redundancy and cost is an ongoing challenge; however, without fault tolerance and redundancy, reliability is just wishful thinking.

Scalability and load management

A reliable system must not only be available when handling a small number of users but must also perform under heavy load as usage grows. Systems should gracefully handle growth and spikes in demand. Scalability is the ability of a system to handle increased workload without compromising performance or reliability, and load management is the set of practices and tools that ensure this scaling happens smoothly and effectively. For SRE, these are design constraints to deliver consistent user experiences, whether the system serves 100 or 100 million users.

Vertical and horizontal scaling

The first step while scaling is to identify the direction in which we need to add capacity. There are two strategies of scaling, vertical and horizontal. Let us look at both of them:

1. **Vertical scaling**: It also means scaling up or down by adding more resources like CPU, RAM, or disk I/O to a single node. This can be done by migrating our application to a larger VM or a much more powerful physical machine and then letting go of the old machine.

   Pros of vertical scaling:

   a. Vertical scaling is simple to implement. It often requires no change in the application architecture. In the case of a cloud application, it is mostly a configuration change in the cloud dashboard.

   b. Since the application remains within a single machine, vertical scaling avoids challenges like network communication, data partitioning, and handling of distributed state.

Cons of vertical scaling:

a. Vertical scaling is limited by the maximum hardware size available, as we cannot scale beyond the largest machine available with the cloud provider or that available with our hardware vendors.

b. Vertically scaled machines are still single points of failure as they are single servers.

c. Vertical scaling is expensive, as larger machines are disproportionately more expensive than smaller machines.

d. Also, scaling vertically may require a reboot, resulting in service downtime.

Vertical scaling is ideal for monoliths or databases that are difficult to shard and distribute across a cluster. It can also be used as a temporary fix for unexpected load and not used as a long-term strategy for modern cloud-native applications.

2. **Horizontal scaling**: It also means scaling out or scaling in by adding more nodes to a system and distributing the load across them. This is generally done by adding more identical instances of our application server behind a load balancer.

Pros of horizontal scaling:

a. Theoretically, horizontal scaling provides infinite scale as we are limited only by the cloud budget or the orchestration platform.

b. Horizontally scalable systems are inherently fault-tolerant, as the loss of one node does not result in a catastrophe.

c. Horizontal scaling is cost-efficient as we can use small commodity machines and add as much capacity as needed gradually.

d. Nodes can be added or removed from the pool without impacting the overall service, resulting in zero downtime.

Cons of horizontal scaling:

a. Horizontal scaling is architecturally complex to implement. Our applications must be designed to run in a distributed environment, which introduces complexity in communication, data consistency, and service discovery.

b. Horizontal scalability is the default choice for modern applications, microservices, and any other systems that need high availability and elastic scalability (scale out or in as per user base).

SREs generally prefer horizontal scalability as this pattern enables reliability, elasticity, and cost optimization. The most important design principle for enabling horizontal scaling is architecting and building stateless services, which are services that do not store persistent client-specific data on the server between requests. This enables any server to handle the request from the client at any time.

Principles of load management

Even with scalability, there will always be peaks where demand exceeds capacity. Load management ensures the system degrades gracefully instead of failing catastrophically. Let us look at some of the principles that help in load management:

- **Load balancing**: The load balancer is a crucial piece of infrastructure that makes horizontal scaling work. It acts as the single-entry point that distributes traffic across the pool of backend instances. Let us look at some of the load balancing algorithms that determine which backend server receives the request:
    - Round robin distributes requests sequentially to every server in the pool. This is a simple algorithm and does not account for varying server load or request complexity.
    - The least connections algorithm sends the request to the server with the fewest active connections. This is better than round robin as it accounts for the current server load, making it excellent for handling requests of varying duration.
    - IP Hash algorithm uses the client's IP address to determine which server handles the request. This ensures that a user is consistently routed to the same server, which can be used for applications that cannot externalize state.

    The load balancer uses health checks to identify dead or unhealthy instances and avoid sending traffic to them. The load balancer periodically sends a health check request (e.g., `GET /health`) to each registered backend instance to see if it returns a `200:OK` response. If any instance fails to return a response or returns a `5XX:error`, the load balancer automatically drains that instance and stops sending new traffic to it. The load balancer keeps rechecking the health of that instance, and once it is back to normal, it is automatically added back to the pool.

- **Autoscaling**: It is a typically threshold based (can also be predictive, depending on the tooling) strategy for load management. It is the practice of automatically adding or removing nodes based on real-time demand. Autoscaling is configured by defining a scaling policy that is tied to a metric like:
    - **CPU utilization**: Example, if the average CPU across the fleet is > 70% for 5 minutes, add two instances.
    - Memory utilization metric is used if applications are memory-bound.
    - Custom application-level metrics can also be used for autoscaling. For example, if the number of messages in our processing queue is > 10000, add five worker instances. This example uses queue length as a custom metric for autoscaling.

Let us look at a real-world example of an e-commerce site during a flash sale. Traffic begins to spike, causing CPU utilization to climb from 30% to 80%. The cloud autoscaler detects this, and within 2-3 minutes, it automatically spins up 50% more web servers to handle the load. After the sale, as traffic dwindles, it scales the fleet back down to save costs.

- **Rate limiting**: It is a reactive measure for load management. Rate limiting protects our API from being overwhelmed by a single client or a group of clients by defining a quota (e.g., 100 requests per hour per API key). This also prevents accidental **denial of service** (**DOS**) from misconfigured clients.
- **Load shedding**: It is an advanced technique to ensure the system remains up during extreme load. This is done by intentionally dropping less critical requests to ensure that the most critical ones are handled. For load shedding to work, we must classify request priority and define a threshold. For example, when CPU crosses 90%, middleware can be configured to start rejecting **`GET /api/notifications`** requests with a **`503: service unavailable`** response to reserve capacity for other critical requests like **`POST /api/orders`**.
- **Caching**: It reduces redundant work, which consumes system resources by storing frequently requested results closer to users. There are multiple ways of caching frequently used resources, as follows:
    - Client-side caching is done at the web browser level to cache static resources.
    - Edge caching is done on **content delivery network** (**CDN**) nodes to serve popular content from nearby nodes.
    - Server-side caching is done using technologies like *Redis* or *Memcached* to store precomputed results.

A real-world example of caching is Netflix, which caches thumbnails and metadata on CDNs to avoid overloading backend services.

Scalable architecture

It is crucial to remember that scalability is not only about the application tier. Our entire stack must scale in unison. A common pitfall that few architectures encounter is that a perfectly scalable web tier is unable to scale due to the monolithic database, which is unable to handle increased query load.

Our scalability architecture must include the following tiers:

- Application tier should be horizontally scalable via stateless web/API servers.
- Caching tier is a key-value store that offloads repeated read requests from the database. The caching tier must be deployed as a cluster so that it can be scaled by adding more nodes if needed.

- Database tier contains the databases. Databases can be scaled vertically by adding more resources or horizontally by adding more read replicas (for read scaling) and shards/partitions (for write scaling).

By designing each layer with scalability in mind and using load balancers and autoscaling to manage capacity, we can build a system that is not only reliable but also efficient and cost-effective, capable of gracefully handling both quiet nights and record-breaking days.

Reliability testing using chaos engineering

In most engineering disciplines, systems are rigorously tested before they go into production. Traditional software testing validates that a system works correctly under ideal and expected conditions. In other words, traditional testing ensures functionality but does not prepare a system for the unpredictable realities of production, which can vary from failing dependencies, network issues, or exhausted resources. Reliability testing is about simulating failures before they happen in production, ensuring systems degrade gracefully instead of collapsing.

Reliability testing focuses on rigorous testing that focuses on different types of failures, ranging from:

- Database node failures.
- Resource constraint due to sudden surges in traffic.
- Cache failures resulting in queries flooding the database.
- Does the system degrade gracefully instead of collapsing?

This type of testing explores failure modes instead of the happy path, thus building confidence that the system can survive chaos.

Types of reliability testing

Traditional reliability testing focuses are categorized into the following types:

- **Stress testing**: This type of testing pushes the system to and beyond its limits to see how it behaves under extreme load. The goal here is to identify breaking points and bottlenecks. Tools like Apache JMeter are used to increase traffic (for example, 10x of normal peak traffic) to test if the system degrades gracefully or collapses.
- **Load testing**: It measures how a system performs under expected traffic levels. The goal here is to ensure that response times and error rates remain within the SLO. An example of load testing is simulating 1000 concurrent users over a 1 hour period on the system to mimic a product launch.
- **Spike testing**: In this type of testing, sudden bursts of traffic are induced to see how the system handles traffic spikes. The goal here is to test if the autoscaling triggers are

working properly. For example, simulating an event where traffic jumps from 10K requests to 100K requests in 5 minutes.

- **Failover testing**: It is used to validate redundancy and disaster recovery mechanisms. The goal here is to ensure that services failover smoothly with minimal downtime. An example of failover testing is shutting down a primary database node to see if the system automatically fails over to a replica.
- **Fault injection testing**: In this type of testing, the idea is to intentionally introduce errors, latencies, or failures in the system to see how the system responds. The goal here is to test error handling, timeouts, and recovery logic. An example of fault injection testing is simulating packet loss or API timeouts within interservice communication.

Chaos engineering

Chaos engineering is the discipline of deliberately injecting failures into production systems to discover weaknesses before real-world failures expose them. It is not about breaking things randomly; it is a rigorous, scientific practice to build confidence in the system's capability to withstand turbulent conditions in production.

Principles of chaos engineering

Chaos engineering is a term popularized by Netflix through their tool, famously known as **Chaos Monkey**. Let us look at the principles of chaos engineering as formalized by Netflix:

- Start by defining a steady state, which is some measurable output of the system that indicates normal behavior (e.g., low error rates or consistent latency).
- Formulate a hypothesis that this steady state will continue in both the control group and the experimental group.
- Introduce real-world events in the experimental group, such as server failures, network latency, or I/O errors.
- Try to disprove the hypothesis by looking at a difference in steady state between the control and experimental groups.

The goal of chaos testing is to uncover hidden assumptions and weaknesses before they cause a customer-facing outage.

Chaos engineering cycle

The following figure shows the cycle of chaos engineering, which is a 4-step process:

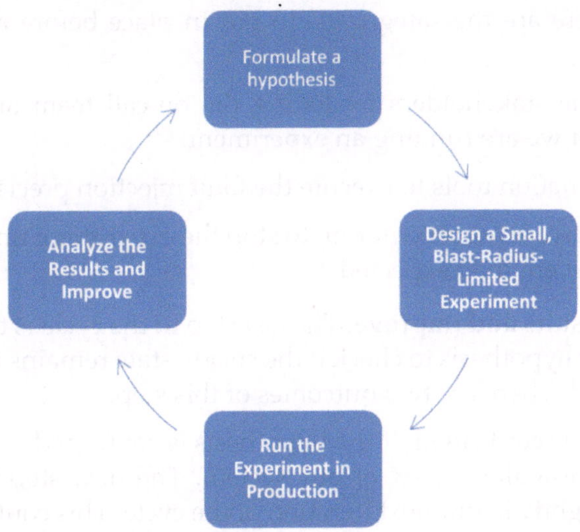

Figure 5.2: *This cycle operationalizes chaos engineering as a repeatable experiment loop*

Let us look at the four steps of the chaos engineering cycle:

1. **Formulate a hypothesis**: The first step is to start with a specific, measurable belief about how a system should behave during a failure. A good hypothesis should be clear and testable and should reference state-ready metrics (SLI/SLO) already defined earlier.

   Example of strong hypothesis: It is believed that if the primary MySQL database in us-east-1a becomes unavailable, the application will automatically fail over to the replica in us-east-1b within 30 seconds, and the P99 latency for write operations will not exceed 2 seconds during the failover.

2. **Design a small, blast-radius-limited experiment**: The second step is to carefully design an experiment. The key principle is to start small. The blast radius is defined as the potential impact of the experiment. We should always start with the smallest possible blast radius.

   Examples of experiments:

   a. **Smallest experiment**: Terminate one non-critical backend worker instance out of 50.

   b. **Medium experiment**: Inject latency between a specific microservice and its cache cluster.

   c. **Large experiment**: Block all network traffic to an entire availability zone.

3. **Run the experiment in production**: This is the most critical step. While we can always run experiments in the staging environment, the staging environment is never a perfect replica of production. The true complex interactions and real user traffic exist only in

production. Here are the safeguards to put in place before running experiments in production:

a. Inform the stakeholders by letting the on-call team and relevant developers know that we are running an experiment.

b. Use automation tools to execute the fault injection precisely and consistently.

c. Always have an abort criterion to stop the experiment immediately if the impact is more severe than expected.

4. **Analyze the results and improve**: The last step in the cycle is to compare the system's behavior to our hypothesis to check if the steady state remains and whether the impact was as expected. There are two outcomes of this step:

    a. **Hypothesis confirmed**: If the hypothesis is confirmed, we have built confidence in that particular aspect of our system. The next step is to increase the blast radius slightly in our next iteration of the cycle. This could also mean expanding the failure modes (e.g., latency, packet loss, dependency errors).

    b. **Hypothesis rejected**: This means we have found a weakness before it caused a real outage. This needs to be fixed. Once fixed, we need to run the experiment again to verify the fix.

Common chaos experiments

Let us look at some of the common chaos experiments that are run as part of chaos engineering:

- Instance termination where servers or containers are randomly shut down to validate autoscaling groups and failover mechanisms.
- Network latency and packet loss are checked by introducing artificial delays and dropped packets to test whether services degrade gracefully during poor connectivity.
- Dependency failure is introduced by killing or slowing down critical dependencies, like the cache, to verify circuit breakers, retries, and fallbacks.
- Simulate a full data center or region outage to test geo-readiness and disaster recovery scenarios.
- Resource exhaustion is introduced by maxing out CPU, memory, or disk to validate autoscaling triggers and backpressure mechanisms.

Chaos engineering and blameless culture

Chaos engineering and reliability testing are not one-time events; they are cultural practices. They foster a mindset that treats failure as normal and resilience as an ongoing pursuit. To build a blameless chaos engineering culture, we should adopt these practices:

- Blameless postmortems should be done after chaos experiments to capture the findings.

- Continuous verification should be done to ensure that reliability is tested regularly (ideally in every sprint) instead of just once a year.
- Cross-team collaboration during chaos testing ensures that reliability is built into each and every layer of the stack.

Chaos engineering tools and benefits

There are a variety of tools that can be used for chaos engineering, ranging from open-source projects to commercial ones. Let us look at some of the tools, as follows:

- Chaos Monkey is an open-source tool developed by Netflix. It is best for getting started and testing basic instance failure resilience.
- Gremlin is a commercial tool with a user-friendly UI and a wide range of attacks on CPU, memory, disk, network, and state. This is generally used by enterprises that want a safe and controlled platform with support.
- LitmusChaos is a tool that is native to Kubernetes, which focuses on testing the Kubernetes infrastructure and cloud-native applications. This is generally used by teams running Kubernetes workloads.
- AWS Fault Injection simulator is a tool native to AWS and can be used to target **Elastic Compute Cloud** (**EC2**), **Relational Database Service** (**RDS**), **Elastic Container Service** (**ECS**), etc. This is used by teams that have systems deployed heavily on AWS.

Chaos testing results in significant benefits for the organization. Firstly, it exposes hidden weaknesses before end users are impacted. It builds confidence in the teams' recovery processes and trains them to respond to incidents more effectively. Following a blameless culture also promotes a culture of resilience at all levels in the organization.

Real-world example of Netflix's Simian Army

Netflix pioneered chaos engineering with its suite of tools, famously called the **Simian Army**. This suite of tools contains the following tools:

- Chaos Monkey is used to terminate random instances.
- Latency Monkey is used to introduce artificial delays in RESTful clients to simulate network degradation.
- Chaos Gorilla can be used to simulate an entire Amazon availability zone failing.
- Chaos Kong is the ultimate test that simulates an entire AWS region going down.

By running this suite of chaos engineering tools continuously in production, Netflix has ensured that every service is built to withstand failures, making its system inherently more resilient.

Summary

Testing for reliability, and chaos engineering in particular, transforms resilience from a hopeful claim into a proven property. It moves teams from a reactive posture to a proactive one. By systematically introducing failure in a controlled manner, we build not just more robust systems, but also more confident and prepared engineering teams. It is a powerful practice for validating that our design for reliability actually works under real-world conditions.

Capacity planning and scalability

Even the most reliable systems will fail if they run out of resources. Capacity planning is the process of predicting future demand for system resources and ensuring that sufficient capacity is provisioned to handle that demand while meeting the SLO. It acts as a bridge between business ambition and technical reality. For SREs, capacity planning is not a one-time exercise. It is a continuous cycle of measurement, forecasting, and provisioning that prevents performance degradation and outages during growth or traffic spikes.

Capacity planning process

Effective capacity planning is a systematic, ongoing process that involves the following steps:

1. **Measure and establish a baseline**: The first step in the process is to thoroughly understand our system's current state. Key metrics to focus on are average and peak traffic, resource utilization levels for CPU, memory, disk I/O, network, etc., and capacity headroom available before hitting saturation. This also involves collecting all application-level performance metrics and infrastructure utilization.

2. **Forecast future demand**: This step involves predicting how demand will change over a specific time horizon (e.g., 3, 6, or 12 months). For forecasting demand, we need to focus on these aspects:

    a. Work with product and marketing teams to understand business growth projections. This can also include new features, product launches, or any upcoming marketing campaigns.

    b. Analyze the past traffic to identify the growth pattern, which can be linear, exponential, or seasonal.

    c. Impact analysis of a new feature is also done to see if it will significantly increase the load.

3. **Model required capacity**: The third step in the process is to translate the demand into concrete resource requirements. The basic formula to forecast resource requirements is:

    Resources needed = (Total forecast demand) / (Performance per unit resource) + Headroom

Let us understand this with an example that predicts that API requests will grow from 1000 RPS to 1500 RPS over a period of 6 months. While measuring the baseline (as in the first step), we identified that an application instance can handle 100 RPS before it degrades. The calculation for future resources is done as follows:

Current instances = 1000 RPS / 100 RPS-per-instance = 10 instances

Future instances = 1500 RPS / 100 RPS-per-instance = 15 instances

Add a 20% headroom to maintain performance during unexpected spikes.

*15 instances * 1.2 (headroom) = 18 instances required.*

4. **Provision and execute**: Once we know the future demand of resources, the next step is to provision the instances either manually or preferably automatically. IaC tools like Terraform can be used to define the target state. The plan to scale the infrastructure should be executed ahead of the projected need.
5. **Monitor and validate**: The last step of the process is to monitor and continuously track the actual usage against our forecast. This includes setting up alerts for when resource utilization exceeds the safe threshold (e.g., CPU over 70% for an extended period) or when the actual growth deviates from the forecast, triggering a re-planning cycle.

USE metrics

The **utilization, saturation, and errors** (**USE**) metrics are a valuable framework for identifying bottlenecks. Let us look at these metrics:

- Utilization is the percentage of time a resource is busy (e.g., CPU utilization is 70%). High utilization is a warning sign but needs further investigation. A CPU can be 100% utilized but still process work efficiently.
- Saturation is the degree to which a resource has more work than it can handle. This is often identified as queue length and is a more critical indicator of performance problems. An example of saturation is when the disk is overwhelmed, and read/write requests are queued. This leads to disk I/O saturation, which directly impacts latency.
- Error rate is the rate at which requests fail. A rising error rate often indicates that a resource is saturated or failing.
- SREs should focus on saturation and error rate as the primary indicators of capacity alerts, while resource utilization can act as a secondary indicator.

Forecasting models

There are different forecasting techniques based on the different types of growth:

- Linear growth projection assumes a constant increase over time.
- Seasonal growth analysis identifies recurring patterns, which are essential for businesses with predictable peak usage.

- Event-based forecasting is used to model the impact of specific known future events—like a flash sale or a product launch.

Scalability planning

The ultimate evolution of capacity planning is full automation via autoscaling. Autoscaling works based on a defined scaling policy, which is triggered when a monitored metric triggers a scale out or scale in event. Autoscaling can be reactive or metric-based, which responds to current load/trigger, or predictive, which uses machine learning to forecast short-term demand and autoscale.

A common mistake made during scaling is that it is planned for the application stack only, ignoring the entire stack, which includes the caching and the data tiers. Hence, while scaling the entire stack must scale in unison, which may include the following tiers:

1. Application tier should be scaled horizontally by using load balancers and stateless applications.
2. The caching tier can be scaled by adding more nodes (for caches like Memcached or Redis). A key metric is to monitor the cache hit ratio and memory usage to identify when to scale.
3. The data tier involves read scaling and write scaling. Read scaling can be done by adding more read replicas, which should be a part of the capacity planning exercise. For scaling writes, data needs to be sharded or partitioned across multiple database instances using a shard key, which needs significant architectural foresight.

Capacity planning and scaling transform reliability from a technical concern to a strategic business function. By systematically measuring, forecasting, and provisioning, SREs ensure that user growth leads to celebration, not catastrophe. It is a continuous dialogue between the business ambitions and the system's capabilities, ensuring that the platform is always ready for what comes next.

Designing for recovery

Even the best-engineered systems will fail. While fault tolerance, redundancy, and scalability reduce the likelihood of failure, they cannot be eliminated entirely. Therefore, a critical aspect of reliability is not just to prevent failures but to ensure that when they happen, recovery is swift, smooth, and minimally disruptive. Recovery is about restoring service as fast as possible with minimal user impact, learning from failures, and ensuring the same issue does not repeat.

Choosing between MTTR and MTBF

Reliability is often expressed as **mean time between failure** (**MTBF**), whereas recovery is measured as **mean time to recovery** (**MTTR**). Traditional engineering often focuses on maximizing the MTBF, which is the average time the system runs before breaking. However, failures are inevitable. Low recovery time ensures that failures are short-lived. A system can tolerate frequent failures if recovery is instant. Conversely, even rare failures are unacceptable if recovery takes hours.

A system that fails once a month for five minutes (low MTBF, low MTTR) provides a better user experience than a system that fails once a year but is down for five hours (high MTBF, high MTTR). Designing for recovery acknowledges this reality and optimizes for the speed of restoration. The art of SRE is to balance both.

Recovery-oriented design

Recovery-oriented design focuses on the principle that failure is expected and hence the team should focus on automating recovery as much as possible. Whenever failure occurs, the blast radius or the impact should be minimal using the SRE design patterns we have discussed at the beginning of this chapter. An acceptable situation is to provide partial functionality during recovery by using graceful degradation, instead of complete downtime. And observability tools must be well setup for quick diagnosis during recovery.

Some of the techniques for recovery are listed as follows:

- Automated failover is a technique where, when a component fails, traffic is rerouted to healthy replica nodes.
- Graceful degradation designs services to degrade without collapsing completely.
- Circuit breakers can be used to cut off requests to repeatedly failing services, thus preventing cascading slowdowns.
- Rollbacks and roll-forwards are used to recover during a software deployment. The idea is to either rollback (revert) to the last known good version or roll forward by applying a hotfix.
- Backups and snapshots should be taken regularly to provide recovery in stateful systems.
- Disaster recovery planning is used to plan for large-scale failures so that the business can continue even during major outages.
- Playbooks and runbooks can be used wherever manual intervention is needed to reduce the panic during outages and ensure consistency, thus reducing the MTTR.

Real-world examples

Let us look at the real-world examples:

1. Netflix uses a multi-region active-active architecture to recover from regional failures.
2. Amazon S3 had a large-scale outage in 2017 due to a typo during a maintenance activity. Recovery took hours. The postmortem for this outage emphasized faster rollback procedures and more automations.

3. Google search can function even if one data center goes offline, as global traffic is redistributed automatically.

Recovery-oriented mindset

Designing for recovery completes the circle of reliability engineering. It acknowledges that perfection is unattainable and instead focuses on resilience and speed. While redundancy and fault tolerance reduce the frequency of incidents, recovery ensures that when outages occur, they are short-lived and minimally disruptive. By automating failover, enabling graceful degradation, planning for disaster recovery, and fostering a culture of learning, SRE teams build systems that not only survive failures but bounce back stronger. When an incident strikes, a recovery-oriented system provides the tools, data, and pathways to restore service quickly, turning a potential disaster into a minor blip. This mindset ensures that our system's reliability is defined not just by its ability to avoid failure, but by its capacity to heal itself.

Conclusion

Designing for reliability is a holistic discipline that integrates architecture, development, and operations. It requires a shift in mindset from hoping nothing goes wrong to knowing exactly what will happen when things inevitably go wrong. By treating reliability as a non-negotiable feature, employing resilient patterns like circuit breakers and bulkheads, planning for scale through rigorous capacity management, and proactively uncovering weaknesses via chaos engineering, we build services that are more than just robust. We build systems that are more resilient, learning from each failure and emerging stronger so they can withstand scenarios like unexpected load, partial failures, network issues, and dependency outages. This reliability foundation empowers teams to innovate faster, deploy with confidence, and deliver the consistent experience that users expect, thus enabling velocity, innovation, and, ultimately, user trust and happiness that leads to business success.

In the next chapter, we will explore how disciplined release engineering practices enable safe, predictable, and automated software delivery. Release engineering is the discipline that bridges the gap between code completion and product deployment. We will examine build pipelines, artifact management, deployment strategies, and release automation. This chapter will help us understand how strong release engineering becomes the backbone of high-velocity and low-failure software teams.

CHAPTER 6
Release Engineering

Introduction

In the early days of software development, the act of releasing a new version was often a monumental and high-stakes event. Engineering teams would coordinate complex merge days to merge changes from various teams into the release branch and then manually run deployment scripts late at night, and hope that a single configuration error or missed dependency would not lead to a catastrophic system failure. This process was slow, stressful, and inherently risky, creating a culture of fear around deployment and slowing down the pace of innovation. The software industry has since undergone a profound transformation, recognizing that the ability to deliver changes reliably and frequently is a critical competitive advantage. Release engineering has emerged as the essential discipline that answers this demand.

In modern software engineering teams, release engineering acts as the backbone of DevOps and agile practices, focusing on the systematic design and implementation of automated processes for building, testing, and deploying software. This move releases from being rare, disruptive events to becoming predictable, routine, and even uneventful occurrences. The core mission is to establish a pathway for delivering software that is not only fast but, more importantly, safe, reliable, and trustworthy. This requires a holistic approach that encompasses tooling, processes, and a collaborative culture. Hence, modern release engineering emphasizes automation, risk mitigation, rollback strategies, and continuous improvement. A well-designed release process reduces human error, minimizes downtime, and instills confidence in both developers and end-users.

Structure

The chapter covers the following topics:

- Release lifecycle
- CI/CD pipelines and automation

- Deployment strategies
- Rollback and recovery
- Culture of safe releases
- Feature flags
- Change management and reliability
- Overview of release engineering tool Jenkins

Objectives

This chapter explores the fundamental principles and practical techniques that underpin the discipline of release engineering. We will go over **continuous integration/continuous deployment** (CI/CD) pipelines and how they can be used to automate the build, test and deployment of software to accelerate delivery while maintaining quality. We will understand some of the key deployment strategies like blue-green, canary and rolling updates to minimize risk while reducing downtime. We will also cover rollback strategies and processes that can be leveraged to quickly recover from any issue that may arise. We will see how feature flags can be used as a powerful tool for decoupling deployment from release, enabling safer experimentation and controlled rollouts. By the end of this chapter, we will understand how to build a robust release engineering workflow that supports rapid deployment while maintaining system stability and user trust.

Release lifecycle

The release lifecycle defines the end-to-end journey of software from development to production, ensuring that each stage adds value, enforces quality, and reduces risk. A software release is not a single action but a structured and repeatable journey that includes planning, building, testing, validation, deployment and monitoring. A well-defined lifecycle introduces clear checkpoints where issues can be detected early and addressed proactively. This provides visibility, establishes accountability across teams and standardizes the release practices. Clear release lifecycles help organizations deliver software in a predictable, reliable and safe manner while continuously improving quality and user confidence.

Stages of the release lifecycle

The release lifecycle is a structured framework that guides software from its initial conception to its final delivery and beyond. Let us understand each stage in detail, so we can design and implement a robust, predictable and high-quality release process. The following figure gives an overview of the stages involved in a release cycle:

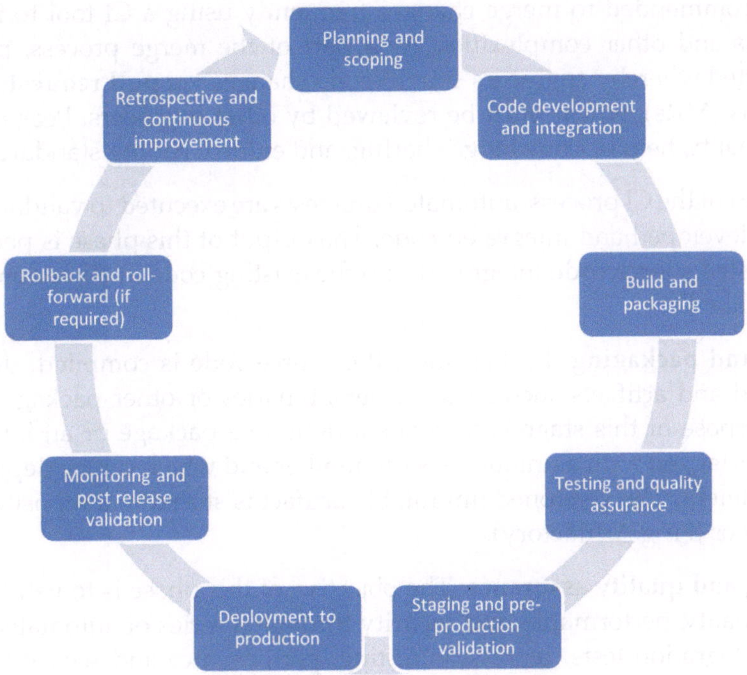

***Figure 6.1**: Stages of the release lifecycle*

The stages of the release lifecycle are as follows:

1. **Planning and scoping**: The objective of this stage is to define the scope of the release including the features, bug fixes, security patches or performance improvements that need to be packaged in this release. This should be decided by collaborating with stakeholders, product managers and users to gather the complete list of items and prioritize them based on business goals, user needs and technical feasibility.

   Once the scope of the release is clear, the next step is to define the success criteria for the release by identifying the key metrics related to user engagement, performance benchmarks or business goals for the release. These metrics are vital for post release validation. The next step is to identify potential challenges, dependencies or compliance requirements as part of risk assessment for the release. The final step is to create a high-level timeline in collaboration with other teams to ensure a smooth launch.

   This stage gives us a well-defined **product requirement document** (**PRD**), a defined scope and a set of measurable success criteria for the release.

2. **Code development and integration**: The objective of this stage is to translate the requirements into functional code while continuously integrating the code into a shared codebase to prevent integration conflicts. In this stage, developers implement changes in short-lived feature branches, which are later merged into the main or release branch.

It is recommended to merge changes frequently using a CI tool to minimize merge conflicts and other complexities. As a part of the merge process, peer reviews are conducted whereby engineers submit code changes via **pull requests** (**PRs**) or **merge requests** (**MRs**), which must be reviewed by other engineers. Peer reviews improve code quality, help in knowledge sharing, and enforce coding standards.

As a part of the CI process, automated unit tests are executed to validate the correctness of the developed and integrated code. The output of this phase is peer reviewed and auto-tested source code integrated into the existing code in a **version control system** (**VCs**) (like Git).

3. **Build and packaging**: In this stage, the source code is compiled, dependencies are resolved and artifacts such as containers, binaries or other packages are generated. The purpose of this stage is to create a definitive package or an immutable artifact which is tagged with a unique version number and which can be deployed across any environment. The versioned immutable artifact is stored in a repository (like Docker registry or JFrog Artifactory).

4. **Testing and quality assurance**: The objective of this phase is to validate the artifact's functionality, performance and security through a series of automated tests (like unit tests, integration tests, regression testing, performance and security tests) to ensure that it meets the quality standards. Manual or exploratory testing can be used to complement automated tests for certain edge cases or usability aspects. Only those artifacts that pass all required quality gates during these validations are allowed to proceed further.

5. **Staging and pre-production validation**: During this stage, the validated artifact is deployed into a production-like environment for final checks before the release. The staging environment generally mirrors production in terms of infrastructure, configuration and data. Following tests are executed in the staging environment:

   a. Smoke testing is a quick set of tests to ensure that the deployment was successful and the application has started correctly.

   b. Final integration validation is done to confirm that the application works with all external dependencies in a near-live setting.

   c. **User acceptance testing** (**UAT**) is done manually by product managers or QA engineers for certain workflows to ensure that they meet the acceptance criteria.

   d. Load tests or canary tests are also performed to ensure system stability in production-like conditions.

   This stage acts as the last line of defense to catch environment-specific issues that may not have appeared in earlier testing phases, thus building confidence that the artifact is ready for production.

6. **Deployment to production**: This is the technical execution of the release to safely and efficiently install the new version of the software into the live production environment with minimal impact on users. To manage risk, deployment strategies like blue-green, canary, or rolling updates are used, which are designed for close to zero downtime deployments and allow for rapid rollback if issues are detected.

   This stage uses automation to ensure consistency and reduce manual errors while making the new software version live in production.

7. **Monitoring and post release validation**: The work is not over once the deployment is complete. Instead, the next step is to use observability tools to verify the health and performance of the new release in production. Automated alerts will flag anomalies in performance, error rates or latency. This is also the stage where the success metrics defined in the planning stage are verified against real-time data. It is also important that the release does not violate the predefined SLOs. This stage helps in confirming the success of the release or early detection of potential issues.

8. **Rollback or roll-forward (if required)**: This is an optional stage. The purpose of this stage is to restore stability if a critical issue is detected in production post release. In case of an issue in production, the team can perform one of the following steps to restore stability:

   a. Rollback the release by reverting the production environment to the previous known stable version. This is the fastest way to restore service.

   b. Roll-forward is another way to restore service by deploying a new version of the application to production that contains a fix for the issue. This requires the team to be able to develop, test and deploy a fix rapidly and is generally done when rollback is complex or not possible.

   The purpose of this step is to ensure a stable production environment by mitigating any incident that can or has happened.

9. **Retrospective and continuous improvement**: The objective of this phase is to learn from the release process (both success and failure) and identify opportunities for improvement. During this stage, the teams will hold blameless retrospective meetings to discuss the following questions:

   a. What went well?

   b. What could have been done better?

   c. What were the root causes of the problems?

   d. What actionable items need to be implemented to improve the next release?

   During this stage, learnings and actionable items are documented to strengthen the release cycle. This practice fosters a culture of psychological safety and continuous improvement, ensuring that each release cycle is more efficient and safer than the last.

CI/CD pipelines and automation

Modern release engineering thrives on automation, and at its core are CI/CD pipelines. They transform the theoretical release lifecycle into a fast, reliable, and repeatable automated process. These pipelines automate the process of building, testing, and deploying software, reducing manual effort while ensuring consistency and reliability.

Continuous integration

CI is the development practice where developers integrate code into a shared repository frequently, typically multiple times a day. Each integration is automatically verified by an automated build and a set of tests.

The primary goals of CI are as follows:

- Early bug detection by identifying and fixing integration errors within minutes, rather than weeks into a development cycle.
- Reduce chances of integration hell by avoiding the massive effort of merging large, long-lived feature branches.
- Maintain a deployable mainline by ensuring that the main branch (like main or trunk) is always in a working state.

As a part of CI, the following steps need to be automated:

1. Automated builds are triggered by every code commit to ensure that the code compiles successfully.
2. Automated tests such as unit tests, integration tests and regression tests are run to validate the correctness of the build and to catch defects.
3. Static analysis and security scans are done to automatically check for style violations, code quality and vulnerabilities.

As an analogy, CI can be thought of as a high-quality automated assembly line that produces a finished car.

Continuous delivery/continuous deployment

While CI ensures that code changes are integrated successfully, CD ensures that those changes are deployed quickly and safely. There are two different types of CDs, explained as follows:

- **Continuous delivery**: This is an extension of CI, which ensures that every change that passes the CI pipeline is always in a state that can be deployed to production safely and quickly. The key differentiator between continuous delivery and CD is that in the former, the final step of deployment to production is a manual, business-triggered decision. The technical capability to release is continuous, but the actual release is gated by human decision.

- **CD**: It is the most advanced stage of automation, where every single change that passes the automation testing phase is automatically deployed to production without any human intervention. This requires an extremely high degree of confidence in the entire pipeline, including the test suite, monitoring and rollback capabilities.

For CD to function, the following steps need to be automated:

1. Automated deployment scripts using **infrastructure as code** (**IaC**) tools (like *Ansible, Terraform*) to ensure reproducible environment.
2. Release orchestration by building pipelines that control the flow of code through development, staging and production environments.
3. Verification gates where automated health checks, smoke tests and monitoring confirm successful deployments.

As an analogy, continuous delivery means that the car is always gassed up, tested and ready to be driven off the lot by a salesperson. Whereas continuous deployment means that the car automatically drives itself to the customer's house the moment it rolls off the line.

Anatomy of CI/CD pipeline

A CI/CD pipeline is a codified, automated sequence of steps that software changes must pass through on their journey from version control to production. It is typically defined as code (e.g., in a `Jenkinsfile`, `.gitlab-ci.yml` file, or GitHub Actions YAML file), making it versionable, reviewable, and reproducible.

The key stages of a CI/CD pipeline are as follows:

1. **Source stage**: This stage is triggered when a developer pushes code to a feature branch or merges a pull request into the main branch. Once the pipeline is triggered, the CI server fetches the latest code from the repository.
2. **Build stage**: Once the code is fetched by the CI server, it is compiled, dependencies are resolved and artifact packaging is done. This ensures that a versioned immutable artifact is stored in the repository.
3. **Test stage**: During the test stage, unit, integration and regression tests are executed. First, a suite of fast, isolated unit tests is executed to verify the correctness of individual components. At the same time, static code analysis is done to analyze the code for style violations, potential bugs and security vulnerabilities. Later integration and regression tests are done to check for functionality correctness.
4. **Deployment to staging**: The validated artifact is now automatically deployed to the staging environment, which mirrors production. A more comprehensive suite of tests run against the staged application, which includes integration tests with other services and end-to-end tests that simulate real user behavior. Automated security scans and performance tests may also be executed in this environment.

5. **Deployment to production**: The deployment to production can be manual for continuous delivery, where a team lead or an automation check must approve the deployment to production, or it can be fully automated in case of CD. The pipeline should execute a safe deployment strategy like blue-green or canary to roll out the changes to production.

6. **Post deployment monitoring stage**: Automated health checks (called **smoke tests**) are run in the production environment to ensure that the deployment was successful. The pipeline can also be used to trigger scripts for monitoring key application metrics for a short period of time to validate the release's health. Also, observability tools check metrics, logs and traces to ensure release stability.

Key components and tools

A robust CI/CD ecosystem relies on several integrated tools, listed as follows:

- VCS (like *Git, GitHub, Bitbucket*) as a single source of truth for the code repository.
- CI/CD orchestrator (like *Jenkins, GitLab CI* or *GitHub Actions*) that acts as the brain of the operation that executes the CI/CD pipeline.
- Artifact repository (like *JFrog Artifactory* or *Docker Hub*) that stores the immutable build outputs.
- Configuration management and IAC tools (like Ansible or Terraform) that help in provisioning and managing infrastructure consistently.
- Monitoring and observability tools (like Prometheus and Grafana), which help in tracking the success of the deployment and application health.

Benefits of CI/CD pipeline

CI/CD pipelines help accelerate time to market by reducing the cycle time from commit to production and automating the manual steps needed for the same. Automated tests, which are a part of the CI/CD pipeline, help in catching bugs early when they are the cheapest to fix. Whereas code review and static code analysis enforce quality standards, thus improving the code quality. Small, frequent releases are easier to debug, while safe deployment strategies and rapid rollbacks help in minimizing the impact of any single failure. Developers spend less time managing builds and deployments in production and spend more time writing code, thus improving their productivity. Finally, since every change is tracked through a pipeline, a clear audit trail is available for compliance requirements.

By implementing a robust CI/CD pipeline, organizations embed speed, quality, and safety directly into their software delivery process, creating a fundamental capability for competing in the modern digital landscape.

Deployment strategies

The method we use to deploy software is critical for managing risk. There are different deployment strategies, which help organizations in balancing risk with speed, as outlined:

- **Recreate deployment**: This is the simplest strategy where the old version is terminated entirely, and then the new version is deployed. This is the safest way to deploy, but it results in significant downtime. Hence, it is not suitable for user-facing applications.
- **Rolling update**: In this strategy, instances of the old version are gradually replaced with instances of the new version across the infrastructure. This is the default strategy in systems like Kubernetes. For example, in a cluster of 10 servers, the update will proceed one server at a time.
  - **Pros**: This strategy is simple to implement and has zero downtime.
  - **Cons**: For this strategy to run successfully, the new application must be backward compatible as both old and new versions of the application run simultaneously during the update.

The following figure shows how rolling updates are done:

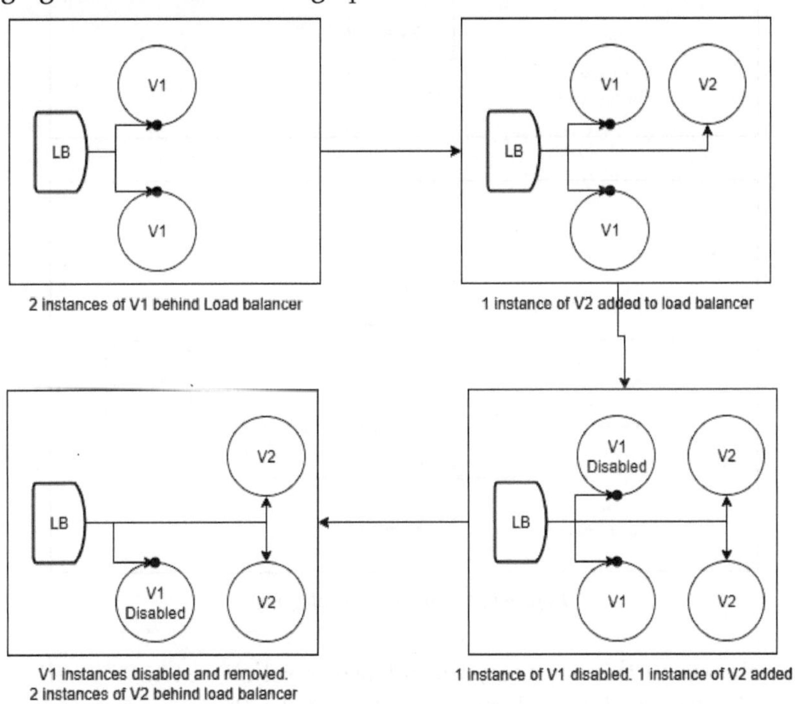

Figure 6.2: *Rolling update*

- **Blue-green deployment**: This strategy requires two identical production environments, labeled *blue* and *green*, where only one environment is live at a time. Assuming that the blue environment is live, we would deploy the new version to the green environment, which is idle, and perform any necessary tests over there. Once verified, we will switch the load balancer to direct traffic from the blue to the green environment, making the green environment live.

- **Pros**: This strategy provides instantaneous rollbacks by switching back to the old environment. Hence, releases are fast with minimal risk.
- **Cons**: This strategy requires double the infrastructure resources and also requires careful management of stateful components (like database or cache).

The following figure shows how blue-green deployments work:

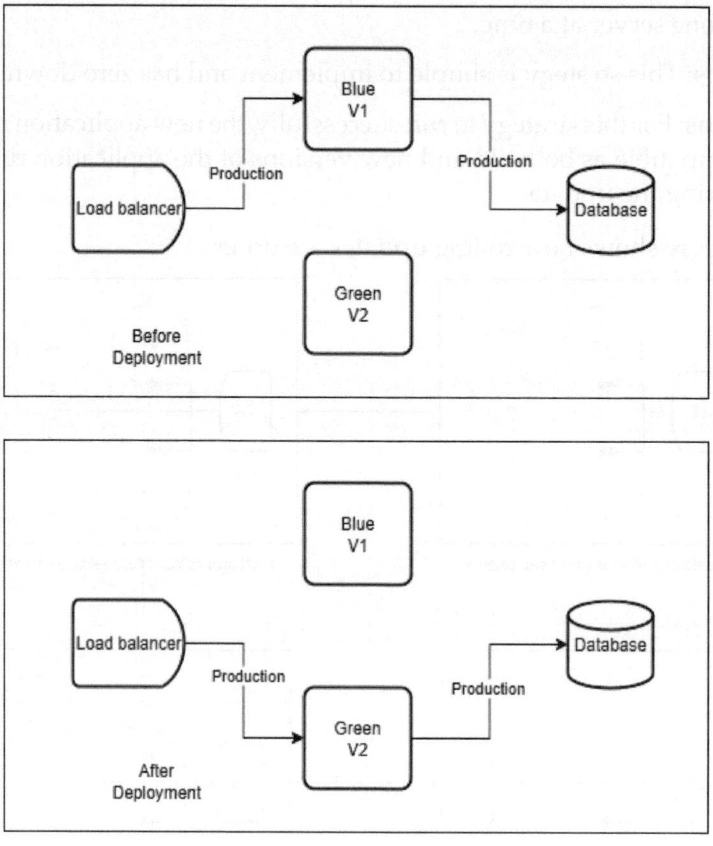

Figure 6.3: Blue-green deployment

- **Canary release**: In this strategy, the release is rolled out to a small subset of users first. If no issues are detected, the rollout is gradually expanded to include all users. So, the new version would be deployed to a small percentage of the production infrastructure (e.g., 5% of servers) and a small percentage of user traffic is directed to these servers. The health and service metrics for the canary instances are closely monitored. If metrics remain healthy, we gradually increase traffic to the new version until it reaches 100%. If problems are detected, traffic can be immediately routed away from the canary deployment.

- **Pros**: This strategy limits the blast radius of a bad release while also allowing for real-world performance testing.
- **Cons**: This is more complex to orchestrate than the blue-green deployment as it requires sophisticated traffic routing and monitoring.

The following figure shows how canary deployments work:

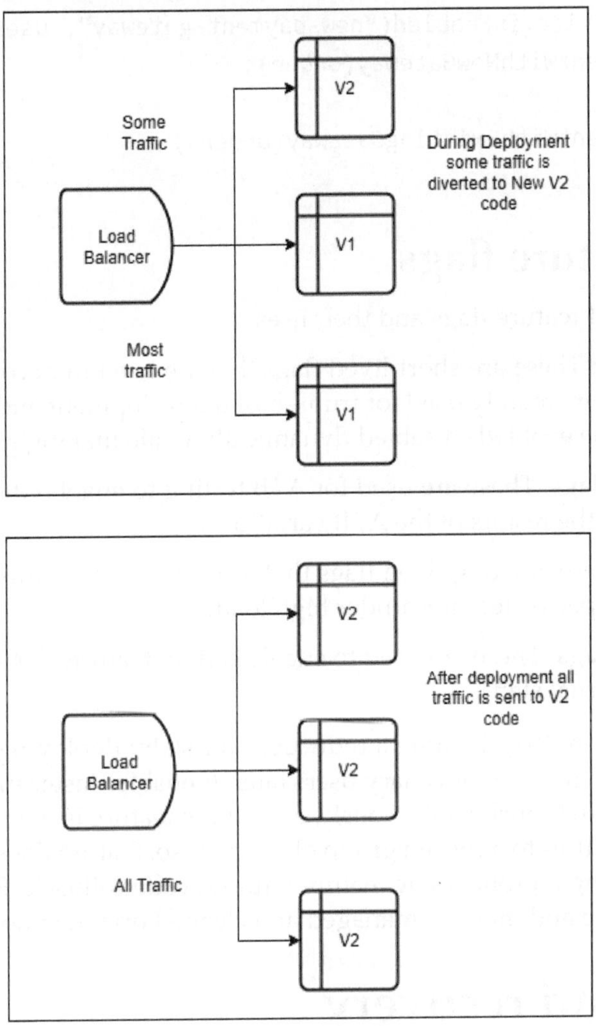

Figure 6.4: Canary deployment

These strategies reduce risk while providing flexibility in how new versions are introduced to users. The deployment strategy should be selected based on the risk tolerance and system architecture to ensure a stable release.

Feature flags

Feature flags (or feature toggles) are used to decouple deployment from release. It is a powerful programming technique that allows teams to modify system behavior without major code changes. It is a conditional statement that checks the status of a condition setting which is often managed by a dedicated service. This helps developers wrap features in flags that can be enabled or disabled dynamically.

Here is a sample code in Java to enable a new payment gateway feature dynamically:

```
if (featureFlagService.isEnabled("new-payment-gateway", user)) {
        processPaymentWithNewGateway(order);
} else {
        processPaymentWithExistingGateway(order);
}
```

Types of feature flags

Let us look at types of feature flags and their uses:

- **Release flags**: These are short-lived flags that are used to decouple deployment from release. They are mainly used for trunk-based development and canary releases where features can be enabled/disabled dynamically while making a release.
- **Experiment flags**: These are used for A/B testing to enable/disable different features and compare the results of the A/B variations.
- **Ops flags**: These are long-lived flags that are used for operational control, like killing or disabling specific features under high load.
- **Permission flags**: These are used to enable certain features for specific users (like beta testers or internal staff).

Benefits of using feature flags include a reduction in risk by deploying code with the flag off and then turning it on for a set of canary users later. It enables faster integration as teams can merge code to the main branch continuously, even if the feature is not ready for release. It can be used to release features to a certain group of users. Also, feature flags function as an instant kill switch by disabling a problematic feature without code rollback. Feature flags introduce complexity in the code and must be managed and cleaned up when no longer needed.

Rollback and recovery

Even with automated pipelines, rigorous testing, and safe deployment strategies, release processes are subject to failure due to bugs that can slip through, performance issues, or issues arising due to unexpected interactions with real-world data. Hence, to maintain the trust and stability of the system, we need to design and implement robust rollback and recovery mechanisms. The purpose of a well-defined rollback and recovery mechanism is to minimize downtime and restore services as quickly as possible, thus reducing the **mean time to recover (MTTR)**, ensuring smooth continuity of the service.

Rollback strategies

The rollback strategies are as follows:

- **Application rollback**: For application rollback, simply revert to the last stable version of the application. In the case of blue-green deployment, rollback can be automated by simply switching back to the stable environment. Whereas in the case of a canary deployment, we can simply route traffic back to the old version of the application. For other deployment strategies, rollbacks work best when builds are immutable and versioned, allowing for quick redeployment of a safe version of the application.
- **Database rollback**: It is more challenging due to schema and data changes. Some techniques that help in database rollback are:
    - Backward compatible schema design (like adding columns instead of modifying or dropping columns).
    - Shadow tables with dual writes to allow seamless cutover and rollback.
    - Feature flags for schema dependent features which can be used to enable rollbacks without breaking functionality.
- **Feature flag rollback**: When an application is deployed using feature flags, teams can instantly disable problematic features using flags instead of redeploying. This allows for rapid mitigation without redeployment cycles, making it a popular recovery strategy in continuous delivery environments.
- **Configuration rollback**: There are scenarios where outages happen due to faulty configuration instead of code. In these scenarios, version-controlled configurations allow quick reversion to stable configurations.

Recovery approaches

Let us now look at the approaches that can be applied to recover from failures:

- **Automated health check and monitoring**: The primary approach is that the CI/CD pipeline should include health checks that continuously evaluate system performance, error rates and response times. If a threshold is breached, automated rollback can be triggered based on the above rollback strategies.
- **Roll-forward**: In complex systems, especially those with database schema changes, rolling back to a previous version can be difficult and dangerous. In such scenarios, a roll-forward strategy is used whereby a new version of the application that contains

the fix is deployed. This is sometimes faster and safer when strong CI/CD automation and rapid validation pipelines are available to deploy a hotfix.

- **Redundancy and failover**: In case of performance issues after a release, load balancers can be leveraged to divert traffic to healthy instances (like replicas or failover systems) while recovery takes place. In cloud-native environments, orchestration platforms like Kubernetes can self-heal by restarting failed pods or replacing nodes.

- **Runbooks and playbooks**: Documentation of step-by-step recovery procedures can guide engineers during incidents. Additionally, common playbook steps should be automated to reduce reliance on manual intervention during high-stress situations.

Best practices for effective rollback and recovery

The best practices for an effective rollback and recovery process include immutable artifacts and regular testing of rollbacks via simulation. Additionally, monitoring and alerting in real-time help detect issues within seconds of deployment. Automation of rollback steps to reduce human interaction reduces the MTTR while also preventing human mistakes. Finally, graceful degradation needs to be built into the applications so that they degrade the service gracefully instead of failing completely.

Rollback and recovery strategies help combine both proactive strategies (like backward-compatible changes, feature flags) with reactive strategies (like automated rollback and playbooks) to recover quickly from incidents and help maintain user trust.

Change management and reliability

Change management in release engineering ensures that modifications are introduced in a controlled and auditable manner. SRE provides a structured framework for managing change, which is a major cause of incidents in production systems. While the traditional change approval process focuses on bureaucracy, modern DevOps-driven change management emphasizes the following:

- Smaller, frequent releases ensure a lesser risk per change.
- Automated approvals, which are based on test results and compliance checks.
- Observability-driven verification using monitoring dashboards and SLO.

Automated pipelines enforce quality gates (via tests, security scans, etc.) and create a clear, auditable trail for every change. This controlled approach is fundamental to achieving high reliability and adhering to SLOs. This approach improves reliability without slowing down innovation.

Culture of safe releases

While tools, automation, and deployment strategies form the technical foundation of release engineering, long-term success ultimately depends on organizational culture. A culture of safe releases encourages practices that prioritize reliability, transparency, and learning over speed-at-any-cost. It emphasizes that releasing software is not just a technical activity but a collaborative, cross-functional effort that requires alignment across development, QA, operations, and business stakeholders. Safe releases are achieved by managing risks intelligently and building resilience into both systems and teams.

The culture of safe releases is characterized by the following:

- **Small, frequent changes**: Encouraging incremental, smaller releases reduces the complexity of the release while making issues easier to diagnose and rollback.
- **Shift left testing and quality ownership**: Shift left testing means that testing should start early in the development cycle. Additionally, developers (and not only QA teams) share the responsibility for ensuring quality through unit tests, integration tests and CI pipelines.
- **Blameless postmortems**: When incidents occur, the focus is on understanding the root cause of the failure in the system and processes and not on assigning blame to individuals. The goal is to learn and improve by sharing postmortem insights across teams, which fosters continuous improvement and prevents repeat failures.
- **Observability and feedback loops**: Safe releases require real-time visibility into system health, error rates, and user experience. Teams need to adopt proactive monitoring, logging, and tracing to detect issues before users report them. Additionally fast feedback loops from production incidents provide guidance on quick fixes and future improvements.
- **Collaboration across teams**: Cross-functional release teams enable shared accountability and smoother communication while removing silos between developers, testers, and operations teams.
- **Psychological safety**: Teams must feel safe to experiment, raise concerns, and admit mistakes without fear of retribution. Psychological safety encourages innovation and ensures that potential risks are flagged early rather than hidden.

Business alignment for safe releases

A culture of safe releases is not only technical, but it also requires business buy-in. Product managers and other stakeholders must understand the value of progressive rollouts and staged deployments, even if it delays feature launches. Leadership must encourage sustainable release velocity instead of pushing for unrealistic timelines that compromise reliability. Finally, the release metrics (like deployment frequency, MTTR, and change failure rate) should be aligned with business goals.

A culture of safe releases transforms release engineering from a purely technical discipline into a strategic enabler of trust and innovation. By promoting small, frequent changes, blameless postmortems, shared accountability, and strong feedback loops, organizations create an environment where reliability is not only a process but also a shared mindset.

Overview of release engineering tool Jenkins

Jenkins is a widely adopted open-source automation server that enables teams to automate every aspect of building, testing, and deploying software. It provides flexibility through plugins, integrates with most VCS, and can automate everything from building and testing code to deploying applications across environments.

Let us look at a quick reference guide to getting started with Jenkins.

Installation and setup

The following steps will help in the installation and setup of the Jenkins server:

1. Download Jenkins from **https://www.jenkins.io/**.
2. Run Jenkins by executing the following command in your command shell:
   `java -jar jenkins.war`
3. This will start the Jenkins server, and it can now be accessed via browser at:
   http://localhost:8080
4. To log in to Jenkins, use the initial admin password, which is displayed in the console.
5. Jenkins also recommends plugins that can be installed for a smooth start.

Key concepts

Let us look at the basic concepts of the Jenkins server:

- Jobs or projects are basic units of automation for building, testing and deploying code.
- Pipelines are multi-step workflows that are defined via code in a `Jenkinsfile`.
- Nodes and agents are used to execute the jobs. These nodes and agents can scale across multiple machines.
- Plugins provide extended functionality such as integration with VCS like Git, or containerization via Docker and Kubernetes.

Creating first job

To create our first job, proceed to the Jenkins dashboard and execute the following steps:

1. Click on **New Item** on the dashboard.

2. Choose the type of job, it can be a **`freestyle project`** or a **`pipeline`**.
3. Next, configure the following for the job:
   a. **Source code management**: Connect to the source code on GitHub or Bitbucket repository.
   b. Next, define how the job will be triggered. It can be via Poll SCM or via GitHub Webhook.
   c. Next, define the build steps for the code. (These can be commands like **`mvn clean install`**, **`mvn test`**, etc.).
   d. Now, at the final stage, we need to define the post build actions. (like archive artifacts or send email notifications).
4. This completes our first job. Click **Save and build now**.

Creating pipelines

Pipelines in Jenkins are built by defining workflows in a **`Jenkinsfile`**. Let us look at a sample **`Jenkinsfile`** which defines the CI/CD workflow as code:

```
pipeline {
    agent any
    stages {
        stage('Build') {
            steps {
                sh 'mvn clean install'
            }
        }
        stage('Test') {
            steps {
                sh 'mvn test'
            }
        }
        stage('Deploy') {
            steps {
                sh './deploy.sh'
            }
        }
    }
}
```

We need to store the **`Jenkinsfile`** in the root of the code repository.

Jenkins automatically detects the **Jenkinsfile** and executes it.

Essential plugins to install

Let us look at the plugins that need to be installed for the smooth execution of Jobs and pipelines via Jenkins:

- Git for source code management.
- Pipeline plugin to enable **Jenkinsfile** usage.
- Docker pipeline for docker container integration.
- Kubernetes for container orchestration integration.
- JUnit for test result reporting.
- Email extension for sending rich email notifications.
- Slack notification for sending notifications on Slack.

Some useful commands and tips

Let us look at some commands that are commonly used in Jenkins:

- **Restart Jenkins**:
  ```
  sudo systemctl restart Jenkins
  ```
- **View Jenkins logs**:
  ```
  tail -f /var/log/jenkins/jenkins.log
  ```
- **List all jobs**:
  ```
  java -jar jenkins-cli.jar -s http://jenkins:8080 list-jobs
  ```
- **Trigger build with parameters**:
  ```
  java -jar jenkins-cli.jar -s http://jenkins:8080 build job-name -p
  VERSION=1.2.3
  ```
- **Get build console output**:
  ```
  java -jar jenkins-cli.jar -s http://jenkins:8080 console job-name 25
  ```

To secure Jenkins, we need to use role-based access control and run Jenkins with HTTPS while restricting admin access.

Jenkins remains a powerful, flexible, and extensible CI/CD tool. With pipelines as code (**Jenkinsfile**), plugins for integrations, and wide adoption, it enables teams to quickly automate their software delivery lifecycle, making releases faster, safer, and more reliable.

Conclusion

Release engineering is the discipline that transforms software deployment from a chaotic, high-risk event into a smooth, predictable, and safe process. It is the essential bridge between rapid development and operational stability.

This chapter encouraged aggressive automation across the CI/CD pipeline, which gives us speed, reliability, and safety during releases. This chapter also guided us to consider which deployment strategy best suits our risk tolerance and helps us choose accordingly. It also told us to decouple deployment from release by using feature flags to turn the release into a controlled process, and while doing this, we should also plan for failure and have a well-defined rollback strategy. Eventually, the culture of blamelessness, shared ownership, and continuous improvement helps us bind the engineers and tools together.

By embracing these principles and practices, organizations can achieve the dual goals of rapid innovation and operational excellence while building a foundation of user trust that allows them to deliver value continuously and confidently.

In the next chapter, we will explore performance optimization that will focus on building systems that are fast, efficient, and resilient under load. We will look at key performance metrics such as latency, throughput, and resource optimization, and understand how to identify bottlenecks using monitoring and profiling techniques. This chapter will also cover strategies for optimizing application code, databases, and infrastructure, along with load testing and capacity planning.

Chapter 7
Performance Optimization

Introduction

Performance optimization is one of the foundational pillars of **site reliability engineering** (**SRE**). In a world where digital systems are expected to respond instantly, performance defines user experience, operational stability, and ultimately, business success. A system that is technically operational but responds with agonizing slowness is, from the user's perspective, fundamentally broken. Performance is not a separate feature; it is a foundational dimension of reliability itself. A delay of even a second can translate into frustrated users, abandoned transactions, and lost revenue. For SREs, ensuring that systems are fast, responsive, and cost-efficient is as critical as ensuring they are reliable or secure.

Performance optimization is about creating systems that deliver speed, scalability, and efficiency under real-world conditions. It involves understanding where time and resources are spent, identifying bottlenecks, and tuning the system to increase work per unit resource while also maintaining reliability. The modern system architecture is composed of microservices, distributed databases, and global networks, where performance becomes a multi-layered discipline spanning not only the application but also the infrastructure and network layers. To deliver the best performance, we might have to work on reducing the latency, increasing throughput, optimizing databases, leveraging cache, and minimizing resource wastage. The benefits are not only limited to user satisfaction but also span across lower cloud costs and faster innovation cycles as a result of better resource utilization.

Structure

The chapter covers the following topics:

- Importance of performance optimization
- Measuring performance
- Application performance optimization

- Infrastructure and network optimization
- Latency vs. throughput
- Efficient resource utilization
- Automating performance optimization

Objectives

This chapter will equip the readers with a comprehensive toolkit for performance optimization. The journey begins by understanding why performance is a non-negotiable business metric with direct ties to user satisfaction, revenue, and competitive advantage. The readers will then master the craft of measurement by learning to track the right metrics, which will range from user-centric latency to system-centric throughput. The core of our exploration will focus on the key levers we can pull across the entire stack, from optimizing application code and database queries, through caching strategies and data design, down to the efficient utilization of infrastructure resources like CPU, memory, and network. Finally, we will see how to automate this process, transforming performance from a reactive firefight into a proactive, engineered outcome. By the end of this chapter, the readers will be prepared to diagnose, optimize, and design systems that deliver unparalleled speed and reliability, all while maintaining a crucial balance with cost.

Importance of performance optimization

Performance optimization is a core function with direct and profound implications across the user experience and operational efficiency, which directly affects the business outcomes. Let us understand the importance of performance optimization from the three core pillars it affects, as explained in the following subsections.

User experience and satisfaction

A fast and responsive application keeps the users engaged. A delay of just 100-200 milliseconds is often perceptible by humans. Studies by *Google* quantified that an extra 500ms of search page load time resulted in a drop of traffic by 20%. At the same time, Amazon reported that 100ms of latency costs them 1% in sales. Also, as per research, 40% of users abandon websites that take more than 3 seconds to load.

Slow performance leads to frustration, abandoned shopping carts, and a tarnished brand reputation. At the same time, speed or low latency builds user trust and reliability.

Operational efficiency

A well-optimized system handles the same load with fewer resources. This directly leads to reduced resource costs as lower CPU, memory, and I/O requirements directly translate to lower cloud or infrastructure bills. When each unit of resource does more work, we need fewer units to handle a traffic spike, thus simplifying scaling and making scaling less frequent with lower risk. Optimized systems also have more headroom, thus allowing them to absorb unexpected load or handle minor resource failures without toppling over.

Business outcomes

Performance acts as a key competitive differentiator. A fast and responsive application not only increases user engagement and retention, but also improves conversion rates (in e-commerce or service-based businesses) while enhancing SEO rankings as search engines like Google use page loading speed as a ranking factor. Thus, performance is a business goal and not merely a technical metric.

Measuring performance

Before any meaningful optimization can occur, SRE teams must establish comprehensive measurement and monitoring practices. This foundational discipline transforms performance management from speculative guesswork into a disciplined, data-driven science. Effective monitoring provides the crucial visibility needed to establish performance baselines, identify bottlenecks, validate improvements, and ensure systems consistently meet their performance objectives over time. For observing system behavior, it is important to implement monitoring that provides maximum insight with minimal overhead. This requires careful selection of metrics, intelligent aggregation, and strategic alerting that focuses on what truly matters for user experience and system health.

Key performance metrics

Performance metrics provide vocabulary for discussing and improving system behavior. So, to avoid being overwhelmed by data, SREs focus on a curated set of metrics that provide comprehensive coverage across user experience, application behavior, and infrastructure utilization. These metrics can be categorized into three different sets: user-facing metrics, Application performance metrics, and System resource metrics. Let us look at these in detail in the following subsections.

User-facing metrics

These metrics directly correlate with how users perceive our application performance. They are categorized between latency and completion metrics as follows:

1. **Latency metrics**: The following is a set of metrics that can help measure user-perceived latency:

   a. **Time to first byte** (**TTFB**) is the time between sending a request and receiving the first byte as a response.

   b. **First contentful paint** (**FCP**) is the time at which the first text or image renders.
   c. **Largest contentful paint** (**LCP**) is the time by which the main page content becomes visible.
   d. **Time to interactive** (**TTI**) is the time by which the page becomes fully responsive to user input. For interactivity, consider **Interaction to Next Paint** (**INP**) as a practical user-perceived responsiveness metric.
2. **Completion metrics**: The following is a set of metrics that help in measuring completion from the business point of view, as follows:
   a. Transaction success rate is the percentage of successful user transactions.
   b. Abandonment rate is the rate at which users leave during a process flow.
   c. Conversion rate is the rate of completed purchases.

Application performance metrics

These metrics measure the performance of the business layer and reveal how efficiently our application code and services are operating. They are categorized into throughput metrics and efficiency metrics, as follows:

1. Throughput metrics are listed as follows:
   a. **Request per second/queries per second (RPS/QPS)** is used to measure the volume of traffic handled by the application.
   b. **Transaction per second** (**TPS**) is used to measure the business-level transaction volume.
   c. Concurrent users/connections are used to measure the current active load on the system.
2. Efficiency metrics are as follows:
   a. Cache hit ratio is used to measure the effectiveness of caching at various layers, like application, database, or **content delivery network** (**CDN**).
   b. Error rates are the frequency of application errors, which can be broken down by error type for better understanding.
   c. Queue length is the backlog of pending work in message queues and buffers.

System resource metrics

These metrics measure the performance of the infrastructure layer, which can help explain the reason behind the application's performance. The following metrics give us this visibility at the infrastructure layer:

1. CPU utilization is the percentage of CPU capacity being used. High sustained CPU may indicate inefficient code or a lack of parallelization. System load can also be monitored, which should be related to the available CPU cores.

2. Memory utilization gives an idea of the active memory usage. Memory leaks or oversized caches can cause **out-of-memory** (**OOM**) errors. We can also look at swap usage and **garbage collection** (**GC**) metrics for more detailed insights.

3. Storage performance can be measured via I/O wait times, I/O operations per second and I/O latency. High I/O wait times can suggest disk or network latency. Disk utilization should also be monitored to understand the percentage of disk capacity available.

4. Network performance is measured via network throughput, packet loss rate, and **Transmission Control Protocol** (**TCP**) connection count.

These metrics should be measured as percentiles instead of averages wherever possible. As an SRE best practice, we should always track and alert on multiple percentiles. For example, P50 can act as a baseline performance where 50% of requests are faster and 50% are slower. In contrast, P95 is essential for ensuring a quality experience for most users, as 95% of requests are faster than this value. P99 can be used to investigate systemic problems as it captures the worst-case outliers, where only 1% of requests are slower than the P99 value. While P50 gives you general performance trends, P95 and P99 reveal the user pain points that need urgent attention.

Measuring performance in practice

Always start with SLOs. The purpose is to define SLOs before building our monitoring. Our SLOs help determine which metrics matter the most and what thresholds require our attention.

Instrumentation

Once we have identified our SLOs, the next step is to figure out the tools that will help in measuring them. Instrumentation involves embedding measurement points inside the application code. We can use:

- Prometheus for metrics; OpenTelemetry for instrumentation and exporting metrics, traces, and logs.
- ELK stack or Splunk for collecting logs that record each event.
- Jaeger or Zipkin for distributed tracing.
- StatsD or Micrometer for application-level metrics.

Instrumentation also helps in correlating system metrics with business metrics.

Benchmarking and load testing

Before deploying to production, it is important to simulate workloads to test how the application will perform. Tools that can be used here are k6, Locust, or JMeter. There are three types of tests for benchmarking and load testing:

- Load tests where the traffic is gradually increased to measure system limits.
- Stress tests where traffic is increased to push beyond system limits to observe degradation and failure behavior.
- Soak tests where systems are run under steady load for long durations to detect leaks or slow memory growth.

Real user monitoring

Real user monitoring (**RUM**) is used to capture actual user experiences from browsers and mobile devices. Most of the user-facing latency metrics that we saw earlier (like FCP, TTI, etc.) are captured via RUM and are valuable for frontend performance optimization. Combining RUM with synthetic monitoring provides a full picture where synthetic tests simulate, whereas RUM validates real-world performance.

Application performance monitoring

Application performance monitoring (**APM**) tools like *Dynatrace* or *New Relic* can be used to collect metrics, logs, and distributed traces to record the complete journey of a user request in the system. These help SREs to follow a request as it traverses multiple microservices. It exposes latency contributions of each service and helps identify slow dependencies. Tools such as AWS X-Ray or OpenTelemetry traces can be used for distributed tracing.

While measuring performance, it is essential to establish a performance baseline. Baseline defines the meaning of normal, allowing us to detect anomalies early through monitoring systems. Monitoring performance includes a continuous feedback loop where alerting rules are set to trigger notifications when SLO thresholds are breached. A mature system eventually evolves from reactive monitoring to proactive optimization.

Application performance optimization

Application performance optimization focuses on improving how efficiently our code and application logic execute to deliver fast, reliable, and scalable services. Application-level performance optimization can deliver the most dramatic performance improvements. A well-optimized application can achieve significantly better performance on the same hardware, reduce operational costs, and provide superior user experiences. At the application layer, every function, query, and **application programming interface** (**API**) call matters. The goal is to reduce unnecessary work, make operations parallel where possible, and design data flow to minimize latency and resource contention.

Let us look at the various aspects of application performance optimization:

- **Code-level optimization**: Code-level optimizations are often the first and most direct way to enhance performance. Efficient code helps in reducing CPU cycles, memory usage, and I/O overhead. These, in turn, contribute to lower latency and higher throughput. Let us look at the different aspects of code-level optimization:
  - **Algorithmic efficiency**: While writing code, it is important to analyze the complexity of algorithms being implemented. The idea is to choose algorithms that provide optimal time complexity for our use case. Also, selecting the right data structures for the computations can yield significant gains (e.g., using hash maps for fast lookups instead of lists). Another factor that helps in improving the efficiency of code is to break out of loops and computations as soon as the result is determined and sometimes we should use lazy evaluations, which delay expensive computations until their results are absolutely determined.
  - **Memory management**: The aim of memory management is to use only the ideal amount of memory. To do this, we can pool and reuse expensive objects instead of creating new instances. We need to reduce GC pressure by avoiding unnecessary object creation. Some languages, like Java and Go, have the option of pre-allocating buffers or using object cache for high-frequency operations.
  - **Reduce I/O blocking**: Instead of using synchronous I/O operations (like file access or network calls), which block threads and degrade performance, we should use asynchronous APIs or background workers to perform these tasks concurrently.
  - **Eliminate redundant operations**: Avoid recomputing results that can be reused. For this, we can cache results of expensive calculations, reduce repetitive logging or data transformations, and collapse loops and unnecessary data conversions. This can drastically reduce the compute needed by the application.

  This works best when we profile before optimizing. We can use profilers like *PyInstrument, pprof,* or *VisualVM* to profile our code and identify bottlenecks, which will point us towards the problem (instead of guessing).

- **Database optimization**: The database is frequently the primary bottleneck in modern applications, hence optimizing the database often yields the greatest performance returns. Let us look at the different aspects of database optimization.

Query optimization

Here are a few steps that can help in query optimization:

1. Execution plan analysis can be done using **`EXPLAIN`** (or similar statements) to understand how the queries are executed and to identify full table scans and costly joins.

2. Instead of using multiple queries to fetch data, use joins or prefetching to fetch all related data in a single query.
3. Select only needed columns instead of doing a `SELECT *` on the entire table.
4. Batch multiple operations together by grouping inserts, updates, and deletes together instead of performing them one-by-one.

Indexing strategy

The idea is to index frequently queried columns while also avoiding over-indexing, and it slows down writes. Indexes should be created strategically on columns that are used in `WHERE`, `JOIN`, and `ORDER BY` clauses. Composite indexes can be created on multiple columns to speed up common query patterns. In order to avoid table lookups, we can create covering indexes whereby all required columns are included in the index. Finally, we need to regularly review and remove unused or duplicate indexes.

Use connection pooling

Creating a new database connection for every request is expensive. Instead, we can use connection pools (like *HikariCP*, *SQLAlchemy pooling*) to reuse existing connections efficiently.

Optimize read and write queries

For read-heavy workloads, we can use read replicas to spread out the workload to more servers. To reduce database hits and improve latency, we can cache the results of frequently used queries in a cache like Redis or Memcached.

For write-heavy workloads, we can use message queues or asynchronous write batching to avoid locking contention. As databases grow, we can shard or partition the data logically or horizontally and distribute the same across multiple nodes to improve query parallelism and throughput. Database sharding and partitioning, however, require careful key design.

Asynchronous processing

The purpose of asynchronous processing is not to make users wait for a response. Many application tasks do not need to block user responses, and not all work needs to happen immediately. Offloading work to background tasks for non-critical or time-consuming operations dramatically improves perceived performance. Let us look at some ways in which asynchronous processing is done.

Event-driven architecture

Instead of performing all logic within a request cycle, we can offload background tasks to message queues (like Kafka, RabbitMQ). These help in creating a publisher-subscriber pattern whereby services are decoupled via event publishing. We can also use priority queues to process time-sensitive tasks before batch operations.

Example: When a user uploads a video, we can return the success response immediately and push the task into a queue, which can be asynchronously processed later.

Background workers

Background workers are used to handle tasks outside the main request-response cycle, thus improving application responsiveness and scalability. These are used for tasks such as sending emails, processing payments, or generating reports, which can be delegated to background queues managed by workers. This ensures that the main thread is free to handle new requests, thus reducing latency and improving user experience. Background workers can also be scaled horizontally to handle variable workloads. Frameworks like Celery in Python and Sidekiq in Ruby can be used to handle background jobs efficiently. We can also use a retry mechanism and idempotent operations to ensure consistency.

Non-blocking I/O

Non-blocking I/O allows applications to perform multiple I/O operations concurrently without waiting for each to complete before starting the next. Instead of blocking a thread until data is read or written, the system continues executing other tasks and handles I/O events asynchronously when ready. This approach significantly improves scalability and responsiveness, especially in networked or high-concurrency environments. Non-blocking I/O reduces thread contention, lowers resource usage, and enables efficient event-driven architectures. Languages like Node.js, Go, and Rust provide asynchronous I/O primitives that allow thousands of connections to be served concurrently with minimal threads.

Common uses of asynchronous processing

The common uses are as follows:

- Email/SMS sending is done asynchronously. Never send these notifications during request processing.
- File processing, like uploads and transformations, is handled asynchronously.
- Report generations, especially processing large reports, are done in background jobs.
- Data synchronization or handling external API calls is also done asynchronously.

Asynchronous processing improves user-perceived latency and enhances throughput under high concurrency. It also has the benefit of decoupling long-running workflows from the request lifecycle.

Concurrency and parallelism

Modern applications must efficiently utilize multi-core systems via their distributed architecture and handle multiple requests concurrently. Concurrency allows our applications to make better use of available resources.

Concurrency refers to the process of managing multiple tasks that are in progress by switching between them. At the same time, parallelism refers to the process of executing multiple tasks at the same time.

Concurrency models

Let us look at the architecture models that help in executing concurrency:

- Multithreading is an architecture that uses fixed-size thread pools to prevent resource exhaustion while executing CPU-bound tasks with shared state.
- Async/wait models are used to leverage non-blocking I/O for high concurrency scenarios.
- An actor and message passing model is used to avoid shared state and locking issues.
- Futures and promises can be used to handle long-running computations cleanly.
- Coroutines are lightweight threads that can be used for massive concurrency (like Go goroutines).

Best practices for concurrent processes are as follows:

- Avoid shared mutable state by using immutable objects where possible.
- Thread pool size should be based on the workload type (CPU or I/O bound).
- Circuit breakers should be used to prevent cascading failures under load.
- Rate limiting should be used to prevent systems from being overloaded.

Parallel processing

Let us look at some of the patterns that are used for parallel processing, as follows:

- MapReduce patterns can be used for distributing work across multiple workers.
- Fork-join frameworks can be used to recursively split and process tasks.
- Data parallelism can be used to process collections in parallel (like Java Streams).

Caching strategies

Caching is a strategy that trades memory for performance. It is the most effective performance optimization technique, which reduces latency and backend load by storing frequently accessed data. Done well, it can reduce backend load and latency by orders of magnitude, whereas done poorly, it can cause inconsistency or stale data issues. Let us look at the various cache placement strategies.

Client-side caching

Client-side caching is done so that browsers or mobile apps can cache static content:

- Leverage cache-control, etag, and last-modified headers in HTTP caching headers to cache required data at the client-side.
- Service workers can also be used to cache API responses and assets at the browser level.
- Local storage can be used to cache user-specific data locally.
- CDN like Akamai or Cloudflare can be used to cache static assets closer to the end user.

Application-level caching strategies include the following:

- In-memory caches like Redis or Memcached are used to cache frequently accessed data.
- Applications can also manage cache population on demand via cache-aside patterns.
- Write-through or write-behind cache is used based on the need for synchronous or asynchronous cache updates. Write-through favors consistency at the cost of write latency, while write-behind favors throughput with eventual consistency risks.

Database caching is as follows:

- Frequent query results can be cached and reused without hitting the database again.
- Expensive algorithms can be pre-computed.
- Read traffic can be offloaded to read replicas.

Cache invalidation strategies

Cache invalidation is one of the most challenging aspects of caching. Incorrect invalidation strategies often lead to serving stale or inconsistent data, which can be harder to detect than outright failures. Cache invalidation strategies include the following:

- Time-based expiry or TTL to automatically expire data after a set duration.
- Write-through is used to update the cache and the database simultaneously.
- Write-behind is used to cache data first and then asynchronously persist it to the database.
- Event-driven invalidation can be done by invalidating the cache upon update events.
- Versioned cache keys can be used to ensure safe updates to the cached data.

Data modeling and optimization

How we structure data significantly impacts performance. Poor schema design often results in costly joins, slow reads, and excessive data transfer. Let us look at some strategies around different aspects of data modeling.

Database schema design

The following are some of the aspects of database schema design that can help in improving data modeling and performance of databases:

- **Normalization vs. denormalization**: Normalization is for consistency, whereas denormalization is for speed. Normalization reduces redundancy but increases join operations and is preferred for write-heavy data. Whereas denormalization (or duplicating some data) can drastically improve speed in read-heavy systems.
- **Use the right data types**: Choosing smaller appropriate data types improves performance. Like using `INT` instead of `BIGINT` when possible. It is also recommended to use `ENUM` or `BOOLEAN` for categorical fields. We should avoid using text fields for IDs or status codes.
- **Data partitioning**: Partitioning large tables by date, user ID, or geography improves query performance and simplifies data lifecycle management.

Efficient data formats are as follows:

- Use binary serialization tools like *protocol buffers* or *Avro* for internal communication.
- Columnar databases like *Parquet*, *ORC*, or *BigQuery* compress efficiently and accelerate analytical queries.
- Apply appropriate compression based on the need to decompress and the time and space complexity of the compression algorithms.

API design for performance

The following are some best practices for API design to improve performance:

- In GraphQL, allow clients to request only needed fields.
- Implement cursor-based pagination for large datasets.
- Let the client specify which field to return in the response.
- Enable response compression for API responses. Compression should be evaluated carefully for CPU-intensive services.

Data lifecycle management

Let us look at the best practices for data lifecycle management:

- Implement archiving policies that move old data to cheaper storage.
- Implement TTL-based deletion to automatically expire transient data.
- Implement data aggregation to roll up detailed data into summaries over time.

Summary

Application performance optimization requires a methodological approach, which includes:

- Using APM tools to identify actual bottlenecks.
- Focusing optimization efforts on the slowest parts of the system.
- Optimize holistically by considering the entire stack instead of individual components.
- Including performance testing in our CI/CD pipeline.
- Monitor in production to track the impact of optimization on real users.

The optimization hierarchy is as follows:

1. Optimize architecture and algorithms.
2. Optimize data access and I/O patterns.
3. Optimize code implementations.
4. Consider infrastructure scaling as the last resort.

By applying these application-level optimization techniques systematically, SREs and developers can build systems that are not just functionally correct but also exceptionally performant, scalable, and cost-effective. The most elegant solution is one that solves the business problem efficiently, using minimal resources while delivering maximum value to users.

Infrastructure and network optimization

While application optimization addresses software efficiency, infrastructure and network optimization ensure the underlying platform delivers maximum performance for every dollar spent. In SRE, this layer of optimization focuses on distributing workloads intelligently, scaling resources automatically, minimizing network latency, and tuning compute, storage, and connectivity resources for maximum efficiency. Proper infrastructure optimization ensures that performance improvements are not just local (per service) but systemic across the environment. Let us look at the different aspects of Infrastructure and network optimization.

Load balancing

Load balancing is one of the most fundamental techniques for improving system scalability and reliability. A load balancer acts as a traffic manager that decides which backend server will handle each client request based on the current load, availability, and other factors, thus optimizing resource utilization and ensuring high availability.

Types of load balancers:

- **Layer 4 (transport layer)**: These types of load balancers make routing decisions based on IP addresses and TCP/**User Datagram Protocol** (**UDP**) ports. These are ideal for non-HTTP traffic and scenarios requiring maximum throughput.
- **Layer 7 (application layer)**: These types of load balancers have the capability to make intelligent routing decisions based on HTTP headers, URLs, and cookies. They enable advanced features like SSL termination, content-based routing, and sticky sessions.

Load balancing algorithms

Let us look at some of the load-balancing algorithms that are configurable in most load balancers:

- Round robin, which distributes requests sequentially across all healthy servers.
- Least connection algorithm that routes requests to the server with the fewest active connections.
- IP Hash algorithm that uses client IP to determine server assignment, which ensures session persistence.
- Weighted routing that assigns traffic based on server capacity or health status.

Advanced features of load balancers

Let us go over some of the advanced features that are configurable in most load balancers:

- Health checks are used to continuously monitor backend instances and remove unhealthy nodes. This provides fault tolerance and high availability.
- SSL termination, which is used to offload CPU-intensive encryption/decryption to the load balancer.
- Content caching is used to cache static content at the load balancer level.
- Path-based routing is used to route different URL paths to different backend services.

Global load balancing

Global load balancing distributes user traffic across multiple geographically dispersed data centers or cloud regions to ensure optimal performance, high availability, and fault tolerance, unlike traditional load balancers that operate within a single region. In case of a regional outage, traffic is seamlessly redirected to other available regions, ensuring business continuity. GLB routes users to geographically closest regions or healthiest regions using DNS-based routing (e.g., AWS Route 53, Cloudflare Load Balancer, Google Cloud GSLB). This minimizes network latency while supporting regional failover.

Autoscaling

Modern systems face fluctuating traffic patterns. Manually provisioning servers for peak load wastes resources, while under-provisioning leads to outages. Autoscaling solves this by dynamically adjusting capacity based on demand.

Scaling strategies

Let us look at the scaling strategies that are available with most cloud and container providers:

- Horizontal scaling is done by adding or removing instances (in a cloud environment) or pods (in a containerized environment).
- Vertical scaling is done by resizing existing resources by adding more CPU or memory. This strategy requires a restart and is useful for short-term spikes, as it is limited by the maximum instance size available.

Scaling triggers

Let us look at the triggers that can be used to autoscale:

- Metric-based triggers like:
  - CPU or memory utilization
  - Queue length or lag
  - Custom triggers like RPS or requests per second
- Triggers based on custom application metrics (like latency > 500ms).
- Schedule-based or predictive triggers can be used to proactively adjust capacity before load increases.

Best practices for autoscaling

Let us look at some of the best practices for autoscaling in production:

- Warm pools are used to keep pre-initialized instances ready to scale, which reduces scaling latency.
- A gradual scaling policy is used to add or remove instances incrementally.

- Multi-zone distribution is used to ensure that scaled instances are distributed across multiple availability zones.
- Cost optimization is done by using spot instances for fault-tolerant workloads.
- Graceful scaling and cooldowns are done by defining cooldown periods and graceful termination hooks so that active requests are served before instances are removed.
- Autoscaling ensures both cost efficiency and performance stability under variable load.

Network optimization

The network is the circulatory system of distributed applications. Optimizing it improves response times, reduces packet loss, and ensures data flows efficiently across clients, services, and regions. Let us look at the different aspects of network optimization.

Latency reduction strategies

Latency is introduced by distance, hops, or poor configuration. The following are some of the key strategies to reduce network latency:

- Deploy services closer to users via multiple regions, CDN, or edge locations.
- Minimize round-trip between client and server by combining API calls.
- Reuse connections (via HTTP Keep-alive and connection pooling) to avoid frequent TCP/**Transport Layer Security** (**TLS**) handshakes.
- Use TLS session resumption to minimize handshake delays.
- TCP tuning is also an option whereby we can optimize kernel parameters for TCP window sizes and buffer management.

Throughput optimization strategies

The strategies are as follows:

- Use larger MTU sizes for high-throughput internal networks.
- Use network card bonding to combine multiple **network interface cards** (**NICs**) for increased bandwidth.
- Prioritize traffic based on application requirements.
- Use binary protocols like gRPC or protocol buffers for internal service calls.

Content delivery optimization

The following are the ways in which content delivery can be optimized for end users:

- Use CDNs to cache and deliver static and semi-static content (like images, CSS, videos) from servers geographically close to users. This not only reduces origin load but also decreases latency while providing DDoS mitigation.
- Use HTTP/2 and HTTP/3 to leverage multiplexing and other performance improvements.
- Compress payloads using gzip or Brotli compression for text-based content.

DNS optimization

DNS optimization focuses on reducing the time it takes to resolve domain names to IP addresses, thus improving overall response times. Every web request begins with a DNS lookup, making DNS optimization crucial for performance.

DNS performance improvement techniques

The performance improvement techniques are as follows:

- Reduce TTL strategically to balance cache duration with change flexibility for faster failover. TTL values should be tuned carefully to avoid excessive DNS query load.
- Enable DNS prefetching to hint browsers to resolve domains before they are needed.
- Implement DNS caching at the client and resolver levels.
- Use low latency DNS providers (like *Cloudflare DNS, Google Public DNS*).
- Use DNS-based load balancing to direct users to the closest regional endpoint. This minimizes round-trip time and balances global traffic efficiently.

Monitoring DNS performance

It is essential to monitor DNS performance. The following are the tips on how to monitor DNS performance:

- Monitor how long DNS lookup takes.
- Track query volume, which is the query rate and patterns.
- Track cache hit ratios to measure the effectiveness of DNS caching.

Best practice is to configure multiple authoritative name servers and use health checked DNS failover for resilience.

Container and VM optimization

Modern applications increasingly run in containerized or virtualized environments, each requiring specific optimizations. Container and VM optimization ensure that applications run efficiently by fine-tuning compute environments for performance and resource utilization. Containers should have well-defined CPU and memory limits to prevent resource contention, while VMs should use the right instance types based on workload patterns. Together, these optimizations improve scalability, stability, and cost efficiency across environments.

Container optimization

The features of container optimization are as follows:

- Ensure proper resource allocation by defining optimal CPU and memory limits in container orchestrators (like Kubernetes) to prevent resource starvation or waste.
- On shared nodes, one container's heavy CPU or memory usage can degrade others. This should be mitigated by using cgroups and namespaces for isolation and assigning dedicated nodes or pools for resource-heavy workloads.
- Container images need to be optimized by:
  - Using minimal base images (like Alpine Linux).
  - Removing unused packages, logs, and built artifacts.
  - Layering cache strategically to speed up deployment.

Kubernetes-specific optimizations

The following are the tips for Kubernetes-specific optimizations:

- Distribute pods across nodes for better resource utilization.
- Enable horizontal pod autoscaling so that pods are scaled based on custom metrics.
- Configure guaranteed, burstable, and best-effort quality of service.

VM optimization

The following are the tips for optimizing **virtual machines** (**VMs**):

- Choose the right instance type for workload pattern (compute-optimized, memory-optimized, or I/O-optimized).
- Enable paravirtualized drivers (virtio) for faster I/O operations.
- Enable dynamic memory reclamation in virtualized environments.
- Enable CPU and memory hotplug to add resources without VM restart, where supported.

CPU, memory, and storage optimization

While CPU, memory, and storage are hardware-level resources, optimizing their usage ensures efficient infrastructure utilization. Let us look at the details:

- **CPU optimization**: CPU optimization involves ensuring processors are utilized efficiently without becoming bottlenecks. The following are the best practices for CPU optimization:
    - Right-sizing of instances by matching instance types to specific workload characteristics. For example, use C-series AWS instances for compute-intensive applications and T-series AWS instances for workloads with variable CPU needs.
    - Pin compute-intensive tasks to specific cores to reduce context switching.
    - Use CPU affinity for latency-sensitive processes.
    - Monitor load averages and if consistently high, scale horizontally.
    - Optimize thread pools to match core count and workload type.
    - Tune sysctl settings in kernel parameters for optimal scheduler behavior.
- **Memory optimization**: Efficient memory usage prevents swapping and ensures optimal application performance. Let us look at the best practices for memory optimization here:
    - Avoid memory overcommitment to ensure sufficient swap or buffer space.
    - Use huge pages for memory-intensive applications to reduce TLB misses.
    - Pre-allocate memory pools for database and application use.
    - Monitor for memory leaks in long-running containers or JVM processes.
    - Enable cgroup memory limits and alerts.
    - Optimize GC for throughput or latency based on application needs by:
        - Setting appropriate initial and maximum GC heap sizes.
        - Selecting an appropriate GC algorithm (e.g., G1, Shenandoah, or ZGC) based on latency requirements.
- **Storage and disk I/O optimization**: Storage performance often becomes the limiting factor in I/O-intensive applications. The following are the best practices for storage optimization:
    - Prefer SSDs over HDDs for transactional workloads.
    - Separate data and logs onto different disks to prevent I/O contention.
    - Enable read-ahead caching for sequential workloads.
    - Monitor I/O per second, latency, and queue depth metrics.

- Use RAID 10 for performance-critical databases or caches.
- Enable compression and deduplication only if CPU overhead is manageable.
- Choose appropriate RAID levels for performance and redundancy.
- Choose an appropriate filesystem like XFS for large files, ext4 for general purpose, and ZFS for advanced features.
- Cloud storage can be optimized by:
  - Using provisioned I/O per second for consistent performance.
  - Leveraging ephemeral storage for temporary data.
  - Automatically moving data between hot, cool, and archive tiers.

Monitoring and observability

Infrastructure optimization must be backed by continuous visibility. We can use node exporters for CPU, memory, and disk metrics. Monitor network bandwidth, packet loss, and RTT. Track load balancer latency, autoscaling events, and DNS resolution time. All these metrics can be visualized using Grafana dashboards for correlation and trend analysis. Automated alerts based on SLOs need to be setup to ensure early detection of degradation before it affects users.

Implementation checklist

We can use the following checklist to systematically optimize our infrastructure:

- Implement appropriate load balancing for our traffic patterns.
- Configure autoscaling with proper metrics and cooldown periods.
- Rightsize instances based on actual workload requirements.
- Monitor and optimize memory usage and garbage collection.
- Select appropriate storage types and monitor performance metrics.
- Optimize network configuration and implement CDN where it is beneficial.
- Tune DNS settings and monitor resolution times.
- Apply container/VM-specific optimizations for your runtime environment.
- Establish comprehensive monitoring for all infrastructure components.
- Regularly review and optimize costs alongside performance.

By systematically addressing each layer of our infrastructure, starting from load balancing and autoscaling to resource tuning and network optimization, we can create a foundation that can scale efficiently, maintain performance under load, and deliver optimal cost-performance ratios for our applications.

Latency vs. throughput

Performance optimization often revolves around two fundamental metrics: latency and throughput, which capture how fast and how much work a system can perform. Understanding their relationship and the inherent trade-offs between them is crucial for making informed architectural decisions and setting realistic performance expectations:

- Latency measures the time taken to complete a single unit of work. It is the delay between initiating a request and receiving the response:
  - **Formula:** *Latency (ms or s) = end-time – start-time*
- Throughput measures the amount of work a system can handle per unit of time. It represents the system's capacity or bandwidth:
  - **Formula**: *Throughput (RPS or QPS) = Work units/time*

Latency and throughput trade-off

A system with low latency can still have low throughput (if it processes requests one at a time). Conversely, a system with high throughput might have higher latency if it processes requests in bulk or queues them. As we push a system towards its maximum throughput, latency typically increases.

Let us understand this with the analogy of cars on a highway:

- **Low traffic (low throughput)**: Cars travel at the speed limit (low latency).
- **High traffic (high throughput)**: As the road becomes saturated, cars slow down due to congestion (high latency).

When optimizing systems, we are often faced with explicit trade-offs between latency and throughput, as follows:

- **Batch processing vs. real-time processing**:
  - Batch processing increases throughput but also increases latency.
  - Real-time processing minimizes latency but reduces throughput.
- **Connection pooling**:
  - Small pools may have lower latency for individual requests, but limit total throughput.
  - Large pools increase throughput but may suffer from connection management overhead.
- **Caching strategies**:
  - Write-through caches maintain low read latency but reduce write throughput.
  - Write-behind caches increase write throughput but risk data inconsistency.

Optimization strategy by use case

Now, that we have seen the trade-off between latency and throughput, we need to understand that each system needs a custom optimization based on the purpose it serves. Let us look at the different optimization strategies for latency-sensitive, throughput-sensitive, and balanced applications.

Latency-sensitive applications

For latency-sensitive applications like gaming, real-time trading, or interactive applications, the following are the strategies for optimizing them:

- Prioritize low percentiles (like P50, P90).
- Use faster, more expensive hardware.
- Minimize serial dependencies.
- Implement request prioritization.

Throughput-sensitive applications

For throughput-sensitive applications like batch processing, data ingestion, or analytics, the following are the strategies for optimizing them:

- Focus on maximizing P99.9 throughput.
- Use batching and buffering extensively.
- Leverage cheaper, higher-density hardware.
- Accept higher latency for cost efficiency.

Balanced applications

For balanced applications like web services, APIs or e-commerce, the following are the strategies for optimizing them:

- Set SLOs for both latency and throughput.
- Use autoscaling to maintain target latency under load.
- Implement quality of service tiers.
- Monitor both average and tail metrics.

Efficient resource utilization

Performance optimization is not only about speed. It is also about the value derived. Efficient resource utilization is where performance engineering meets cost optimization. For SRE, it is not enough to make systems faster; they must also be cost-efficient, ensuring that the organization gets maximum performance per dollar spent.

There is always a trade-off between performance and cost. A system designed for a P99 latency of 10ms will cost more than one designed for 100ms. The SRE's job is to work with the business and define SLOs that balance user expectations with budgetary constraints.

Identifying waste

There are idle resources or resources that are running at 1-5% of CPU for days that are burning money. Another scenario is where an instance is over-provisioned with 32 GB of RAM, whereas it uses only 4 GB. There are orphaned resources like unattached disks, unused load balancers, and old snapshots that need to be taken care of. Finally, inefficient software (like an unoptimized query) will require larger and more expensive resources to handle the load. SREs need to identify such scenarios and take appropriate measures to remedy them.

Best practices are as follows:

- SREs need to find the bottleneck, fix it, and then rightsize the resources to make it more efficient. Rightsizing is the continuous process of matching instance type with workload requirements.
- Most APMs can be configured to trigger alerts on resources under usage, which need to be reviewed on a periodic basis.
- Cost awareness should be a part of the engineering culture. Teams should make cost a metric that needs to be tracked. SREs should educate teams and incentivize efficiency that motivates teams to build a cost-sensitive culture.
- Spot instances can be leveraged to use spare cloud capacity at a significant discount for fault-tolerant and interruptible workloads (like batch processing).

Automating performance optimization

Manual optimization is difficult to scale, whereas automation reduces human error and ensures consistency. SREs need to build automation to make performance a continuous and integrated process by following these steps:

1. **Continuous performance testing**: Integrate performance testing into the CI/CD pipeline to handle load testing, stress testing, and soak testing. These tests will help identify and prevent slow code from being deployed into production.
2. **Continuous profiling**: By continuously collecting profiling data (CPU, memory, I/O) from production systems using tools like Pyroscope or Google's Cloud Profiler, we can provide an always-on, low-overhead view of where our application spends its time, making it easy to pinpoint new inefficiencies.

3. **Automated capacity planning**: Using historical metrics, we can forecast future needs. Tools can be used to automatically recommend scaling profiles or rightsizing changes based on trends, thus ensuring we have capacity when we need it before we need it.
4. **Chaos engineering for performance**: Introducing controlled features to test whether performance degrades gracefully will help uncover hidden coupling and assumptions that can lead to performance issues during partial outages.

Conclusion

Performance optimization is not a one-time project but a continuous cycle of measurement, analysis, and improvement. It is a core SRE discipline that sits at the heart of user satisfaction, operational excellence, and financial efficiency.

As SREs, we need to measure everything, optimize the application first, cache aggressively and wisely, rightsize our infrastructure, reduce network round-trip times, compress data, and automate the complete process to build a performance engineering culture.

With this mindset, we move from fighting fires to building systems that are inherently fast, resilient, and cost-effective. In doing so, we transform performance from a technical concern into a tangible business advantage. In the next chapter, we will explore and learn about DevSecOps, automation, and AIOps.

CHAPTER 8
Automation, DevSecOps and AIOps

Introduction

There is one word that captures the evolution of **site reliability engineering** (**SRE**) and its automation. Many SRE teams begin in a reactive (or firefighting) mode, handling incidents, patching servers, and responding to alerts. However, over time, teams realize that many of those tasks repeat in slightly different forms every day. These tasks can range from restarting a service, updating a configuration file, deploying code, or checking metrics. That is when SREs, instead of doing the same thing manually, write a small script, setup an automation rule, or build a workflow, to help the system take care of itself. This defines the essence of automation, which is doing more by doing less manually.

Automation in SRE is not only about convenience, but it is also about reliability, consistency, and speed. When humans repeat a task, we make mistakes, whereas when code repeats a task, it does it the same way every single time. The outcome is predictable, measurable and version controlled.

Modern SRE practices have evolved far beyond simple bash scripts. They now include **infrastructure as code** (**IaC**), self-healing systems, continuous delivery pipelines, **policy as code** (**PaC**) and even AI-driven operations. Each of these approaches provides a deeper level of automation with the single goal of building reliable systems that run themselves as much as possible.

Automation also frees up precious human bandwidth. So instead of manually tending infrastructure, engineers can spend more time improving the architecture, refining monitoring, or experimenting with new technologies. This shift from manual toil to strategic work improves the impact of SRE teams.

Structure

The chapter covers the following topics:

- Automation principles
- Infrastructure as code
- Auto-healing
- Measuring automation success
- AIOps
- Identifying areas of automation
- Automating workflows
- Reducing toil
- DevSecOps

Objectives

This chapter explores the role of automation in SRE, which focuses on reducing manual effort while improving system reliability. We will understand how IaC can be used to provision and manage infrastructure through version controlled repeatable scripts. We will learn how automating workflows by leveraging tools like Ansible can accelerate changes in production while reducing human error. This chapter will also cover how to design and build auto-healing systems that will detect and recover from failures without any human intervention, thus improving **mean time to recover** (**MTTR**) and uptime. We will understand why automating repeated tasks is important and how it improves team capacity by reducing toil and enabling strategic engineering work. Finally, we will look at the evolving frontiers where automation meets security (DevSecOps) and **artificial intelligence operations** (**AIOps**), creating a future where systems are not only automated but also intelligent and secure by design. By the end of this chapter, we will understand how to strategically leverage automation across the application lifecycle to improve efficiency, reliability, and scalability while reducing human intervention and operational overhead.

Automation principles

Behind every great automation lies a strong foundation of principles that keep it reliable and sustainable. These principles guide our decisions and ensure our automation efforts yield maximum value. These principles that form the DNA of everything we automate are as follows:

- **Eliminate toil**: It is manual work tied to running a production service and is repetitive, tactical, devoid of enduring value, and scales linearly as a service grows. SREs aim to spend no more than 50% of their time on toil. Automation is the primary weapon against toil. Every script that reduces manual effort is a direct reduction of toil.
- **Repeatability**: It ensures that a task yields the same outcome every time it is executed. A script (like a deployment script) should work every time it is triggered, irrespective of the day or time it was triggered. Good automation ensures this and removes uncertainty around scripts that would fail because they are not truly repeatable.

- **Idempotence**: Running the same automation script multiple times should not cause unintended side effects. For example, if our automation script creates a server, running it twice should not create two servers; the script should recognize that the server exists and do nothing. Idempotence ensures that the automation is safe to run anytime (like manually, scheduled, or triggered automatically). This is what separates a quick script from a reliable automation.
- **Version control and traceability**: Every automation script, playbook, and IaC template should be treated as code and should reside in a **version control system (VCS)**, so that it is reviewed, tracked, and auditable. Version control provides change history, rollback capability, and collaboration. When our automation runs changes in production, it is invaluable to trace its effects while running in production.
- **Observability and feedback loops**: Every automated process must have visibility so that it reports its outcome, like success, failure, or partial execution, via logs, metrics, or alerts. This will help provide the necessary feedback loop to validate that automation behaved as expected. Proper feedback ensures that we observe and refine the automation over time.
- **Fail-safe design**: Automation can amplify mistakes. For example, a misplaced variable or an incorrect loop can wipe out entire environments. Hence, it is essential to design fail-safe automations by:
    - Requiring explicit confirmation before running destructive actions.
    - Using dry-run or plan modes.
    - Validating input and boundary conditions.
    - Implementing rollback or compensating actions.
- **Human intervention**: It is essential in some cases to implement a hybrid approach, especially in some actions that impact production. This hybrid approach may involve human approval so that automation does not replace humans but assists them. An example of a hybrid approach is when automation auto-detects incidents but lets the engineers decide escalation paths. A hybrid approach preserves control while reducing toil.
- **Continuous improvement**: An automation is a living system that is continuously refined, optimized, and extended. For this, SREs review automation performance periodically, gather feedback from on-call engineers, and remove obsolete steps. This is done to ensure that the automation does not grow without structure.
- **Simplicity and clarity**: The best automation scripts and pipelines are simple, readable, and modular. Automations should be well-documented and clearly structured so that anyone on the team can understand everything. Clarity prevents future errors while improving maintainability.
- **Security by design**: Automations are used to execute powerful tasks like provisioning infrastructure, deploying code, and modifying config files; hence, they must be

designed with security in mind by using least privilege principles, encrypting secrets, and validating all inputs. Security should be a part of automation design and not added as an afterthought.

Identifying areas of automation

While SREs are tempted to automate everything, that is neither realistic nor efficient. Automation should focus on areas where it adds maximum value by reducing toil, improving reliability, and accelerating delivery. Let us look at some high-impact areas of automation:

- **Infrastructure provisioning and management**: Spinning up servers, networks, databases, and load balancers manually is slow and inconsistent. SREs should use IaC to automate the creation of entire environments, which ensures consistency across development, staging, and production, rapid recovery and scaling, while providing version controlled infrastructure changes. Terraform and CloudFormation are tools that are used here.

- **Incident response**: During an incident, when time is critical, automation can be used to detect, classify, and even remediate partially in some cases. For example, automation can be used to trigger escalation to the right on-call team based on the error type. Automated paging, routing, and contextual alert messages can reduce noise and improve the on-call experience. This does not eliminate human effort in incident response, but reduces manual overhead so humans can focus more on decision-making.

- **Software deployment and releases**: Manual deployments are a major source of outages. Instead, automating build, test, and deployment processes through CI/CD pipelines ensures fast, safe, and repeatable releases. This also ensures execution of security scans and rollbacks on failure, which makes releasing code a routine event and not a war-room situation.

- **Configuration management**: Maintaining consistent configurations across hundreds of servers or containers is nearly impossible to manage manually. Instead, automation tools like *Ansible*, *Chef*, and *Puppet* can be used to ensure that every instance runs the exact same settings, packages, and permissions.

- **Monitoring and alerting**: Monitoring can also be automated by using dynamic alerting systems, which can discover new services, apply default rules, and auto-tune thresholds by using historical data. Tools like *Grafana*, *Prometheus*, or *Dynatrace* integrate with automation scripts to register or deregister metrics as infrastructure changes.

- **Change management**: Change is often a major cause of most incidents. Hence, by automating change approvals, rollouts, and rollbacks, we can minimize that risk. For example, automation can be used to generate change requests when new commits are merged and to validate changes through automated tests. We can also roll back automatically if metrics degrade post-deployment.

- **Compliance and security checks**: Compliance rules (like ensuring encryption, access policies, or patch levels) can be codified and continuously validated using automation tools like *Checkov* or *AWS Config*. This will result in continuous compliance without the need for manual audits. Security scans for detecting vulnerabilities in code and dependencies can be automated against compliance policies.
- **Backup and disaster recovery**: Automating backup ensures that data is protected instead of relying on human memory. Scripts or workflows can be used to automate the execution of snapshots, replicate data, and validate recovery periodically. Testing recovery is an important task, and automation can be used to make it repeatable and predictable.
- **Routine maintenance and housekeeping**: Simple cron jobs or Lambda functions can be used to eliminate recurring manual efforts needed for routine tasks like rotating logs, archiving old data, patching systems, and renewing certificates.

Automation is not only about tools, but also a mindset change where every repeatable manual task becomes an opportunity to learn, automate, and scale.

Infrastructure as code

In earlier days of operations, we used to run commands manually on physical or **virtual machines (VMs)** (for installing software, editing configuration files, creating users, etc.) to setup new servers and environments. It worked fine when the number of servers was low (ideally in single digits), but now with more than 100 servers, it would be impossible to do the same without missing a step.

This is where IaC helps, where we define our IaC, which is version controlled, repeatable, and auditable.

IaC is the practice of managing and provisioning computing infrastructure through machine-readable definition files, rather than physical hardware configuration or interactive configuration tools. It is similar to writing a blueprint for our infrastructure.

In IaC, we write declarative configuration files that describe what we want the environment to look like, and the IaC tool picks up the file, compares it to our current state of the environment, and makes the necessary changes automatically.

Benefits of IaC are as follows:

- IaC is less about convenience and more about reliability. It aligns with the following SRE goals:
    - **Speed and simplicity**: We can execute a script to build a full environment in minutes.

- o **Consistency**: Every environment (development, staging, and production) can be identical. Also, this eliminates configuration drift.
- o **Accountability**: Every change can be tracked via version control. They can also be reviewed and are reversible.
- o **Testing**: We can test our infrastructure changes before applying them in production.
- o **Documentation**: The IaC code itself becomes the living documentation of our infrastructure.
- o **Disaster recovery**: In case of a disaster, we can re-create the entire environment from our code without missing a single step.

Types of IaC

There are two philosophies in IaC as follows:

- Imperative, where SREs write step-by-step commands describing how to reach a state.
- Declarative, where SREs describe the desired end state and the tool computes the path.

Declarative IaC is idempotent and predictable, and hence is preferred. Declarative systems are capable of detecting drifts automatically and can bring them back in line automatically.

Tool overview of Terraform

Terraform by HashiCorp is one of the most powerful IaC tools, which is supported by almost every cloud provider (AWS, Azure, **Google Cloud Platform** (**GCP**), etc.). It can be used to manage everything ranging from compute instances to DNS records.

Terraform core concepts are as follows:

- **Declarative language**: Terraform uses its own declarative language called **HashiCorp Configuration Language** (**HCL**) through which we can define the desired end state. Terraform then figures out the changes and API calls needed to achieve the end state.
- **Providers**: Terraform's extensibility is powered by providers. A provider is a plugin that interacts with the APIs of a cloud platform, SaaS service, or other API. The major cloud providers (AWS, Azure, GCP) have officially supported providers, but there are also Terraform providers for everything from DNS (Cloudflare) to databases (MySQL) and monitoring tools (PagerDuty).
- **Resources**: The most important element in Terraform's configuration. A resource block is used to define one or more infrastructure objects.
- **State file (terraform.tfstate)**: It is a critical JSON file that Terraform uses to map our configuration to the real-world resources in our cloud. It tracks the resource

ID and metadata. This state must be stored and shared securely when working in a team to avoid conflicts.

- **Execution plan (terraform plan):** It is a safety feature. This command computes and displays the proposed execution plan, outlining exactly what actions Terraform will take (like create, update, destroy) without making any critical changes. This is used by SREs to review and validate the changes before execution.
- **Apply (terraform apply):** It is used to apply the changes required to reach the desired state of configuration, as shown in the plan.

Terraform example

Let us look at a sample Terraform example to provision an AWS EC2 instance:

```
provider "aws" {
  region = "us-east-1"
}

variable "instance_count" {
  description = "Number of EC2 instances to create"
  type        = number
  default     = 3
}

resource "aws_instance" "web" {
  count         = var.instance_count
  ami           = "ami-0c55b159cbfafe1f0"
  instance_type = „t3.micro"

  tags = {
    Name = "SRE-Web-Server-${count.index + 1}"
  }
}
```

To execute this, we will run the following commands:

1. **terraform init**: This will initialize the working directory, download the required providers, and setup the backend.
2. **terraform plan**: This will generate the speculative execution plan. The SRE needs to review this plan carefully.
3. **terraform apply**: After typing yes to confirm, Terraform will make the API calls to AWS to create all the defined resources (in our case, three instances). It then writes the created resource IDs and metadata to the state file.

4. **terraform apply -var "instance_count=5"**: Is the command used to scale up the number of instances from the default `3` to `5`. We can check the plan using **`terraform plan -var "instance_count=5"`**, which will show that only two new instances will be added and the existing infrastructure will remain untouched.
5. **terraform destroy**: Will instruct Terraform to destroy all the resources defined in the configuration, in the correct dependency order, ensuring a clean teardown.

Terraform best practices

Let us look at some of the best practices using some advanced concepts in Terraform:

- **Use modules**: As infrastructure grows, we should break it into modules. A module is defined as a container for multiple resources that are used together (e.g., AWS VPC module or Kubernetes cluster module). This will help in reuse, simplicity, and maintainability.
- **Separate environments**: Use workspaces to manage multiple distinct state files for the same configuration (e.g., development, staging, and production). Some teams also prefer to keep separate directories for different environments.
- **Store state separately**: We should use remote backends (like S3 or Terraform Cloud) with state locking to avoid conflicts.
- Always review the plan before applying the changes.
- Version everything so module and provider versions are linked to prevent unexpected updates.

Terraform beautifully integrates with our CI/CD pipelines (like Jenkins or GitLab CI), so infrastructure changes can go through the same change management process as code. This brings change management discipline to infrastructure as well. Terraform can detect drifts when we run **`terraform plan`** and show discrepancies, which can be reviewed and automatically corrected while applying the changes.

There are other IaC tools (like *AWS CloudFormation*, *Google Cloud* deployment manager, and *Azure Resource Manager* templates). However, Terraform is cloud agnostic, which makes it ideal for multi-cloud SRE teams.

Automating workflows

While IaC tools like Terraform excel at provisioning the shell of our infrastructure (like VMs, network, databases), the next critical step is to configure what runs inside these shells. This is managed by configuration management or orchestration tools, which include deploying software, configuring services, patching systems, rotating logs, and managing user access. The goal of automating workflows is to make routine operations predictable, repeatable, and fast.

Objectives of configuration management

Automating workflows helps in day-to-day tasks such as deployment, verification, patching, restarting, and rollback. Automating them means fewer human errors, consistent and auditable changes, faster recovery and releases, and eventually happier engineers. Let us look at the key objectives of configuration management, where automation can help:

- Software installation and configuration, where automation can ensure that the correct version of software (e.g., Nginx) is installed and configured consistently across all servers.
- File management where automation can help in distributing configuration files (like `nginx.conf`) to the right locations with the correct permissions.
- Service management where automation can ensure that specific services (like Nginx) are running, are configured to enable on boot, and are restarted automatically if they fail.
- User and access management, where automation can help in creating user accounts, managing **Secure Shell** (**SSH**) keys, and controlling sudo access across our fleet of servers.
- Orchestration where automation can help coordinate complex multi-step workflows across multiple servers, such as performing a rolling application deployment or managing a database schema upgrade.

Ansible

There are multiple configuration management tools like Ansible, Puppet, and Chef, which help in automating the configuration, deployment, and orchestration of servers and services. Among them, Ansible has emerged as a preferred tool due to its simplicity and agentless nature.

Ansible is a powerful agentless automation tool that uses human-readable YAML playbooks and does not require the installation of agents on servers, as it connects over SSH or via API.

Ansible core characteristics

Let us look at the core characteristics of Ansible that make it stand out as the preferred tool:

- **Agentless architecture**: Ansible does not require any software to be installed on the target nodes it manages. It connects remotely via **`SSH`** (on Linux/Unix) or **`WinRM`** (on Windows), using the existing credentials and access methods. This makes it incredibly easy to start automating existing servers without a complex setup process.
- **Simple, human-readable language**: Ansible configurations are written in YAML, called Playbooks, which is much easier to read and write than custom DSLs or JSON, making automation accessible to the entire team.

- **Idempotency**: Like Terraform, Ansible modules are designed to be idempotent. We can run a playbook multiple times, and it will only make changes if the current state does not match the desired state defined in the playbook. This makes playbooks safe and predictable.
- **Inbuilt module library**: Ansible ships with hundreds of built-in modules that act as tools for everything, including managing packages (using apt or yum), managing files (copy, template), and services (using systemd) to interact with cloud providers, network devices, and APIs.

Ansible core components

Let us look at the core components within Ansible:

- Control node is the machine where Ansible is installed and from where we can run the automation commands.
- Managed nodes are the servers or network devices that we manage or configure with Ansible.
- Inventory is a file (usually `.ini` or `.yml`) that defines our managed nodes and is often grouped for convenience (e.g., `[webservers]`, `[dbservers]`).
- Playbooks are the core of Ansible automation. A playbook is a YAML file containing a list of one or more plays that define a set of automation tasks to be run against a group of hosts.
- Plays are maps of a set of tasks for a set of hosts. It is the bridge between inventory and the tasks to be executed. Tasks are the units of action in Ansible. Each task calls a specific Ansible module (like user, copy, or service).
- Modules are reusable, standalone scripts that Ansible executes on our behalf.
- Roles are a predefined way for organizing playbooks and other files to facilitate sharing and re-use. Roles allow us to break a complex playbook into multiple smaller, manageable components (e.g., an Nginx role, a Java role).

Ansible practical example

Let us automate the installation and startup of Nginx on two web servers using Ansible via the following steps:

1. **Create the inventory file (hosts.ini)**: Create a file named **`hosts.ini`** that lists the IP addresses or hostnames of our web servers. Group them under **`[web_servers]`** for easy targeting:

```
# hosts.ini
[web_servers]
```

```
web-server-1.example.com
web-server-2.example.com
```

2. **Create the Ansible playbook (setup_nginx.yaml)**: Create a file named **`setup_nginx.yaml`**. This is where we define what we want Ansible to do:

```
# setup_nginx.yaml
---
- name: Ensure Nginx is installed and running
  hosts: web_servers  # This targets the group from our inventory file
  become: yes         # This tells Ansible to use sudo/root privileges

  tasks:
    # Task 1: Install the latest version of Nginx
    - name: Install Nginx package
      apt:
        name: nginx
        state: latest
        update_cache: yes
      # This uses the 'apt' module for Debian/Ubuntu systems.
      # For RedHat/CentOS, you would use the 'yum' or 'dnf' module
instead.

    # Task 2: Ensure the Nginx service is started and enabled
    - name: Start and enable Nginx service
      systemd:
        name: nginx
        state: started
        enabled: yes
      # This uses the 'systemd' module to manage the service.
      # 'started' ensures it is running now.
      # 'enabled' ensures it starts automatically on boot.
```

3. **Run the playbook**: Let us execute the following command in our terminal from the same directory where our previous files are located:

```
Ansible-playbook -i hosts.ini setup-nginx.yaml
```

When the previously mentioned command is run, the execution happens as follows:

Ansible reads the inventory (**`hosts.ini`**) and connects via SSH to each server listed under **`[web_servers]`**.

For each server, it executes the two tasks:

a. **First task**: It updates the package cache (**`update_cache: yes`**) and installs the latest version of the nginx package. If Nginx is already installed, Ansible does nothing. This demonstrates idempotency.

b. **Second task**: It ensures that the Nginx service is running (**`state: started`**) and configures it to start automatically when the server boots (**`enabled: yes`**).

We get a summary on our terminal showing if each task was **`ok`** (no change needed) or **`changed`** (Ansible made a change) for each server.

If the command is run for the first time and Nginx is not installed on the web servers, the output would show that Ansible successfully connected to both the servers and made changes on both. If we run the exact same command again, the output would show **`ok`** instead of **`changed`**, proving that the configuration is idempotent and our servers are already in the desired state.

Automated deployment with Ansible

To automatically deploy a new version of our application using Ansible, we need to create an Ansible playbook that captures the following steps:

1. Pull the latest code from Git.
2. Build and package the app.
3. Copy the artifacts to the target servers.
4. Restart services.
5. Verify health.

These steps within a playbook would become a single, predictable command that can be easily integrated with our CI/CD pipeline.

It is very common in SRE teams to use Terraform and Ansible together. Terraform handles infrastructure provisioning, and Ansible configures the servers and deploys the software.

Ansible automation best practices:

- Keep playbooks small and predictable.
- Use variables and templates for flexibility.
- Use Ansible Vault for encrypting sensitive data like passwords, API keys and certificates so that they can be stored safely in version control along with our playbooks.
- Instead of a static file, we can source our inventory dynamically from cloud providers (like AWS EC2, Azure VM) so our automation always targets the correct running servers.
- Use collections to distribute Ansible content (like roles, modules, or plugins) to the Ansible community and vendors.
- Use blocks with rescue and always sections for handling errors gracefully. For example, the automatic rollback of a failed deployment.

- Always validate syntax with **`ansible-lint`**.
- Use **`dry-run (--check)`** to verify before applying the changes.
- Avoid Ansible automation for:
  - o Rare and high-risk operations.
  - o Situations that require contextual judgment.
  - o Unstable or rapidly changing systems.

By integrating Ansible into the SRE toolkit, teams can move beyond one-off server configuration and embrace a model of declarative, repeatable, and auditable system management. This is the engine that powers consistent, large-scale operational workflows, from daily patching to complex, zero-downtime deployments.

Auto-healing

Auto-healing is the capability of a system to automatically detect its own degradation or failure and initiate a recovery process to restore itself to a healthy state, all without human intervention. It represents a fundamental shift from a reactive operation model (where engineers are paged to diagnose operational problems) to a proactive and resilient one, where the system manages its own health.

We can draw an analogy to the human immune system. When we get a cut, our body does not wait for us to consciously notice it and apply a bandage. Instead, it automatically detects the breach, clots the blood, and sends white cells to fight the infection. Auto-healing works in a similar way and can be termed as the digital immune system for our applications.

Auto-healing directly impacts one of the key metrics of SRE, which is reliability. By automating recovery, we can reduce the MTTR from minutes or hours to seconds.

Key components of auto-healing system

Every auto-healing system, regardless of its complexity, is built on three core components, given as follows:

- Detection, which is the monitoring and observability layer that identifies the problem. Detection must be fast, accurate, and specific. Some of the detection methods are listed as follows:
  - o Health checks are the most common method. A lightweight frequency check (e.g., HTTP GET **`/health`** endpoint) should return **`200 OK`** if the service is healthy. If we do not get a **`200 OK`** response, it signals a problem.
  - o Synthetic transactions simulate real human actions (like adding an item to the cart and doing checkout) to verify if critical business workflows are functioning.

    - Metric-based alerts from monitoring systems (like CPU utilization > 95% for 5 minutes or a spike in 5xx HTTP errors) can indicate an impending or current failure.
    - Automated scanning of application logs for specific error patterns or exceptions can also indicate if a failure happens.
- Decision logic (like scripts, policies, or event-driven automation) that helps in choosing the remediation action. Once a problem is detected, the system must use logic like simple if-then rules or complex machine-learning-driven decisions to decide what to do. Let us look at some sample logics:
    - Simple rules, like if the health check fails 3 times in a row, restart the container.
    - Escalation remedies like first restarting the process, and if it still fails 2 times in a row, replace the entire VM.
    - Context-aware logic, like when the database connection is failing. If restarting the web server does not help, re-route the traffic away from this region.
- Remediation is the action that fixes the problem. This is the execution of the recovery action, which must be safe, idempotent, and effective. These actions can include the following:
    - Restarting the process, container, or service can clear stuck states and transient issues.
    - Recreate by terminating an unhealthy compute resource and letting the orchestration launch a new, fresh instance.
    - Traffic routing by updating a load balancer to stop sending traffic to the unhealthy node.
    - Scaling the system horizontally by launching new healthy instances to replace the faulty ones or to handle increased load.

Auto-healing example

Let us look at how Kubernetes can be used to auto-heal a web application. The following Kubernetes configuration file is used to setup the web application with two replicas, along with a health check every 10 seconds:

```
apiVersion: apps/v1
kind: Deployment
metadata:
  name: webapp
spec:
  replicas: 2
```

```
template:
  spec:
    containers:
    - name: webapp
      image: nginx:latest
      livenessProbe:
        httpGet:
          path: /health
          port: 80
        initialDelaySeconds: 30
        periodSeconds: 10
        failureThreshold: 3
```

The following are the steps that detect and auto-heal based on the above configuration:

1. Kubernetes checks **/health** endpoint every 10 seconds.
2. If the health check fails 3 times in a row, the container is marked as unhealthy.
3. Kubernetes has a built-in rule that unhealthy containers must be restarted.
4. Kubernetes remediates the issue by killing the bad container and starting a new one.

From the user's perspective, the user would see slow requests for a few seconds, and the system would recover before most users notice. Also, with auto-healing in place, no engineers are paged in this case.

Auto-healing has a direct and measurable impact on the MTTR metrics. Reducing MTTR means our system's availability improves, which helps us to stay within our error budget and eventually gives us more budget for innovation.

Let us look at the impact on different metrics with auto-healing:

Metric	Without auto-healing	With auto-healing
Detection time	Manual (minutes)	Automated (seconds)
Response time	Manual (minutes)	Automated trigger (seconds)
Recovery time	Minutes to hours	Seconds to minutes
MTTR	High	Significantly reduced

Table 8.1: *Impact of auto-healing on SRE metrics*

Auto-healing acts as a bridge between automation and reliability. In the real-world, auto-healing leads to fewer outages and better experience for end users, fewer after-hours pages and firefighting for engineers, and reliable service and happier customers for the business.

Reducing toil

In the SRE context, toil is the kind of operational work that is manual, repetitive, reactive, devoid of enduring value, and scales linearly as the service grows. In short, most of the repetitive operational tasks are toil. Some examples of toil are:

- Restarting servers after crashing.
- Manually scaling infrastructure up or down for expected traffic.
- Rotating credentials and certificates across servers.
- Rotating logs.
- Manually running database backups.
- Manually deploying application versions.
- Running ad-hoc scripts for minor fixes.

These and similar tasks burn out engineers, prevent strategic work, and make systems less reliable due to human error; hence, they are prime cases for automation.

Automation reduces toil

Every time engineers automate a repetitive task, they free uptime for strategic work like improving architecture, observability, and performance. Let us look at the automation steps that SREs can take to reduce toil:

1. Identify repetitive and manual work by tracking the most frequent on-call tasks or runbook actions.
2. Prioritize the tasks by the amount of time they consume or by the amount of friction they cause.
3. Automate the top task from this list by converting it into scripts or workflow automations.
4. Integrate the automations with alerting to auto-remediate and notify.
5. Review the automation periodically so that it is maintained as the system evolves.

Reducing toil improves team morale, focus, and team efficiency, which gives engineers more bandwidth to innovate and also improves reliability. This is a repetitive cycle and is shown in the following figure:

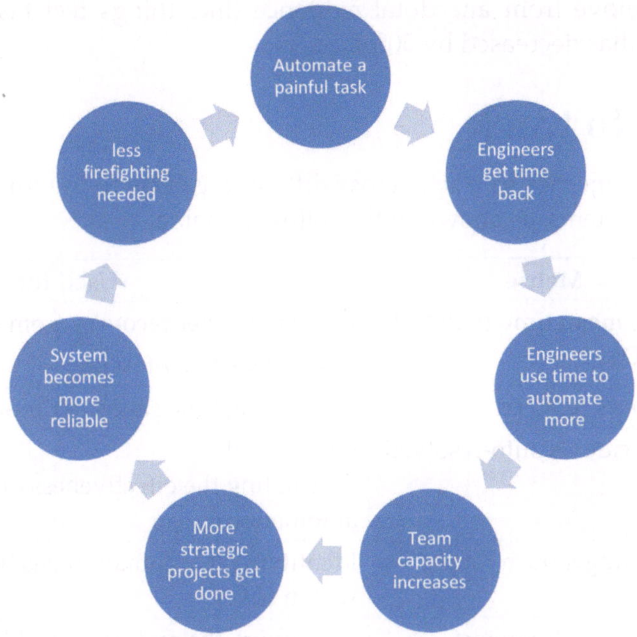

***Figure 8.1**: Ripple effect of reducing toil*

Toil reduction example

Let us look at an example of how toil reduction improves reliability and team morale, while also benefiting the business.

Let us say that the team spends 20 hours per week on manual deployments:

- **Cost**: *20 hours * 50 weeks * $100 per hour = $100,000 per year.*
- **After automation**: The team would spend 1 hour per week on monitoring.
- **Savings**: 19 hours per week = $95,000 per year in recovered engineering time.
- **Benefits**: Fewer deployment failures, faster time to market, happier engineering team.

By systematically identifying and eliminating toil through automation, SRE teams transform from reactive firefighters to proactive reliability engineers, creating more value for the business while building more sustainable careers.

Measuring automation success

As SREs, we cannot improve what we cannot measure. Without clear measurement, we cannot prove value, justify further investment, or know whether the efforts are making the system more reliable. Hence, it is extremely essential to measure the impact of our automation efforts. Measurement transforms automation from a technical exercise to a strategic capability.

The goal is also to move from anecdotal evidence (like things feel faster) to data-driven decisions (like MTTR has decreased by 50%).

Key metrics to track

Let us look at the key metrics to track across different aspects to identify if automation has helped improve our systems, as shown in the following table:

Category	Metric	Used for
Reliability	MTTR, **mean time to detect (MTTD)**	Detecting faster recovery from incidents. Faster detection of issues
Efficiency	Toil hours reduced % of incidents auto-resolved	Calculating time saved per month due to automation Calculating the effectiveness of self-healing automations
Quality	Error budget burn rate	Identifying if automation has helped keep uptime within SLOs
Throughput	Deployment frequency	Identifying the maturity of CI/CD systems

Table 8.2: *Metrics for measuring automation benefits*

For example, if our MTTR drops from 40 minutes to 5 minutes after implementing auto-healing, it is a measurable success. Similarly, if 60% of incidents are automatically resolved, it shows a massive improvement in reliability and engineer productivity.

Example

Let us look at an example where we quantify the benefits of an automated deployment pipeline. In this scenario, the team manually deploys their service once a week. The process is fragile and often requires rolling back:

- **Before automation**:
    - **Deployment frequency**: Once a week
    - **Lead time for changes**: 3 days to merge and deploy
    - **Change failure rate**: 30% (3 out of 10 deployments have issues)
    - **Time spent per deployment**: 4 engineer hours (2 engineers for 2 hours)
- **After automation (implementing CI/CD)**:
    - **Deployment frequency**: 5 times per week (can also deploy on-demand)
    - **Lead time for changes**: 2 hours (since it is an automated pipeline)

- o **Change failure rate**: 5% (dropped drastically)
- o **Time spent per deployment**: 0.5 engineer hours for monitoring only

From the previous example, we can quantify the following benefits:

- **Time saved**:
  - o **Before automation**: *1 deployment * 4 hours = 4 hours*
  - o **After automation**: *5 deployments * 0.5 hours = 2.5 hours*
  - o **Net time saved per week**: *1.5 hours*
  - o **Annual time savings**: *1.5 hours/week * 50 weeks = 75 engineer hours*
- **Quality improvement**:
  - o **Before automation**: *30% of 52 deployments failed = ~16 failures/year*
  - o **After automation**: *5% of 250 deployments failed = ~12.5 failures/year*
  - o **Benefit**: Despite 5x more deployments, we have fewer failures
- **Business agility**:
  - o Features can now reach customers in hours instead of days.
  - o The team can experiment and iterate much faster.

Automation and error budget

The error budget is the calculated amount of unreliability a system can tolerate over a period (like a month). It is defined as: 100% - availability SLO. So, if our SLO is 99.9%, our error budget is 0.1%, which is 43 minutes in a month.

Automation directly preserves and protects this error budget. Let us understand in the context of the previous example of automating deployments on a monthly budget:

- **Before automation**:
  - o Manual deployments are risky and have a high failure rate (30%). Hence, each failed deployment burns a larger chunk of the error budget. Monthly:

    *4 deployments * 30% failure rate = ~1 failed deployment/month*

  - o Slow recovery (high MTTR) means that when failures occur, the service stays broken for a longer duration, thus burning through the error budget quickly.

    60 minutes to fix failure = 60 units spent

    Remaining budget = 40 units

- **After automation**:
  - Deployments have become more reliable with only 5% failure rate, so each deployment burns very little from the error budget. We can deploy 5 times more often while having fewer incidents.

    *20 deployments * 5% failure rate = ~1 failed deployment/month*

  - Faster auto-recovery means that when failure happens, it is fixed in minutes instead of hours. So, a 5 minute outage burns less budget than a 60 minute outage.

    5 minutes to fix failures = 5 units spent

    Remaining budget = 95 units

Benefits are as follows:

- With 95 units of error budget remaining instead of 40, the team has strategic freedom. They can deploy more frequently and confidently, take calculated risks on performance improvements, conduct game days and chaos engineering experiments, and roll out major features with lower anxiety.
- Hence, automation not only prevents going over budget but also creates a surplus of reliability that enables innovation and velocity.

Automation dashboard

It is recommended to build a simple dashboard to track the following key metrics over time. This will help us visualize and showcase the benefits of automation to everyone:

- MTTR trend should be going down.
- Deployment frequency should be going up, and lead time should be going down.
- The change failure rate should be going down.
- Toil ratio should be going down.
- Error budget consumption should be slower than before.

By consistently measuring these indicators, we can clearly demonstrate that automation is not a cost center, but a strategic investment that directly fuels reliability, velocity, and innovation.

DevSecOps

DevSecOps is the cultural and technical practice of integrating security practices and tools throughout the entire **software development lifecycle** (**SDLC**). It moves security from being a gatekeeper at the end of the process to being a shared responsibility embedded in every phase, from design to deployment and operation.

The traditional model of having a separate security team perform a final review before release is too slow for the modern development practice. It results in bottlenecks and lapses in security practices to meet deadlines. Instead, DevSecOps shifts security left by introducing security considerations at the very start of the development process.

In the DevSecOps model, every stage of the software lifecycle, from code commit to deployment, has security checks automated and integrated seamlessly.

Importance of DevSecOps

The mission of SRE is to keep systems reliable, available, and secure. Security directly impacts the previously mentioned three objectives. Let us see how DevSecOps supports the goals of SRE as shown in the following table:

Goal	DevSecOps supports it by
Reliability	Preventing outages caused by security breaches or vulnerabilities.
Scalability	Ensuring security policies are automated and scale with the infrastructure.
Toil reduction	Reducing manual audit work as security scans are automated.
Compliance	Ensures that the system meets regulatory requirements by continuous monitoring.
MTTR and error budgets	Minimizing impact on availability due to faster detection and mitigation of security incidents.

***Table 8.3:** DevSecOps and SRE principles*

Thus, integrating security in our automation keeps our reliability metrics healthy and our systems trustworthy.

Pillars of DevSecOps

Let us break down DevSecOps into three pillars that directly align with automation and SRE practices:

- **Culture and collaboration**: Security is everyone's job. Developers, SREs, and security engineers work together as one team with shared goals. Security is shifted left and starts during commit. By integrating static code analysis, dependency scanning, and container checks in the CI/CD pipeline, vulnerabilities are caught before they hit production.
- **Continuous security monitoring**: Automating runtime monitoring with tools that scan for threats, privilege escalations, or unauthorized configuration changes without human intervention makes security a seamless and continuous part of the delivery pipeline.

- **Automated remediation**: When something does go wrong, security automation can isolate the threat, rotate credentials, or roll back vulnerable deployments automatically.

Integrating security into CI/CD pipeline

Injecting security at every stage of the CI/CD pipeline creates a continuous security feedback loop. Before DevSecOps, the CI/CD pipeline would look like this:

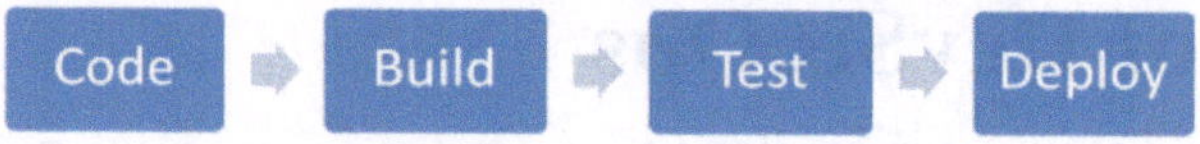

Figure 8.2: Traditional CI/CD pipeline

After including DevSecOps in the CI/CD pipeline, the pipeline would look as shown here:

Figure 8.3: CI/CD pipeline with DevSecOps

Let us look at all the security stages in the CI/CD pipeline in detail.

Code commit phase

Static application security testing (**SAST**) tools are used to scan the source code for vulnerabilities. This helps the team catch bugs early when they are the cheapest and easiest to fix. This prevents vulnerable code from ever being merged. Let us look at the details:

1. **Build and test phase**: **Software composition analysis** (**SCA**) tools are used to scan software dependencies for known vulnerabilities. This prevents deploying applications with known, exploitable open-source vulnerabilities, reducing the attack surface of production services.

2. **Artifact storage phase**: Container or image scanning tools are used to scan for OS-level vulnerabilities, misconfigurations, and secrets. This ensures that the final deployable artifact is secure, which is critical for the integrity of the production environment.

3. **Deployment phase**: IaC scanning tools scan Terraform, Ansible, or CloudFormation scripts for security misconfigurations. This prevents misconfigured or insecure infrastructure from ever being provisioned.

4. **Runtime phase**: Tools like **dynamic application security testing** (**DAST**), **web application firewall** (**WAF**) are used to monitor the application in production for security attacks and anomalous behavior. This provides a last line of defense and detection for vulnerabilities that were missed in earlier stages.

Secrets management

Hardcoding API keys, passwords, and certificates in source code is a primary cause of security breaches. DevSecOps encourages centralized, automated secret management via tools like:

- HashiCorp Vault, which encrypts and dynamically rotates secrets.
- AWS Secrets Manager/ Azure Key Vault that helps in managing a separate secret per environment.
- Sealed secrets in Kubernetes can be used to encrypt and store secrets safely in VCS like Git.

Let us look at a sample code for using Vault with Terraform:

```
provider "vault" {
  address = "https://vault.example.com"
}

data "vault_kv_secret_v2" "db_creds" {
  path = "secret/data/database"
}

resource "aws_db_instance" "secure_db" {
  username = data.vault_generic_secret.db_creds.data["username"]
  password = data.vault_generic_secret.db_creds.data["password"]
}
```

With vaults, even our infrastructure code can remain secure and compliant without exposing sensitive credentials. Applications and scripts retrieve secrets dynamically from the vault at runtime. The vault provides auditing, automatic rotation, and fine-grained access controls. This also eliminates a major security risk and operational headache of manually rotating credentials.

Automating compliance and policy enforcement

Manual compliance audits are slow, expensive, and often point-in-time. DevSecOps helps in defining security and compliance policies as code using tools like:

- **Open Policy Agent** (**OPA**) that enforces fine-grained policies on resources.
- Terraform Sentinel that checks IaC configurations against compliance rules.
- Conftest that runs OPA-based checks on YAML/JSON/Kubernetes manifests.

We can write rules in high-level language (like Rego for OPA) that can be used to enforce policies (like *no storage buckets can be public* or *All EC2 instances must have a specific tag*).

Example: Preventing S3 buckets from being public using OPA policy:

```
package s3.security

deny[msg] {
  input.resource_type == "aws_s3_bucket"
  input.acl == "public-read"
  msg = "S3 bucket should not be publicly readable"
}
```

These policies are automatically evaluated against infrastructure code or running environments to ensure continuous compliance. The pipeline automatically blocks non-compliant changes, turning a periodic, stressful audit into a seamless, automated process.

Secure deployment workflow

Let us look at a secure deployment workflow in a mature SRE setup:

1. Developer pushes code, which triggers the CI pipeline.
2. Code and secret scanning (via SAST tools like SonarQube) is done. If any vulnerabilities are found, the build fails instantly.
3. Dependency checks (via SCA tools) run.
4. The application is built into a Docker image.
5. The container image is scanned by Trivy for OS and library vulnerabilities, which, if found, stop the build.
6. Before deploying, the Terraform code is scanned by Sentinel policies (like **Terraform security** (**Tfsec**)), which block deployments if it finds a publicly accessible database or any other misconfigurations.
7. Deployment is triggered only if all checks pass.
8. During deployment, the application retrieves its database password from a vault (like Hashicorp Vault), so no secrets are stored in the code.
9. Continuous monitoring in production ensures that alerts are raised for any anomalies.

As each step is automated without human intervention, security becomes a part of the release speed instead of a blocker.

Measuring DevSecOps success

For SREs, the success of DevSecOps is measured by tangible improvement in reliability, velocity, and operational overhead. Here is a table that shows which metrics can be used to measure different aspects of DevSecOps success:

Metric	Measures	Meaning
Vulnerability detection rate	% of issues found before production.	A high number indicates security is catching issues early, before production.
Mean time to patch (MTTP)	How quickly vulnerabilities are fixed.	Shorter times mean less window of exposure and less operational debt.
Number of security incidents	Number of incidents caused by security flaws.	Directly impacts service reliability and should reduce overtime with automation.
Secrets exposure incidents	Number of incidents caused by the exposure of secrets.	It should ideally be zero after automation, which also reduces the risk and operational toil of credential rotation.
Policy violations blocked	Number of policy violations causing build failures.	Shows proactive enforcement effectiveness.

Table 8.4: DevSecOps metrics to measure SRE success

So, if our vulnerability patch time drops from 10 days to 2 days after automation, this could be measured as a success of DevSecOps and SRE.

Security incidents are some of the most severe and error-budget-consuming events a service can face. A successful ransomware attack or data breach can mean 100% unavailability for an extended period of time, completely obliterating the error budget. With DevSecOps, automated scans and policies prevent vulnerable code and misconfigured infrastructure from ever reaching production. This proactively protects the error budget from being consumed by preventable security failures. DevSecOps also helps in reducing human toil and helps us in automatically staying compliant. It gives confidence in reliability by building systems that are fast, safe, and reliable by default.

AIOps

Modern systems generate an overwhelming volume, velocity, and variety of data, which includes logs, metrics, traces, alerts, tickets, and more. The human brain struggles while correlating these millions of data points in real-time. Hence, traditional monitoring and rule-based automations cannot keep up.

This is where AIOps comes in. AIOps is the application of **machine learning** (**ML**) and data science to IT operations challenges. The AIOps platform ingests all our operational data and uses algorithms to detect incidents and anomalies proactively, correlate related events to find the root cause, and automate responses and predictions.

The SRE journey commonly evolves from manual operations to automated to intelligent operations (AIOps). Here is a table describing the operations maturity stage and its benefits:

Maturity stage	Description	Outcome
Manual operations	Reactive troubleshooting	High toil and high MTTR
Automated Ops	Using scripts and CI/CD automation	Reduces toil and faster recovery
Intelligent Ops (AIOps)	Provides ML-driven insights and predictive actions	Self-healing and proactive reliability

Table 8.5: SRE maturity stage and outcome

AIOps has the following benefits for the SRE team:

- It helps the team to detect anomalies in real-time.
- It predicts incidents before they impact end users.
- It reduces alert fatigue through intelligent noise reduction.
- It helps correlate data across observability, CI/CD, and infrastructure.
- It can recommend or trigger automated remediation actions.

Core pillars of AIOps

Let us look at the core pillars that help in building AIOps:

- **Data aggregation**: AIOps starts by ingesting massive amounts of data from multiple sources, including logs, metrics, traces, events, alerts, CI/CD pipeline data, and incidents and tickets (from JIRA or ServiceNow). The first challenge for AIOps is to centralize data by building a unified data layer from which all intelligence flows.
- **Pattern discovery and correlation**: ML algorithms are used to analyze the unified data to find patterns, relationships, and dependencies. It discovers generic patterns and correlates them to events (such as when metric A spikes, log pattern B usually appears 30 seconds later in service C).
- **Noise reduction and intelligent alerting**: Traditional alerting can flood on-call engineers with thousands of events. Instead, AIOps uses pattern recognition to group related events into a single incident, suppress duplicate or irrelevant notifications, and identify causal event chains. AIOps then clusters these events into a single meaningful incident, drastically reducing alert fatigue and improving focus.
- **Anomaly detection and prediction**: Instead of relying on static thresholds, unsupervised ML models learn the normal, dynamic behavior of our systems. They can flag subtle deviations that might indicate an emergency problem long before it triggers a traditional alert.

  Example:

  - If our API latency usually spikes at 8 am due to traffic increase, AIOps will not alert unnecessarily.

    - However, if the latency spikes at 2 pm without any historical precedent, it is flagged as an anomaly.

- **Root cause analysis (RCA):** AIOps can correlate logs, metrics, and changes to identify the root cause of incidents. By linking change data to incidents, AIOps can shorten the RCA from hours to minutes.

  Example: AIOps can say that 95% of incidents where latency exceeded 2 seconds were preceded by the deployment of build-178 to the authentication service.

- **Predictive insights**: AIOps can predict failures before they occur by learning:
    - When resource usage trends indicate imminent saturation.
    - When anomaly clusters precede downtime.
    - Which services are likely to degrade under certain load patterns.

These insights can be used to automatically trigger preemptive scaling, rollbacks, or maintenance actions.

Automated remediation

Now that the system is able to understand and predict issues, it can also self-repair. AIOps platforms can be integrated with automation tools like Ansible, Terraform, or Kubernetes controllers to execute corrective actions automatically (like restarting pods, scaling nodes, rolling back deployments, clearing cache, re-routing traffic via load balancers, etc.). It can also automatically execute runbooks for known problems.

With auto-remediation, AIOps, and auto-healing can be bridged together to form a closed feedback loop, as shown in the following figure:

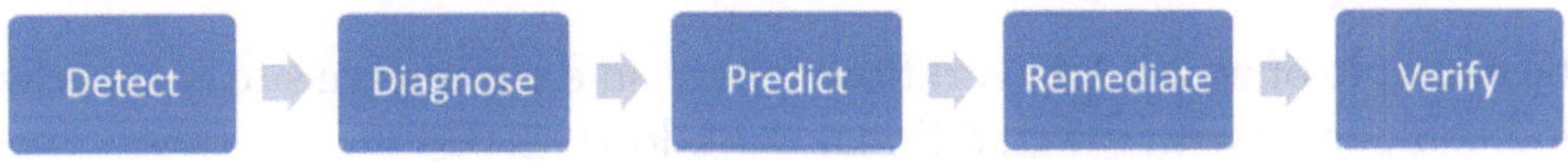

Figure 8.4: *AIOps and auto-healing bridge*

AIOps pipeline

Let us look at the AIOps pipeline. It consists of multiple stages where each stage performs a certain set of actions and feeds the next stage. The AIOps pipeline can be visualized as shown in the following figure:

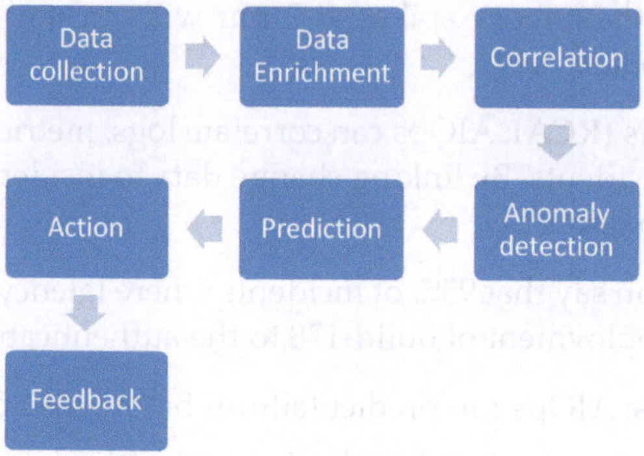

Figure 8.5: AIOps pipeline

The following are the actions that happen at each stage of the AIOps pipeline:

- **Data collection**: Gather all data from logs, metrics, traces, and events.
- **Data enrichment**: Add metadata like service name, version, region, and deployment ID.
- **Correlation**: Group related signals into incidents.
- **Detection**: Identify deviations from normal patterns.
- **Prediction**: Forecast future anomalies or capacity issues.
- **Action**: Trigger automated workflows for resolution.
- **Feedback**: Learn from outcomes to improve future predictions.

Example AIOps workflow

Let us see the example of an AIOps workflow where an e-commerce site is experiencing slow checkouts and compare it with the traditional workflow:

- **Traditional workflow**:
  1. PagerDuty fires multiple separate alerts, including high CPU on three web servers, high error rate on the payment service, high latency from the database, etc.
  2. The on-call engineer logs in and spends 20 to 30 minutes manually correlating these alerts and checking dashboards.
  3. They eventually trace the root cause to a misconfigured database index.
- **AIOps-powered workflow**:
  1. The AIOps platform ingests all data, metrics, and logs. The data is enriched with relevant metadata.

2. Its correlation engine immediately recognizes that all these symptoms are related to having a common root cause. Hence, it suppresses the multiple noisy alerts and creates a single incident titled *Probable database performance degradation impacting checkout*.
3. It automatically attaches relevant data like the specific database query that slowed down, the impacted service topology, and similar past incidents.
4. It suggests execution of a runbook to kill the problematic query or trigger database failover. It can also be empowered to automatically execute the runbook.
5. The engineer gets paged with a clear contextual incident identifying the root cause and actions taken by the system automatically. This drastically reduces the **mean time to acknowledge** (**MTTA**) and MTTR.
6. Once the system has recovered, it automatically logs the incident with relevant data and updates the ML pattern for future pattern recognition.

AIOps tools and platforms

The AIOps landscape can be categorized into domain-specific AIOps tools that tie the ML to a specific domain and pure play AIOps platforms that are designed as a central correlation and analysis engine.

Domain-specific AI

These are tools that bring ML to a specific data domain. The following are some categories and examples of some tools within those categories:

- **APM**: Dynatrace, New Relic, AppDynamics
- **Log management**: Splunk ITSI, Elastic ML
- **Infrastructure monitoring**: Datadog, ScienceLogic

Pure play AIOps platforms

These are platforms designed as a central correlation and analysis engine serving a specific purpose, as follows:

- **Moogsoft**: Specializes in noise reduction and incident correlation.
- **BigPanda**: Focuses on event correlation and enrichment.
- **PagerDuty operations cloud**: Integrates AI into the incident response workflow.

AIOps impact on SRE metrics

AIOps has a direct and measurable impact on the SRE metrics, as shown in the following table:

SRE metric	Impact of AIOps
MTTR	Drastically reduced. Faster root cause identification and automated remediation, reducing resolution time
MTTA	Reduced as intelligent alerting pages, the right person with the right context immediately
Alert volume	Drastically reduced as AIOps turns hundreds of alerts into a handful of actionable incidents
Change failure rate	Reduced as predictive analytics can flag risky deployments before they cause outages
Error budget consumption	Slowed as fewer incidents and faster recovery mean that the error budget is burned much more slowly
Toil	Significantly reducing triage, correlation, and initial diagnosis by automating frees up SREs for engineering tasks

Table 8.6: *Impact of AIOps on SRE metrics*

Building AIOps culture

Adopting AIOps is not only a tool decision. It is more of a cultural challenge than a technical one, and here are the strategies that can be used to succeed in implementing AIOps:

- Start with a painful and specific problem. Start with a clear goal (like reduce false positive pager alerts by 50%) as a focused pilot project, which will be able to demonstrate tangible value.

- Focus on transparency. Choose platforms that explain why the decision was made to build trust. E.g., a platform that says *Anomaly detected: CPU is 75%, which is 3 standard deviations above the normal baseline for this time of day, correlated with a deployment 10 minutes ago,* is better.

- Augment, do not replace. Position AIOps as a tool that augments an SRE's intelligence, not replaces it. The goal is to handle the tedious work of sifting through data so the engineer can focus on high-level problem-solving.

- Invest in data quality. AIOps depends on quality data. Ensure that we have consistent, high-quality data streams from our monitoring tools before expecting reliable insights.

Future of AIOps

AIOps is evolving from a reactive tool to a proactive and predictive partner. In the future, AIOps can deliver the following:

- Self-optimizing infrastructure that auto-tunes CPU and memory based on patterns.
- Adaptive error budgets which adjust SLOs dynamically based on historical reliability.

- AI-generated runbooks that provide contextual remediation suggestions based on past incidents.
- Conversational Ops like chatbots that are powered by **large language models** (**LLMs**) that understand incidents and execute fixes.

AIOps is not a futuristic fantasy but a practical evolution of the SRE toolkit. By delegating the task of data synthesis and initial analysis to machines, SREs can scale their impact, protect their cognitive load, and focus on the engineering work that truly improves system resilience. The future of SRE is not just automated, but intelligent.

Conclusion

Automation is not just a set of tools; it is a cultural mindset. An automation-first culture encourages questioning every manual process and automating processes that are beneficial. It celebrates the creation of a script that saves 10 minutes a day as much as a major new feature, because the cumulative effect of these small automations is profound.

The journey from manual operations to fully autonomous, self-healing systems is iterative. We start with the principles, identify our biggest sources of toil, and begin building with the powerful tools at our disposal. By weaving automation, security (DevSecOps), and intelligence (AIOps) into the fabric of our SRE practice, we can build systems that are not only more reliable and scalable but also more secure and ultimately, more human-friendly.

The next chapter explores how SRE and security work together to build systems that are resilient, trustworthy and scalable. It explains how security controls can be embedded into automation, monitoring, and incident response without slowing teams down. We will see how concepts like least privilege, secure defaults and continuous compliance align naturally with SRE principles like error budgets and SLOs. The next chapter will help us understand why secure systems are reliable systems and why modern SRE must think like secure engineers as well.

CHAPTER 9
Security and SRE

Introduction

Security is a foundational aspect of reliable systems. For **site reliability engineers** (**SREs**), who are tasked with ensuring the scalability, reliability, and performance of modern distributed systems, security is intrinsically linked to these core objectives, as security failures burn the same error budget via downtime and degradation. This chapter explores the critical intersection of SRE practices with the complex demands of enterprise security and compliance standards. We will dissect how SREs can architect and operate systems that are not only resilient to failures but also resistant to malicious threats.

We begin with the security fundamentals for SRE, covering the fundamentals that every SRE must know. Next, we explore secure system design, focusing on building systems that minimize vulnerabilities from the ground up. This chapter then details **identity and access management** (**IAM**) practices, including least privilege, **role-based access control** (**RBAC**), and automation of credential management.

A significant portion is dedicated to handling security incidents, providing a clear framework for detecting, mitigating, and recovering from large-scale attacks, such as **distributed denial of service** (**DDoS**), through techniques such as rate limiting, intelligent traffic filtering, and scalable architecture design.

We will also examine the viral relationship between SRE and compliance, outlining strategies to meet requirements for both data protection, auditability, and access control. Beyond reactive measures, we will emphasize proactive security, including regular audits, penetration testing, and patch management. The chapter also discusses how SRE teams can align with compliance frameworks and cultivate a security-first culture, integrating security checks into **continuous integration/continuous deployment** (**CI/CD**) pipelines and operational reviews. We also introduce Falco as an example tool for runtime threat detection in cloud-native environments. By the chapter's conclusion, you will understand the essential strategies to safeguard systems, protect user data, and maintain trust in an evolving threat environment.

Structure

The chapter covers the following topics:

- Security fundamentals for SRE
- Identity and access management
- SRE and compliance
- Falco
- Secure system design
- Handling security incidents
- Security culture in SRE teams

Objectives

This chapter aims to equip SREs with the foundational knowledge and practical strategies to integrate security seamlessly into their work, ensuring systems are both reliable and resilient against threats. It aims to build awareness of security as a shared responsibility between development, operations, and reliability teams. We will explore how core SRE practices directly support key compliance requirements for data protection, auditability, and access control. The chapter provides a rigorous framework for handling security incidents, with a focused analysis on detecting, mitigating, and recovering from large-scale DDoS attacks through rate limiting, traffic filtering, and resilient design. Furthermore, we will detail proactive measures, including security audits, penetration testing, and patch management. By its conclusion, we will be able to implement the necessary controls, foster a robust security culture within our team, and utilize tools like Falco to safeguard infrastructure, protect user data, and maintain trust in a dynamic threat landscape while aligning with evolving industry standards and best practices.

Security fundamentals for SRE

Security forms the backbone of reliability. No matter how redundant and fast our systems are, a single security breach can destroy trust, compromise availability, and lead to catastrophic financial and reputational loss. Hence, it is crucial to internalize the core principles that guide a security-conscious SRE.

The SRE role is not to replace the dedicated security team but to act as a force multiplier. While the **security operations center** (**SOC**) focuses on broad threat intelligence and monitoring, and the product and technology teams work on secure coding practices, the SRE strongly influences and operates the runtime environment. SRE controls the infrastructure, the configuration, the deployment pipeline, and the monitoring, which places them at a strategic vantage point to enforce security. This puts SRE in the best possible position to implement, enforce, and validate security controls where they matter most.

CIA triad

The foundational model of information security is the **confidentiality, integrity, and availability** (**CIA**) triad. Hence, every SRE should understand this model. The CIA triad consists of the following principles:

- **Confidentiality**: This ensures that only authorized users and systems can access data. Hence, SREs should focus on encryption and access control.
- **Integrity**: Which ensures that data and systems are accurate and unaltered. Here, SREs need to focus on immutable infrastructure, secure supply chain, and checksum verifications.
- **Availability**: Which ensures that systems are accessible when needed. Here, SREs need to focus on redundancy, scaling, and incident response.

All of these must coexist. A breach in any one of the above will affect the others due to the interdependent nature of these principles. For example, for SRE, a DDoS attack is primarily an availability issue, whereas a data breach is a confidentiality failure. And a compromised software package undermining a deployment is an integrity problem. However, all of these are security incidents that impact reliability.

Shared responsibility model

In today's distributed, cloud-native world, security is a shared responsibility; hence, no single team owns it completely. The shared responsibility model is the fundamental security framework governing cloud computing. It clearly delineates the security obligations of the **cloud service provider** (**CSP**) from those of the cloud customer. The model can be summarized as follows:

- The cloud provider is responsible for the security of the cloud. This encompasses the protection of the global infrastructure that runs all of the services offered in the cloud.
- The customer is responsible for the security in the cloud. This covers the security of anything you put on or connect to the cloud infrastructure.

However, the division is not static and shifts dramatically depending on the cloud service type we are using, such as on-premises, **infrastructure as a service** (**IaaS**), **platform as a service** (**PaaS**), and **software as a service** (**SaaS**). The following table illustrates how the security responsibilities evolve across these service models:

Service model	Cloud provider responsibility	Customer (SRE) responsibility
On-premises	N/A	All layers, including facilities, physical servers, virtualization, operating system, IAM, data, and applications

IaaS	Physical security, network infrastructure, hypervisor	Operating system, network configuration, firewall, IAM, application, data, and client-side encryption
PaaS	Everything in IaaS, operating system, runtime, and platform management	Application, data, IAM for access, network traffic controls
SaaS	Everything in PaaS, application, identity, and directory infrastructure	Customer data, endpoint devices, user access management

***Table 9.1:** Security responsibilities across different service models*

In general, the cloud provider is responsible for the physical security of data centers, hypervisor isolation, host patching, and network perimeter protection. They are responsible for ensuring compliance of the infrastructure via certifications (like SOC 2) for the underlying infrastructure. The customer's responsibility includes securing configurations, monitoring and logging for suspicious activity, managing secrets and encryption keys safely, and ensuring incident response readiness. The developers are responsible for writing secure code, updating dependencies and libraries regularly, and integrating security scans in the CI/CD pipelines.

The shared responsibility model empowers SRE but also demands vigilance. We must understand the service model under which we operate and where our control begins and ends. The provider gives us a secure foundation, but it is our responsibility to build a secure house on it.

Secure system design

Secure system design is the practice of architecting and building systems where security is an intrinsic property, not an afterthought. For SREs, this means creating environments that are not only operationally robust but also inherently resistant to threats. Secure design ensures reduced attack surface area, predictable and auditable system behavior, resilience against both external and internal threats, and compliance with organizational and regulatory requirements. Let us explore the core principles, patterns, and practical implementations that define secure architecture.

Core architectural principles

Secure system design is founded on core principles that embed resilience from the ground up. It begins with Zero Trust networking, which is reinforced by defense in depth. This is followed by the **principle of least privilege** (**PoLP**) and minimal attack surface. Finally, auditability helps in tracing and maintaining compliance.

In this subsection, we will learn about these core principles for designing a secure application and infrastructure.

Zero Trust networking

The Zero Trust principle assumes that no one and nothing is trusted by default, and trust is earned per-request/session. It assumes that a threat exists both inside and outside the network and hence focuses on continuous verification. Here are the key tenets of Zero Trust networking:

- Identity is the new perimeter. Every access request, whether from a user, service, or device, must be authenticated and authorized based on identity and context.
- Micro segmentation. Enforce fine-grained security policies to control traffic flow between different parts of the network (even within the same subnet). This ensures that if an attacker compromises one component, they cannot easily move laterally to higher-value targets (e.g., database).
- Explicit verification. Grant access to individual resources on a per-request or per-session basis, depending on the architecture.

SREs can ensure Zero Trust by implementing the following:

- **Service mesh (like Istio)**: Service mesh automatically encrypts all service-to-service communication (using **mutual TLS** (**mTLS**)) and enforces access policies based on service identity.
- **Software-defined perimeters**: Tools like *BeyondCorp*-style or cloud-native solutions make applications inaccessible from the public internet until user and device identity are verified.

Defense in depth

Relying on a single security control is a single point of failure. Defense in depth employs multiple, redundant defensive layers. If one layer is breached, the next layer stops the attack. The layers can include network isolation (like **virtual private clouds** (**VPCs**), subnets, and firewalls), application firewalls (like **web application firewalls** (**WAFs**) that block malicious traffic), identity protection (like **multi-factor authentication** (**MFA**) or RBAC), data encryption (both at rest and in transit), and runtime protection (Falco/IDS).

Let us look at an example of how layered security protects a web application:

- **Layer 1**: DDoS protection (like Cloudflare or AWS Shield), which absorbs volumetric attacks.
- **Layer 2**: WAF, which filters malicious http requests (like SQLi, XSS).
- **Layer 3**: Authentication and authorization (using Oauth 2.0 or JWT), which ensures the user is who they say they are and has the right permissions.
- **Layer 4**: Input validation and output encoding, where the application itself sanitizes all inputs.

- **Layer 5**: Operating system and container hardening, where the underlying host is stripped of unnecessary components.
- **Layer 6**: Runtime security (like Falco), which detects malicious activity within the running host or container.

Each layer should have independent telemetry and alerting.

Principle of least privilege

The PoLP states that every process, service, and user should operate with the minimum permissions required to perform its task. This reduces the risk if any attacker is able to gain access to any process, service, or user.

SREs can ensure PoLP by implementing the following:

- For Kubernetes Pod security, pods should be configured to use Kubernetes security context, run as a non-root user, and security context settings should be used to drop Linux capabilities and make the root filesystem read-only.
- For IAM roles and services in the cloud, narrowly scoped IAM roles should be assigned to our EC2 instances, Lambda functions, or EKS pods instead of using a powerful, shared role.

For example:

- A logging service needs only read access to logs and not to the database.
- A CI/CD runner should deploy code but not modify IAM roles.

Minimal attack surface

The principle of minimal attack surface focuses on reducing the number of potential entry points that an attacker can exploit.

The following are some strategies that can be used to ensure minimal attack surface:

- **Network exposure**: Only services that are absolutely necessary to the public internet should be exposed. Private subnets and **network address translation** (NAT) gateways should be used for internal services.
- **API design**: A minimal and well-defined API should be exposed. Exposing unnecessary HTTP methods should be avoided (e.g., do not allow PUT or DELETE if only GET is needed).
- **Default-deny**: Firewalls and security groups should be configured with a default-deny policy. And later, only the required traffic should be explicitly allowed.
- **Avoid verbose errors**: Error messages returned to the users should not reveal system internals (like stack traces, database schema, or file paths).

Auditability

The auditability principle states that every security-relevant event (like login, config change, privilege escalation, etc.) should be logged and traceable.

The following are the best practices for auditability:

- Logs should be stored centrally (e.g., in CloudWatch, ELK).
- Immutability should be enabled for audit logs.
- Events should be correlated across services using unique IDs.
- Review audit trails during and after incidents.

Design patterns for secure systems

Let us look at the design patterns that help in building secure systems. These patterns serve reliability and security, where we focus on the security framing:

- **Immutable infrastructure**: Instead of patching and configuring long-lived servers, we replace them entirely with new, versioned images that are deployed from a known, secure state. This eliminates configuration drift and reduces the risk of attack persistence.
- **Sidecar pattern for security infrastructure**: Security features must be decoupled from the main application logic by deploying helper containers (or sidecars) alongside our application container in the same pod. Sidecars can be used for TLS termination, Authentication proxy, and log shipping and monitoring.
- **Bulkhead isolation pattern**: It ensures that a failure or attack in one component does not impact the entire system. This can be achieved by separating workloads by function or risk level, using dedicated queues, caches, or databases for high-risk services, and applying per-tenant or per-region resource quotas.
- **Circuit breaker pattern**: The circuit breaker pattern protects systems from cascading failures by stopping traffic to unhealthy services instead of letting them degrade upstream systems. It can be used in the security context to help isolate unhealthy or suspicious components by reducing the blast radius.

The following is a table that lists security threats and design patterns to mitigate them:

Threat	Mitigation pattern
Unauthorized access	PoLP, Zero Trust architecture, MFA
Lateral movement	Bulkhead isolation
Configuration drift	Immutable infrastructure
DDoS/cascading failure	WAF, **content delivery network** (**CDN**), circuit breaker, rate limiting
Insider threat	Auditability

Table 9.2: *Mitigation patterns for security threats*

Designing for DDoS resilience

A DDoS attack is fundamentally an attack on a system's availability. So, secure system design should focus on ensuring that the system is resilient to such attacks. The following are the strategies that can be used for designing and mitigating DDoS attacks:

- **Architecting edge/layer 3 and 4 mitigations**:
  - **Using a CDN with managed DDoS protection system**: Services like *Cloudflare, Akamai, AWS CloudFront*, and iare designed to absorb massive, volumetric attacks (SYN floods, UDP reflection attacks) at the network layer. They have the bandwidth and scrubbing capacity that individual companies cannot afford.
  - **DNS protection**: Using a DNS provider that has DDoS resilience. Route 53, Cloudflare DNS, and Google Cloud DNS are built to handle high-volume query attacks.
- **Architecting application/layer 7 mitigation:**
  - **WAF**: We can configure WAF rules to block sophisticated application-layer attacks that mimic legitimate traffic. This includes rate limiting by IP, geo-based controls where appropriate, and detecting bad bots.
  - **Autoscaling and load shedding**: Applications should be designed to be scalable and allow for horizontal scaling. We can configure aggressive autoscaling policies to add backend capacity. Eventually, we can implement load shedding to gracefully degrade functionality if the system is overwhelmed rather than failing completely.
  - **Capacity and redundancy planning**: We need to understand our normal traffic patterns and provision capacity with significant headroom to handle unexpected spikes, whether they are legitimate or malicious. For critical services, we can distribute load across multi-region, multi availability zones and global load balancing. If one region is under attack, global load balancers can direct traffic away from it, preserving availability.

By integrating these principles and patterns from the outset, SREs transition from being firefighters who respond to breaches to architects who build systems that are fundamentally harder to breach. This proactive approach is the cornerstone of modern, secure, and reliable operations.

Identity and access management

IAM is the foundational security discipline that ensures the right identities (users, services, or systems) have the right access to the right resources at the right time and for the right reasons. For SREs, a robust IAM strategy is the most critical control for preventing catastrophic security incidents.

IAM is a framework of policies, technologies, and processes that manages digital identities and controls access to resources. It answers four fundamental questions:

- **Authentication**: Who are you?
- **Authorization**: What are you allowed to do?
- **Authorization scope**: On which resources can you do it?
- **Credentials and verification**: How can you prove your identity (credentials/token, etc.)?

In cloud environments, IAM systems (like AWS IAM, Azure AD, or GCP IAM) are centralized services that govern access to every API, service, and piece of data.

Role of IAM in SRE

From the perspective of SRE, IAM helps in achieving the following:

- **Operational safety**: Prevents accidents or malicious system changes.
- **Auditability**: Every access can be traced.
- **Scalability**: Access control can be automated through policies.
- **Compliance**: Helps meet organizational and regulatory requirements.

SREs manage production credentials, CI/CD pipelines, and automation bots, all of which require secure access controls to prevent leaks or misuse. IAM not only restricts access but also records every access request and action.

Core IAM concepts

The following are the core concepts for IAM:

- **Identities**: These are used by:
    - o **Users**: It represents a person and should be used exclusively for human interaction with the cloud console or CLI.
    - o **Groups**: It represents a collection of users and can be used to assign permission to groups/teams.
    - o **Roles**: An identity that can be assumed by a user, service, or resource. Roles are the preferred mechanism for granting access as they are short-lived credentials or security tokens that are dynamically generated.
- **Resources**: These are cloud objects that we interact with, like EC2 instances, S3 buckets, and databases.
- **Policies**: These are JSON documents that formally define permissions for an identity or resource. Policies are attached to identities or resources.

- **Authentication**: This is the process of verifying an identity. This is typically done by the following:
  - o Passwords and MFA for human users and short-lived tokens/role credentials for services (avoid static access keys).
  - o MFA, which is a mandatory second factor for human users.
  - o Federated identity, like using a corporate identity (e.g., SAML 2.0) to log into the cloud.
- **Authorization**: This is the process of determining what an authenticated identity is allowed to do and is enforced by evaluating IAM policies.

Managing secrets and credentials

Secrets such as API keys, tokens, and passwords are often the weakest link in the automation systems. SREs must prevent static credentials and move towards dynamic secret management. The following are some of the best practices for secret management:

- Secrets should never be hardcoded in the source code.
- Centralized secret manager (like *AWS Secrets Manager* or *Hashicorp Vault*) must be used.
- Credentials must be rotated automatically.
- Access should be environment-based (e.g., separate credentials for prod/staging).
- Git repositories should be monitored for leaked credentials.
- Encrypt secrets at rest and in transit and restrict access via least privilege.

Role-based access control and policy as code

RBAC is the standard model for authorization in modern systems. Access is granted to roles (like *prod-deployer* or *log-viewer*), and then identities are assigned to these roles.

The following are some examples of RBAC for SREs:

- **SRE-readonly**: Permission to view logs, metrics, and resource states, but not modify anything.
- **SRE-developer**: Permissions to deploy to staging environments.
- **SRE-admin**: Powerful permissions for incident response in production.

Policy as code is the practice of defining, versioning, and managing security and compliance policies using code. This brings the benefits of DevOps, like version control, peer review, automated testing, and CI/CD, to security policy. Tools like **Open Policy Agent** (**OPA**) or AWS IAM Policy Generator are used.

Just-in-time access

Rather than giving engineers permanent admin access, SRE teams can use **just-in-time** (JIT) elevation, which is temporary access approved and logged automatically.

Example of JIT access: An SRE needing to debug a production database would request elevated access through a JIT/PAM system integrated with on-call/approval workflows. The system grants the required role for a short duration (e.g., 1-2 hours) and then automatically revokes it. This drastically reduces the attack surface and the risk of accidental misuse.

IAM is the first line of defense in modern distributed systems. It is essential to automate identity assignment and revocation while also applying least privilege, short-lived access, and centralized audit to IAM. Integration of IAM validation into the CI/CD pipeline can also be done. By mastering these IAM concepts and practices, SREs move from being mere consumers of access to being architects of a secure, auditable, and least-privileged access model that forms the bedrock of a reliable system.

Handling security incidents

A security incident is a type of production outage with potentially more severe and long-lasting consequences, as they have a higher blast radius and regulatory impact as compared to availability incidents. For SREs, handling security incidents is an extension of the traditional incident response. The same principles of detection, escalation, and postmortem analysis that guide availability and performance incidents also apply to security incidents, but with an added layer of sensitivity and urgency.

Security incident response lifecycle

A security incident is any event that threatens the CIA of our systems and users. Examples of security incidents include unauthorized access or privilege escalation, malware or ransomware infection, data breach, DDoS attacks, and configuration tampering. Security incidents often have added legal, compliance, and regulatory implications.

A security incident lifecycle can be broken down into the following:

- **Preparation**: This is the most critical phase. This includes having a defined incident response plan, a trained team (including SREs, security, and PR/legal), and the right tools (communication channels, forensics kits).
- **Detection and analysis**: SRE tools can be used to correlate alerts from monitoring systems, security tools, and user reports to identify a potential incident. It is essential to identify if it is an operational flaw or a malicious act. SREs need to classify the security incident by impact and scope to determine the right escalation path, as shown in the following table:

Severity	Description	Example
P0 – Critical	System-wide compromise or service outage	Ongoing DDoS or active data breach
P1 – High	Isolated but confirmed intrusion	Compromised service account
P2 – Medium	Potential vulnerability, but not yet exploited	Publicly exposed endpoint
P3 – Low	False positive or internal misconfiguration	Expired certificate or log alert

***Table 9.3**: Security incident severity decision table (Note: P0/P1 | Sev0/Sev1)*

Containment, eradication, and recovery

Let us look at the different strategies for containment, eradication, and recovery as follows:

- **Short-term containment**: Limit damage by acting immediately. Containment strategies can include revoking compromised API keys or credentials, disabling affected IAM roles or service accounts, quarantining affected servers, containers, or pods, blocking malicious IP addresses at the firewall or load balancer, and temporarily reducing the attack surface by restricting routes or disabling non-critical endpoints.
- **Eradication**: This focuses on finding and removing the root cause of the incident. This may involve patching a vulnerability, removing a backdoor, or rotating compromised credentials.
- **Recovery**: The next step is to restore systems to a known good, secure state and resume normal operations. This may require restoring from a clean backup or deploying new, patched infrastructure.

After the incident, the team needs to conduct a rigorous and blameless postmortem to identify and document the learnings and action items to prevent recurrence. Monitoring, automation, and design patterns should be updated accordingly.

DDoS attack mitigation

A DDoS attack aims to make a service unavailable by overwhelming it with requests. The different types of DDoS attacks are as follows:

- Volumetric, where UDP or amplification attacks are used to flood the bandwidth.
- Protocol where SYN floods and ping of death are used to exhaust network resources.
- Application layer (layer 7), where web servers are overloaded with complex HTTP requests.

Let us apply the incident response lifecycle to an example scenario of a large-scale DDoS attack.

Scenario: Our monitoring alerts show a massive, sustained spike in traffic to your public API. Latency is skyrocketing, and error rates are climbing. Legitimate users are starting to report timeouts. Let us look at the details:

- **Detection and analysis**: The following are the steps taken to detect and analyze the traffic spike to figure out if it is a DDoS attack:
  - **Correlate data**: Our monitoring dashboard (on Grafana) shows the traffic spike, and our WAF log shows that the traffic is coming from a distributed set of IPs worldwide, which is a hallmark of DDoS.
  - **Declare an incident**: Based on the impact on availability, the on-call SRE or the incident commander needs to declare a security incident and activate the response team.
- **Containment and mitigation**: The following are the steps that are taken to contain and mitigate the DDoS incident:
  - We need to immediately engage our upstream DDoS mitigation provider (e.g., AWS Shield Advanced), which can also be automated.
  - SRE works with the security team to filter traffic by identifying malicious traffic patterns in the WAF and creating rules to block them.
  - We need to scale horizontally to preserve availability while mitigation is going on. For this, we need to ensure that our autoscaling policies are functioning to add backend capacity to handle the load.
- **Eradication and recovery**: Once the incident has been mitigated, the eradication and recovery are done by following the steps:
  - In case of a DDoS attack, eradication often means waiting it out while our mitigation holds and we continue to monitor and adjust our filtering rules as the attacker's tactics change.
  - Communicate the status to internal stakeholders and update the public status page.

Post-incident

Analyze the traffic logs after the incident subsides to identify improvement areas like new traffic patterns, faster autoscaling, and adjusting the rate limiting. The data captured during the attack should be used to improve the architecture and runbooks and update capacity models and alert thresholds for future attacks.

SRE and compliance

Modern systems must be compliant with regulations that protect users, organizations, and data. Compliance for SRE represents a formalized set of requirements for security and operational integrity and provides an objective checklist for many security best practices.

SRE practices that support compliance

Let us look at SRE best practices that inherently support compliance, listed as follows:

- **Data protection**: Immutable infrastructure and automated deployments ensure systems are built from a known, secure base image, reducing configuration drift that can lead to data exposure.
- **Auditability**: The entire SRE workflow is naturally aligned with audit requirements. This can be understood from the points mentioned as follows:
    - **Infrastructure as code (IaC)**: Terraform or CloudFormation templates provide a definitive record of what was deployed and when.
    - **Version control**:
        - All changes to code and configuration are tracked in version control systems (like Git), providing a perfect audit trail.
    - **CI/CD pipelines**: They can be used to enable continuous compliance monitoring by enforcing security scans (like **static application security testing** (**SAST**) and **dynamic application security testing** (**DAST**)) and policy checks (like OPA) automatically, providing evidence of due diligence.
- **Access control**: As discussed in IAM, SREs enforcing least privilege and using secrets management directly satisfy access control requirements for standards like SOC 2, ISO 27001, and **General Data Protection Regulation** (**GDPR**).

Handling compliance incidents

Sometimes compliance can fail, and SRE should have a playbook to handle such incidents. The following is an example of an SRE response playbook for compliance incidents:

- Detect using automated scanners or monitoring tools and flag non-compliance.
- Triage by assessing the impact.
- Remediate by fixing the issue immediately and documenting corrective actions.
- Report if required by notifying the stakeholders (internal or external).
- Review by updating automation and policy rules to prevent recurrence.

Security culture in SRE teams

Security culture refers to the collective mindset, behaviors, and practices within an organization that prioritize the protection of systems, data, and users. A robust security culture ensures that every team member is an active participant in defending the systems they build. For SREs, it means embedding security into reliability and performance workflows, treating security issues with the same urgency as reliability issues, automating preventive and detective security measures, and continuously learning from failures, vulnerabilities, and incidents.

Fostering proactive security measures

In modern SRE practices, security is proactive and preventive and a part of the engineering lifecycle. The following are the steps that can be taken to ensure proactive security measures:

- **Regular security audits**: Recurring internal reviews of the infrastructure should be scheduled. Automated tools should be used to scan for misconfigurations, and manual deep-dive reviews of critical services should be done.
- **Third-party penetration testing**: External experts should be engaged who can try to break the system, as they would bring a fresh perspective and find flaws that are blind to the existing teams. The SRE's role is to facilitate the tests and then prioritize the findings.
- **Patch management**: SRE should establish a clear and risk-based policy for applying patches. Critical vulnerabilities should be patched immediately using automated deployment pipelines. Lower risk patches should be batched into regular release cycles.
- **Threat modeling**: This should be incorporated into the design phase of new projects or major features. The purpose is to shift security left in the development process and address things that can go wrong early in the development lifecycle.
- **Integrate security into daily operations**: Security can be integrated into day-to-day engineering operations like code reviews, CI/CD pipelines, monitoring dashboards, runbooks, and postmortems.

Blameless postmortem for security incidents

The rigorous, blameless analysis applied to operational outages must be extended with equal discipline to security incidents. The primary goal of a post-incident investigation is to uncover the underlying systemic factors, like a flawed process, a missing safeguard, or a tooling failure, which created the conditions for the incident to occur. Punishing an individual for an incident does nothing to prevent recurrence; it only ensures that future errors will be hidden. Fostering a culture of psychological safety, where team members can speak openly about mistakes without fear of reprisal, is therefore a strategic imperative. It is the bedrock upon which true learning is built, enabling teams to implement robust countermeasures, harden systems, and ultimately break the cycle of recurring security failures, transforming each incident into a catalyst for a more resilient defense.

Security awareness and training

To ensure that security awareness is a part of the team's DNA, awareness programs must be regularly scheduled. The following are examples of such awareness programs:

- Monthly security meetings, which can act as 10-minute refreshers.
- Phishing simulations to help the team identify social engineering risks.
- Onboarding checklist to introduce security best practices to new engineers.
- Internal newsletters sharing real-world vulnerabilities and how they were mitigated.

A culture thrives when good behavior is acknowledged. Hence, senior leaders must recognize SREs who champion secure practices. In addition to this, SREs can track the maturity of secure practices in the team by measuring awareness (as % of team completing security trainings), proactivity (as % of security issues found pre-release), automation (% of manual vs. automated remediations), and collaboration. These metrics should be trend-based and not absolute targets.

When security awareness and automation meet reliability discipline, organizations achieve the true goal of SRE, that is, systems that are not only available and scalable but trustworthy by design.

Falco

While many tools are in the SRE arsenal, Falco deserves special attention as the widely adopted standard for runtime security in cloud-native environments. Falco is an open-source cloud-native runtime security project. It was originally created by *Sysdig* and is now a **Cloud-native Computing Foundation** (**CNCF**) incubating project. It monitors **system calls** (**syscalls**) at runtime and detects abnormal or unauthorized behavior in containers, Kubernetes, and Linux hosts.

Falco internals

Falco taps into the Linux kernel using *eBPF* (or a kernel module) to get a deep, real-time stream of syscalls like every file opened, every network connection made, every process spawned. It then compares this stream against a powerful set of customizable rules. If an activity violates a rule, Falco triggers an alert. Falco provides the following features, which are essential for SREs:

- **Deep visibility**: It sees everything happening inside our containers and hosts, far beyond what standard metrics can provide.

- **Kubernetes-aware**: It understands Kubernetes concepts like namespaces, pods, and services, allowing for very specific rules.
- **Proactive detection**: It can detect malicious behavior as it happens, not just in retrospect.

Falco in action

Let us look at some out-of-the-box Falco rules that are directly relevant to SRE workflows, as follows:

- **Detecting unauthorized process execution**:
  - **Rule**: Run shell inside container.
  - **Scenario**: An attacker exploits a vulnerability in our web application and gains a shell inside a running container. This is almost always malicious.
  - **SRE detection**: Falco immediately alerts the team, allowing SRE to isolate the container, terminate the pod, and investigate the root cause.
- **Detecting sensitive file access**:
  - **Rule**: Read / Write to `/etc/shadow` file or read file from `/etc/` secrets directory.
  - **Scenario**: A compromised application attempts to read the host's password file or a mounted Kubernetes Secret to escalate privileges.
  - **SRE detection**: Falco detects the attempt to steal credentials, triggering an incident before the attacker can move laterally.
- **Detecting network anomalies**:
  - **Rule**: Unexpected outbound network connection.
  - **Scenario**: Malware inside a container establishes a connection to a known malicious command-and-control server.
  - **SRE detection**: Falco alerts on the suspicious outbound traffic, allowing SRE to block the IP and contain the compromised container.

Integrating Falco

Falco can be run as a DaemonSet on our Kubernetes clusters, ensuring every node is monitored. Deploy Falco as a Kubernetes DaemonSet using the official Helm chart, ensuring a pod runs on every node, including the new ones provisioned by autoscaling. For practical implementation, we can configure its output to connect to our existing monitoring stack. This typically involves setting the Falco sidecar or direct output to forward alerts in a format that Prometheus can scrape. These alerts are then defined in Prometheus Alertmanager rules, routing critical security events like a shell in a container or unauthorized file access directly to PagerDuty. This ensures they trigger an immediate on-call response, enforcing the principle that a security threat is a direct threat to service reliability and must be acted upon with equal urgency.

Conclusion

The journey of integrating security into SRE is continuous and begins with a mindset shift. Every decision about reliability, from a load balancer configuration to an autoscaling policy, has security implications. By embracing secure design principles, enforcing strict access controls, and treating security incidents with the same disciplined rigor as operational failures, we elevate the resilience of our systems to a new level.

The tools and practices outlined in this chapter, from Falco for runtime visibility to IaC for auditable compliance, are the building blocks of a modern, robust engineering culture. As threats evolve, so must our defenses. The most reliable systems of the future will be those built and maintained by SREs who have fully internalized their role as guardians of both uptime and integrity.

While robust systems and secure code form the technical backbone of reliability, it is the human element that brings it all to life. This next chapter shifts our focus from the machines we operate to the teams we build, exploring the critical dynamics that empower SREs to excel. We will cover the SRE roles and cultural pillars of blamelessness, effective collaboration with development, and sustainable on-call practices. Ultimately, a high-performing SRE team is not just built on tooling, but on trust, clear communication, and a shared commitment to resilience.

CHAPTER 10
Team Dynamics

Introduction

Site reliability engineering (**SRE**) is often discussed in the language of systems, algorithms, and metrics. Yet, beneath the sophisticated tooling and complex architectures lies the human foundation that fundamentally shapes operational resilience. Behind every system, every alert, and every postmortem document, there is a human being. While systems scale via infrastructure, organizational resilience scales through empowered teams.

This chapter moves beyond the technical playbook to explore the human core of SRE. We will discuss the structures that make teams effective, the intense pressures they face, particularly during on-call rotations, and the very real risk of burnout. We will confront the emotional toil that comes with maintaining complex, business-critical systems and demonstrate that the ultimate measure of a team's success is not just uptime, but the sustainability and health of its people.

SRE teams operate in high-pressure environments where minutes of downtime can translate into significant business impact. The demands of constant vigilance, late-night incidents, and escalating expectations can take a psychological toll if left unaddressed. Behind every alert and postmortem is a team of engineers managing fatigue, balancing workloads, and striving to maintain their sense of purpose.

Through practical guidance and real-world examples, we will examine how to build and lead SRE teams that are not only highly effective but also resilient, collaborative, and psychologically safe. We will learn how to balance hard metrics like **service level indicators** (**SLIs**) and **service level objectives** (**SLOs**) with qualitative aspects like team morale and continuous learning. The goal is to align our technical ambitions with human needs, creating an environment where both systems and engineers can thrive.

Structure

The chapter covers the following topics:

- Roles within SRE teams
- Collaboration across teams
- On-call process and fatigue management
- Handling burnout
- Knowledge sharing for SRE teams
- Conflict resolution and feedback loops
- Defining and measuring KPIs for SREs
- Career path for SREs

Objectives

This chapter explores the human side of SRE, focusing on the team dynamics, collaboration, and challenges in maintaining a healthy work-life balance in high-pressure environments. We discuss the on-call process, the challenges and realities that engineers face while highlighting the emotional toil, stress, and the chance of engineer burnout. We will look at some strategies to mitigate burnout through sustainable practices such as balanced rotation and proactive incident management, including how auto-healing can help in certain situations, like reducing on-call load. Additionally, we will examine how to define and measure the **key performance indicators (KPIs)** for SRE teams for balancing reliability goals with human sustainability. We will look at how to balance SRE metrics like error budgets, incident response times, and toil reduction with human qualitative aspects like team morale, psychological safety, and continuous learning. Through practical guidance and real-world examples, this chapter will help leaders and practitioners in creating healthier, more effective SRE teams by aligning technical goals with human needs.

Roles within SRE teams

A well-structured SRE team is a balanced blend of individuals who bring a diverse set of skills and specializations to the task. A successful SRE team is a strategic assembly of complementary roles, each with a clear scope and career trajectory. The specific titles may vary across organizations, but the essential functions and the progression of responsibility remain consistent. This structure ensures that operational duties, long-term engineering projects, people leadership, and strategic direction all receive the focused attention they require. The following are the broad roles and responsibilities within SRE teams.

SRE practitioner or engineer

They are the backbone of the team as they are software engineers who focus on operations or systems administrators who have embraced software engineering. They take up roles like on-call, incident commander, automation implementor and toil reducer. Their day-to-day work involves the following:

- Designing, deploying and maintaining scalable and reliable systems.
- Creating and refining automation tools to eliminate toil.
- Participating in on-call rotation.
- Conducting blameless postmortems for incidents.
- Contribute to capacity planning and load testing strategies.
- Working with product development teams to define SLOs and error budgets.
- They may also act as the incident commander if they encounter an incident during on-call.

Senior or staff SRE

These are technical leaders and domain experts. They possess deep, systemic knowledge and guide the technical direction of the team. They take up the roles like reliability analyst and lead tooling and automation initiatives. Their responsibilities include the following:

- Architecting complex and distributed systems for maximum availability.
- Mentoring junior SREs and upleveling the entire team's skills.
- Leading the response to high-severity incidents.
- Driving long-term strategic projects to improve platform resilience.

SRE team lead or manager

This role bridges the technical and people-management worlds. It ensures balance between engineering velocity and reliability targets and owns team health, performance, and coordination. While this role may involve hands-on work, they are also responsible for the following:

- People management, including career growth, performance reviews, and the wellness of the team members.
- Process and project management like prioritizing work, managing the on-call roster, and ensuring that the team has the resources it needs.
- Stakeholder management by acting as the point of contact for other engineering teams and leadership, translating business needs into technical priorities.

SRE technical program manager

In larger organizations, the SRE **technical program manager** (**TPM**) helps coordinate complex, cross-functional initiatives that span multiple SRE and development teams. While engineers focus on technical execution, the TPM owns the programmatic framework, including defining project scope, managing intricate timelines, identifying critical path dependencies, and ensuring transparent communication across all stakeholders. By absorbing the administrative and logistical overhead of large projects, they shield engineers from distraction, enabling a deeper focus on technical design, coding, and operational excellence. This role is essential for executing strategic platform migrations, multi-quarter reliability roadmaps, and other initiatives where coordination is as vital as engineering talent itself.

Real-world example

Let us look at an example of a startup. The startup would hire its first SRE engineer as a full-stack practitioner. However, as the company grows, it would need to hire a senior SRE to design a new service mesh or improve its existing architecture. As the company grows further and the SRE team expands, they will need to hire an SRE team lead to manage the growing team's workload. Eventually, they would need to hire an SRE TPM to coordinate the migration of all services to a better architecture or to the cloud.

Collaboration across teams

In modern engineering teams, collaboration lies at the very heart of reliability. SRE teams exist as a connective tissue between development, operations, security, and product features. The ability of these teams to communicate effectively, share ownership, and align on reliability goals often determines whether a system thrives or struggles under real-world pressures.

Shared ownership model

The most effective collaboration model is one of shared ownership. The development team owns the feature's functionality and performance, while the SRE team owns the platform's reliability and scalability. They collaborate to define mutually agreed SLOs. They jointly define SLO and error budgets by negotiating acceptable downtimes and operational risks. Shared ownership transforms reliability from an afterthought into a core design principle. It ensures that every feature shipped is both functional and sustainable in production.

Embedded SRE model

Many mature organizations have the practice of embedding SREs directly within the product or service teams rather than working as a separate centralized function. This allows the SREs to gain intimate knowledge of the service's architecture and failure modes. Developers and SREs can work side by side during feature design, leading to earlier detection of reliability issues. It also allows developers to learn SRE best practices, thus fostering a culture of operational awareness across teams. This model allows SREs to understand product-level nuances and tailor reliability practices accordingly.

However, embedded SREs must balance being part of the team with maintaining their reliability-first perspective. Over-embedding can dilute their ability to act as neutral reliability advisors.

Production readiness review

A crucial collaboration touchpoint is the **production readiness review** (**PRR**), which is a formal checkpoint before any new service or a major change goes live. During the PRR, the development team presents the changes to the SRE team, and the SRE team reviews its monitoring, runbooks, fault tolerance, and scalability parts. The PRR ensures the following:

- Services meet reliability baselines (including monitoring, alerting, and rollback mechanisms).
- Documentation, dashboards, and runbooks are complete.
- Ownership, escalation paths, and SLOs are clearly defined.
- Security and compliance checks are in place.

Since SRE and development teams jointly evaluate the readiness criteria during PRR, it minimizes incidents post-deployment and also builds a shared sense of responsibility for production health, thus ensuring a smoother launch.

Regular syncs and communication cadence

SREs need to establish weekly or bi-weekly syncs with the dev teams. They should create forums for discussing incident trends, SLO performance, and capacity planning. The structured recurring interaction with the development team creates a healthy collaboration between both teams, preventing silos, aligning priorities, and ensuring that reliability discussions are ongoing and not just reactive.

The following are some touchpoints that can be setup between the SRE and developer teams:

- Weekly sync meetings to review reliability metrics, open incidents, and operational risks.
- Monthly reliability councils to review SLO adherence and incident learnings.
- Joint retrospectives after every major incident or deployment cycle to identify systemic improvements.
- Regular office hours and consultation slots for discussing architecture, scaling, and monitoring.

Collaboration challenges and their solutions.

Even with the best intentions, collaboration between SRE and other teams often faces friction. This can be mitigated by framing the SRE relationship as a *force multiplier* for development, helping the teams ship faster and more reliably by building resilience from the start.

The following table lists some common challenges and possible resolution ideas:

Challenge	Impact	Possible resolution
Conflicting priorities like speed vs. stability	Tension between release velocity and reliability goals	Define shared objectives, key responsibilities, and error budgets that balance both
Unclear ownership boundaries	Incidents fall through gaps	Maintain clear escalation paths and ownership maps
Resistance to postmortems or a blameless culture	Defensive response to incidents	Train leads to model openness and empathy
Tooling fragmentation	Misaligned visibility into metrics	Adopt unified observability platforms
Alert noise and fatigue	Reduced responsiveness	Jointly tune alert threshold (SLO based) and use automation for triage.

***Table 10.1**: Collaboration challenges and possible resolutions*

On-call process and fatigue management

The on-call function is one of the most defining and emotionally demanding aspects of SRE. While tools and automations can drastically improve the alerting and operational response, human beings still remain a significant first line of defense. An effective on-call strategy must balance swift incident response with long-term engineer well-being, ensuring that reliability does not come at the cost of engineer burnout.

Designing healthy on-call rotation

On-call ensures rapid detection and mitigation of issues, continuous service reliability, and reduced **mean time to recover** (MTTR), and hence needs structured responsibility instead of constant availability. A thoughtfully designed on-call process should include the practices discussed in the following subsections.

Balanced rotations

A one-week rotation is standard. Shorter rotations cause context-switching overhead, whereas longer rotations increase fatigue. In addition, each rotation should have 4-6 engineers, along with seasonal load balancing (during major releases or sales). Engineers should not spend more than 25% of their time on on-call. Also, leads should ensure that the on-call load is evenly distributed across the team, considering skill level and domains. They can use data from the incident manager to track pages per engineer.

Clear escalation paths

There should be a clear primary on-call (first responder) and a secondary (backup for escalation or to handle a second simultaneous incident). In addition, engineers must know when to escalate and whom to escalate to. They should have clarity on what constitutes a P0 or a P1 incident and what actions are mandatory and what are optional. This reduces cognitive load and panic during high-stress situations.

Follow-the-sun model

For global teams, structure rotations across time zones to ensure no one is regularly woken up in the middle of the night. Specific regions can take on-call responsibilities during their daytime hours to avoid waking engineers during the night. This not only reduces fatigue but also increases alert responsiveness and improves the quality of an incident triage due to daytime availability. The goal is to have on-call be a regular part of the job, not a life-disrupting event.

Robust runbook and auto-remediation

Runbooks should include common failure patterns, step-by-step mitigation procedures, escalation contacts, automated scripts, and rollback instructions. Auto-remediation tools can help reduce human intervention, especially during off-hours. In addition to this, high-quality monitoring and alerting can help reduce noise and page engineers only when auto-remediation does not mitigate the incident.

Combating on-call fatigue

The following are some strategies that can be used to combat on-call fatigue:

- **Post-on-call recovery day**: After a week on-call, especially if they handled significant incidents, engineers should be given a mandatory day off from their regular duties. They can use this time to learn, work on projects, or simply recover. This acts as a critical investment in preventing burnout.
- **Compensation**: On-call duty is a disruption to personal life, and hence it should be compensated either through extra time off (like a recovery day) or financially.
- **Proper on-call handoffs**: A structured handoff prevents miscommunication and reduces burden. During the handoff, the on-call engineer must share the current incident state, document known issues, highlight risky deployments or upcoming

load events, provide a short summary of recent alerts, and clarify ongoing escalations, if any. Good handoff prevents duplicate work and reduces anxiety.

- Leads can play a crucial role in maintaining team well-being by protecting the team from process flaws that create unnecessary toil by doing the following:
  - Enforcing the maximum number of on-call shifts per month.
  - Providing tools and training to reduce manual work.
  - Encouraging honest feedback from engineers.
  - Adjusting schedules based on the engineer's capacity.
  - Investing in automation and better monitoring.
  - Track on-call health metrics and take actions accordingly.

Metrics for on-call health

Leads need to proactively monitor fatigue within the team so they can take corrective actions before it impacts the team and the application's reliability. In order to monitor the team fatigue, leads need to monitor the following health metrics so they can ensure the sustainability of the team, as follows:

- Number of alerts per shift
- Percentage of false positives
- Frequency of escalation
- After-hours incidents per engineer
- Time spent on repetitive tasks
- Engineer satisfaction surveys

For the team to be healthy, they should have low alert volume, a high signal-to-noise ratio, predictable incident patterns, and increasing automation over time. The health of our on-call process is a direct reflection of the health of our systems and our team culture. By tuning alerting systems, investing in automation, enforcing healthy rotations, and prioritizing the emotional health of the team, organizations can create an SRE culture where both people and systems thrive.

Handling burnout

Burnout is one of the most significant risks in the SRE profession due to the always-on mindset, unpredictable workloads, and emotional weight of incident management. It is a state of emotional, physical, and mental exhaustion caused by excessive and prolonged stress. Burnout is a systemic failure. While infrastructure failures can be restored with code, human burnout requires deliberate cultural, organizational, and psychological support.

Early warning signs of burnout

Identifying burnout early allows the team to intervene before it becomes severe. Let us look at the common symptoms of burnout:

- **In self**:
  - Chronic fatigue and insomnia.
  - Increased cynicism and negativity towards work.
  - Feelings of detachment and ineffectiveness.
  - Difficulty concentrating and increased mental errors.
  - Using unhealthy coping mechanisms.
- **In our teammates**:
  - Withdrawal from team discussions and social interactions.
  - Noticeable drop in productivity and code quality.
  - Difficulty concentrating during outages.
  - Delayed response to alerts due to mental fatigue.
  - Increased errors during troubleshooting.
  - Increased irritability and emotional volatility.
  - Expressing a feeling of being stuck or that their work does not matter.

Practices for burnout mitigation

Preventing burnout is more effective than treating it. Teams should adopt proactive and systemic measures to avoid burnout. The following are some sustainable practices that can help:

- **Leadership role**: Managers must be the first line of defense. They need to actively monitor team workload, encourage time off, and model healthy work-life boundaries themselves. They must create an environment where taking a mental health day is as acceptable as taking a sick day. They need to normalize discussions about stress and provide psychological safety to the team. Mini retros after each on-call week can build micro-feedback loops and prevent long-term burnout.
- **Balanced ticket and rotation**: Explicitly split the team's focus between operational work and engineering work so that no more than 50% of the time is spent on operational work. The other 50% must be protected for engineering project work, like automation, improvements, and new features. This gives engineers a sense of agency and forward momentum, counteracting the reactive nature of ops work.
- **Proactive incident management**: The following steps can help in proactively reducing load at the source:
  - **Auto-healing**: Where possible, build systems that can recover from failure without human intervention. For example, if a node fails, the orchestrator (like Kubernetes) can automatically terminate it and spin up a new one. Another example is if a service is returning errors, a circuit breaker can stop traffic and

allow it to recover. Auto-healing reduces the number of pages and turns *incidents* into self-resolving events.

- **Toil elimination**: Aggressively identify and eliminate toil, such as manual, repetitive, automatable tasks. Every minute spent on toil is a minute not spent on making the system more reliable and less stressful to manage.

Support system for burned-out engineer

Even with all the burnout prevention steps in place, burnout may still occur. The response in such situations should be compassionate and structured to help the engineer recover. The following steps can help support recovery:

1. Provide immediate relief by temporarily removing or reducing the engineer's on-call duties.
2. Rebalance workload by shifting project responsibilities or reducing operational tasks.
3. Have a managerial one-on-one discussion to provide personalized support.
4. Encourage use of mental health resources and provide access to counseling or employee assistance programs.
5. Reintegrate at a healthy pace once the engineer has recovered by a gradual return to on-call with more automation-focused tasks and avoiding critical shifts initially.

Handling burnout is about building a culture where engineers can operate at peak performance without sacrificing their mental or physical well-being. By combining systemic fixes, thoughtful leadership, and emotional intelligence, SRE teams can remain not only resilient under pressure but also humanely sustainable in the long run.

Knowledge sharing for SRE teams

Knowledge sharing is one of the most critical pillars of a successful SRE organization. A team's resilience is directly proportional to its ability to distribute critical knowledge across all its members. Effective knowledge sharing ensures that reliability is never the responsibility of a single expert but an organizational capability.

Criticality of knowledge sharing

The following are the reasons why knowledge sharing becomes critical for SRE teams:

- **Reduces single point of human failure**: When only a single engineer knows how to resolve a recurring issue or debug a particular service, the system becomes dependent on him, and hence it becomes fragile. Knowledge sharing distributes expertise across the team, thus reducing risk.

- **Faster incident resolution**: During an outage, the on-call person may not be the domain expert; however, access to well-structured knowledge allows them to act effectively. This reduces the downtime and directly impacts the MTTR and overall availability.
- **Supports onboarding and upskilling**: SRE roles involve a steep learning curve. Structured knowledge sharing helps junior members to learn faster and allows senior members to delegate effectively. Teams with strong learning cultures also retain talent better.
- **Builds a culture of psychological safety**: When information is openly shared, engineers feel valued and supported. Knowledge sharing encourages transparency, collaboration, and open communication. Thus, strengthening the team morale.
- **Enables consistent operational standard**: Good and structured documentation is a security blanket for the on-call engineers. In large multi-region SRE groups, standardized knowledge ensures consistent incident handling, uniform debugging approaches, and predictable operational quality.

Effective knowledge sharing mechanisms

Now that we know that structured knowledge sharing is important for SRE teams, let us look at effective mechanisms for knowledge sharing. Mechanisms range from having good documentation systems to day-to-day real-time knowledge sharing and having rituals and events that promote knowledge sharing. Some of these mechanisms are listed here:

- **Runbooks and playbooks**: These are living documents. They should contain step-by-step instructions for common incidents, troubleshooting flows, migration procedures, and escalation paths. They must be regularly tested and updated. They reduce cognitive load during stressful incidents.
- **Blameless postmortems**: Postmortems are powerful knowledge artifacts. The primary goal of a postmortem is to share the lessons learned from a failure. The document should be widely accessible, and the key takeaways should be socialized across all relevant teams.
- **Game day exercises**: These can be conducted periodically, deliberately breaking things in the staging environment by simulating a database failure or network partition, etc. This forces the team to use their runbooks and practice their incident response in a safe environment, turning theoretical knowledge into muscle memory.
- **Lunch and learn rituals**: These can be short, informal presentations on topics like new tools, debugging techniques, recent incidents, and architecture evolutions. They help the team create an internal learning culture.
- **Pairing and shadowing**: Leads should encourage pair programming on automation scripts where multiple engineers work together to resolve an issue, facilitating real-time knowledge transfer. Additionally, during incidents and critical operational

tasks, junior engineers can shadow seniors. Later, the pairs can swap responsibilities, enabling knowledge transfer organically. This strengthens team readiness.

- **Weekly open sessions and monthly summaries**: SREs can hold weekly open sessions where developers can ask reliability and architectural questions, share best practices, and clarify ambiguous ownership questions. Monthly summaries can include a curated digest containing new lessons learned, system changes, performance trends, and automation updates. This keeps everyone informed asynchronously.

Most knowledge sharing happens via tools like an internal wiki (such as Confluence, a Git-based wiki, or version controlled documentation). Observability dashboards are widely used to discuss patterns, historical incidents, and operational metrics during knowledge sharing sessions. ChatOps tools like *Slack*, *Microsoft Teams*, or *Discord* are also used during incidents to preserve troubleshooting history, which can act as real-time documentation. ChatOps encourages transparency.

Conflict resolution and feedback loops

With high pressure and the cross-functional nature of SRE work, business demands frequently collide, leading to conflicts. This leads to disagreements, misalignments, or tension between individuals and teams. Healthy conflict resolution and strong feedback loops are essential not only for team harmony but also for operational excellence, as unresolved conflicts directly impact reliability, decision-making quality, and team morale.

The difference between a good team and a great team is not the absence of conflict, but how it is handled. A well-functioning SRE organization cultivates structured communication, psychological safety, and mechanisms to surface issues early, ensuring that conflicts become opportunities for improvement rather than sources of disruption.

Common sources of conflicts

The sources are as follows:

- **Priority conflicts**: Development teams push for rapid release and feature velocity, whereas SREs emphasize controlled rollouts, SLO adherence, and operational safety. This leads to tension if not openly addressed.
- **Error budget disputes**: Development wants to launch a new feature, but SRE is advocating for stability, citing a nearly exhausted error budget.
- **High-pressure incidents and blame culture**: Incidents resulting in outages generate stress, urgency, and strong opinions. If a team lacks a blameless culture, this can result in disagreements and conflicts.
- **Communication gaps and silos**: Remote teams, distributed ownership, and asynchronous communication often lead to misunderstandings. Additionally, missing documentation or a lack of visibility into decisions further strains relationships.

- **Emotional fatigue and burnout**: Overloaded engineers or those recovering from tough incidents may react emotionally or become defensive in discussions. Further fatigue amplifies small disagreements into major conflicts.

Strategies for conflict resolution

The strategies are as follows:

- **Focus on shared goals**: The idea here is to reframe the conflict. Instead of development vs. SRE teams, the conflict needs to be reframed as the team vs the problem of achieving both feature and velocity. Shared SLO can act as the objective arbiter. SRE leaders or TPMs can act as neutral facilitators who can help clarify each party's needs, identify root causes, and mediate towards shared goals.
- **Practice blameless problem solving**: The blameless principles used in postmortems can also be applied to interpersonal conflicts by focusing on the process and the situation and not on the personal character. Learning from the problem must be the guiding principle. This prevents defensive communication and keeps the discussions fact-based.
- **Establish clear feedback loops**: It is essential to establish clear and continuous feedback loops, which can help in continuous improvement, reduce misunderstandings, and strengthen trust. Feedback loops can include SLO reviews, Error budget meetings, post-incident reviews, and reliability councils, which ensure that the goal of reliability stays aligned across teams. The following are some sample feedback loops that can be setup:
    - **Retrospectives**: Retrospectives are one of the most powerful conflict-resolution mechanisms in SRE. Leads should hold regular team retrospectives (in addition to incident retrospectives) to discuss what is working and what needs improvement in the team's processes and interactions.
    - **360-degree feedback**: This is to ensure that feedback flows in all directions. This can be done by setting up weekly or bi-weekly syncs with the developer, program manager, and architecture teams. In addition, managers should setup 1:1 private feedback session with the team members to resolve interpersonal conflicts that require private intervention.
    - **Stakeholder feedback**: This is a proactive approach where SREs can reach out to their stakeholders, like the development or product teams, and ask for improvement areas.

The SRE manager or team lead must act as a facilitator by creating a safe container for difficult conversations, ensuring that all voices are heard, and guiding the team towards a resolution that strengthens trust.

Handled correctly, conflicts become collaboration opportunities that strengthen the team bonds, improve processes, reveal blind spots, increase operational maturity, and clarify shared goals.

In the long run, conflict resolution and continuous feedback loops form the backbone of high-performing SRE teams. When psychological safety is upheld, communication is structured, and learning is prioritized over blame, teams can navigate high-pressure environments with resilience, trust, and operational harmony.

Defining and measuring KPIs for SREs

While measuring the performance of an SRE engineer, the goal is to measure the impact, ownership, and growth in a way that aligns with sustainable SRE practices. A performance framework for SRE should balance quantitative outputs and qualitative behaviors, assessing how the engineer contributes to both system reliability and team health.

SRE performance scorecard

The performance scorecard focuses on the quantitative outputs of an SRE engineer. There are two primary dimensions of performance as listed as follows:

- **Operational excellence and impact**: This dimension assesses an engineer's effectiveness in handling the core, reactive responsibilities of the role. The following table lists the KPI area and how to measure it:

KPI area	Measurement and significance
On-call performance	• **MTTR during their shifts**: An indicator of the engineer's troubleshooting efficiency and use of runbooks. • **Escalation rate**: Indicates the need for additional help. A low rate can indicate brilliance or dangerous heroics, whereas a high rate can indicate a need for training. • **Post-incident documentation**: The quality and timeliness of their contributions to postmortems and runbook updates.
Quality of incident management	• **Leadership**: Gather peer feedback to identify if the engineer effectively leads or coordinates response during incidents. • **Communication**: Clarity of communicating updates and root cause analysis during and after the incident. • **Actionable alerts created and resolved**: Identify how many noisy or useless alerts were proactively identified by the engineer and fixed to reduce toil on the whole team.
System ownership and hygiene	• **SLI/SLO contributions**: Identify if the engineer actively participates in defining and refining SLOs of the services that they own. • **Runbook accuracy**: Identify if the runbooks that the engineer is responsible for are clear, accurate, and properly tested.

Table 10.2: Measuring operational excellence and impact

- **Engineering and initiative**: This dimension assesses an engineer's proactive work to improve the platform, reduce toil, and advance their skills. This is the other 50% of the project work for SRE engineers that helps prevent burnout and drives innovation. The following table lists the KPI areas and how to measure them:

KPI area	Measurement and significance
Toil elimination	• **Toil reduction metrics**: Helps quantify the impact of their automations. • **Automation projects completed**: The number and complexity of scripts / tools built to automate manual operational tasks.
Platform improvement	• **Reliability projects**: Successful delivery of projects that directly improve system resilience. • **Impact on key metrics**: Measuring improvement in key system metrics from their project work.
Knowledge sharing and mentorship	• **Documentation created and reviewed**: Volume and quality of technical documentation, architecture diagrams, and runbooks. • **Mentoring and pairing**: Gather feedback on help given to junior team members or cross-training of peers.

***Table 10.3**: Measuring engineering and other initiatives and their impact*

Human-centric KPIs

Measuring the human-centric KPIs ensures that high-performance is not achieved at the cost of team health and sustainable practices. The following are some human-centric KPIs and ideas on how to measure the same:

- **Collaboration and communication**: This can be measured by gathering 360-degree feedback from development partners, other SREs, and managers.
- **Proactive problem solving**: This can be measured by tracking the engineer contributions that helped identify potential issues before they caused incidents.
- **Continuous learning and growth**: Does the engineer have a personal development plan with tangible goals?

Performance narrative

The idea is to avoid the trap of reducing the engineer's performance to a dashboard of numbers. The most accurate picture comes from a narrative that synthesizes this data. The following are the focus areas for such narratives for engineers across different roles:

- **Junior SRE**: The narrative might focus on their growing independence during on-call, their eagerness to learn, and their successful contributions to smaller automation tasks.

- **Senior SRE**: The narrative should highlight their technical leadership during major incidents, their mentorship of others, and the strategic impact of the platform improvements they drove.
- **Staff/Principal SRE**: The narrative must demonstrate organization-wide impact, such as defining new reliability standards, solving complex architectural problems, and elevating the entire SRE practice.

By focusing on this balanced scorecard and weaving together operational impact, engineering initiative, and collaborative behaviors, we can create a fair and comprehensive framework for evaluating SRE performance that rewards the very actions that make a team sustainable and successful.

Career path for SRE

A common fear for SREs is being labeled as just the on-call person. So, a clear, dual-track career ladder is essential for retaining top talent and providing a sense of purpose and progression. There are two different tracks for SRE engineers mentioned in the following subsections.

Individual contributor track

This track focuses on engineers who want to contribute more on the technical side of SRE and create an organization-wide impact. The following are the roles available in this track:

- **Junior SRE**: Focuses on learning the systems, handling straightforward on-call alerts, and contributing to runbooks and small automation scripts.
- **SRE**: A fully contributing member of the team. Capable of handling most on-call incidents independently and driving small-to-medium projects.
- **Senior SRE**: A technical leader. They design resilient systems, lead incident response, mentor junior engineers, and drive large, strategic projects that significantly improve the platform.
- **Staff/Principal SRE**: An organization-wide expert. They set technical strategy, solve the most complex and ambiguous problems, and their work often defines the future of reliability for the entire engineering organization.

Managerial track

This track focuses on people management; however, it also needs to be technical and hands-on to mentor, coach, and interact with different stakeholders. The following are the roles available in this track:

- **SRE team lead**: A player-coach role, still technically hands-on but taking on people-management responsibilities for a small team.

- **SRE manager**: Focuses on people management, project prioritization, resource allocation, and stakeholder management for one or more teams.
- **Senior manager or director of reliability**: Manages managers and sets the strategic direction for the entire SRE practice across the company.

Considerations

The following are some considerations that should be provided to help SREs grow in their role:

- **Flexibility**: Allow for movement between tracks. For example, a senior SRE might try a team lead role and decide to move back to the IC track without stigma.
- **Explicit criteria**: Each level must have clear, documented expectations for technical scope, leadership, and impact. This removes subjectivity from promotions.
- **SRE rotation program**: Encourage software engineers from development teams to do a 6–12 months rotation in SRE. This will spread reliability thinking across the organization and give SREs a fresh influx of product perspective.

Conclusion

The journey of an SRE is a continuous one. The systems we build will always be complex, and they will always fail in unexpected ways. Therefore, the ultimate asset of any SRE organization is not a specific tool or a piece of code, but the resilience, wisdom, and cohesion of its people.

We have explored the structures that enable effective teams, from clear roles to deep collaboration. We have confronted the human cost of this work, which is the stress, the fatigue, and the risk of burnout, and outlined sustainable practices to mitigate it, from balanced rotations to proactive auto-healing. We have explored a balanced scorecard of KPIs, where team morale and psychological safety are valued as highly as error budgets and MTTR.

The most reliable system in the world is useless if the team maintaining it is burned out, disengaged, and turning over every 18 months. Conversely, a motivated, well-supported, and continuously learning team can navigate any technical challenge and guide any system towards greater stability.

In the next chapter, we will explore the adoption ideas for SRE in small and large organizations and how the culture varies across different organization sizes. We will discuss the challenges of scaling reliability as the organization grows and cover effective strategies for communicating reliability to stakeholders and leaders.

Join our Discord space

Join our Discord workspace for latest updates, offers, tech happenings around the world, new releases, and sessions with the authors:

https://discord.bpbonline.com

Chapter 11
SRE in Small vs. Large Organizations

Introduction

The principles of SRE that blend software engineering with system administration to create scalable and reliable software are widely applicable. However, the practice of SRE is not a one-size-fits-all blueprint. The way we implement and cultivate an SRE culture is significantly shaped by the size, structure, and maturity of the organization.

A small startup with 10 engineers cannot practice SRE in the same way as a global enterprise running thousands of services across multi-cloud ecosystems. The startup battles resource constraints and the need for extreme agility, while the enterprise wrestles with organizational complexity, legacy systems, and distributed decision-making. Trying to impose a large-enterprise SRE model on a startup would overburden it. Conversely, applying a startup's ad-hoc approach to a vast enterprise would lead to chaos.

This chapter will guide us through the nuances of adopting SRE across the organizational spectrum. We will explore the cultural dynamics, team models, and operational strategies that succeed in small teams versus large and structured enterprises. We will also walk through hybrid and embedded SRE models, navigating complexity in distributed systems, and effective techniques for communicating reliability risks and trade-offs to leadership. This will help us tailor our SRE practices to suit our organization's unique context, ensuring that the pursuit of reliability directly supports our business objectives.

Structure

The chapter covers the following topics:

- SRE team models
- SRE culture in small organizations
- SRE culture in large organizations

- SRE culture in small vs. large organizations
- Embedding SRE in engineering teams
- Managing complexity in distributed systems
- Communicating reliability to stakeholders and leaders

Objectives

In this chapter, we will see how SRE can be adopted in organizations of different sizes, from small startups to large-scale enterprises. We will focus on how SRE culture will vary in small organizations where SRE engineers in smaller teams will wear multiple hats, and in large enterprises where structured SRE practices are needed to manage complexity across distributed systems. This chapter introduces centralized and distributed SRE models and examines how each scales with organizational growth. We will discuss the challenges of scaling reliability, from microservices dependencies to cross-team coordination, and how automation and standardization help mitigate risks. This chapter will also cover effective strategies for communicating reliability metrics, risks, and trade-offs to stakeholders and leadership, ensuring alignment between technical efforts and business objectives. By contrasting approaches, this chapter provides insights for adopting SRE principles and practices for organizations of any scale.

SRE team models

SRE teams can be structured in multiple ways depending on the organizational size, maturity, and service complexity. So, before diving into the cultural differences, it is crucial to understand the fundamental organizational model for the SRE function. Most organizations will have to make the choice between a centralized, decentralized, embedded, or hybrid model. This is a strategic decision for the organization that sets the stage for how SRE principles will be implemented and practiced. Let us explore these SRE team models.

Centralized SRE team

In this model, a centralized SRE team manages reliability for all products and services. All SREs report to a single, dedicated organizational unit (SRE department), which is separate from the product and development teams. The SRE department acts as an internal consultancy or shared service provider.

Workings

Development teams build and own their services. When a service reaches a certain level of maturity or requires specialized reliability support, the centralized SRE team is engaged. The SRE department then takes on the operational responsibility of these services, often through an error budget policy, and works to improve the service's reliability, scalability, and operational processes. All reliability tooling, incident management, observability platforms, and automation pipelines originate from this central SRE team.

Analogy

A centralized team can be thought of as a city's fire department. They respond to incidents within the city, maintain standard equipment and enforce consistent training and processes. They ensure that everyone follows the safety protocols. However, if the city becomes too large, the department can become overloaded.

Pros and cons

The centralized team ensures consistency of tools and processes across all teams. They maintain deep reliability expertise in one place, and it is great for early-stage organizations that are building foundational practices. Clear ownership for reliability responsibilities is maintained.

However, as the services multiply, the centralized team can become overwhelmed and act as a bottleneck. Also, a centralized SRE team may not understand the intricacies of the product. There is also a risk of reduced developer ownership, as reliability will be considered an SRE job.

Decentralized or embedded SRE team

In the decentralized or embedded model, SREs sit directly within the product or services team and report to the product team or business unit. There may be minimal central SRE governance, as each SRE is a full-fledged member of their product team.

Workings

Each engineering team has one or more SREs embedded as part of the development squads who work side-by-side with the developers on a daily basis. These SREs contribute to the same code base and participate in design reviews, sprint planning, deployments, and post-incident analysis while also sharing on-call rotations. They build domain-specific reliability tooling and work closely with the developers, thus integrating reliability practices into daily workflows.

Analogy

Imagine a large manufacturing company with multiple factory units. Each unit has its own resident engineer responsible for maintenance, efficiency, and safety. These engineers understand the machines in their units better than anyone else, and when an issue arises, they can fix it immediately without waiting for a central team to arrive. However, different units may have their own processes and tools that help them to boost agility, but cause inconsistencies across the company.

Pros and cons

Since the team is embedded with the product team, they have high product alignment and deeply understand the system they support. This also leads to faster incident response and feature reliability support. Product teams share ownership with SREs, so the team has a better reliability culture, and this model scales better for larger organizations.

However, such a model has a high risk of fragmentation, whereby tools and processes can largely differ across teams. They have higher staffing needs as each product team needs dedicated SRE capacity within it. Since the SREs are distributed across different teams, some may adopt stronger SRE practices, leading to differences in quality. Also, this requires engineering teams to value and support the SRE role.

Hybrid central and embedded SRE model

The hybrid SRE model combines a central SRE governance team with embedded SREs aligned to product teams. This is a common model in practice and often effective, especially for mid-to-large-sized organizations, as it attempts to capture the benefits of both centralized and decentralized approaches.

Workings

A central SRE (core SRE) team exists, which builds shared tools, defines standards, and runs organization-wide reliability initiatives. Meanwhile, other SREs are embedded into key product teams to provide direct, hands-on guidance. Central and embedded teams collaborate via guilds, playbooks, design reviews, and incident processes. During incidents, embedded SREs handle product issues while central SREs own platform-level failures.

Analogy

The central + state government is a good analogy for the hybrid SRE model. The central government sets policies like standards, laws, and frameworks, whereas the state government adapts these policies to local needs and executes them. Both work together to maintain order, safety, and consistency. This ensures national consistency while retaining regional autonomy.

Pros and cons

This model provides the best of both centralized and decentralized models as it provides a global standard with local flexibility. This model scales well for mid-size and large organizations. It ensures organization-wide reliability, vision, processes, and tooling, and encourages wide collaborations.

This model needs strong leadership to ensure alignment between the central and embedded SRE teams. The communication becomes complex as there are more cross-functional meetings, councils, and governance. With higher complexity, this model takes time to mature into a stable operating model. Also, if boundaries are hazy, this model can lead to disagreement on ownership.

Summary of three models

The following table provides a quick summary of the three models discussed previously:

Model	Suited for	Strengths	Weaknesses
Centralized	Small organizations or early-stage startups	Consistency, efficiency, and deep expertise	Does not scale well. Bottlenecks
Decentralized or embedded	Mature teams or mid to large companies	High ownership and faster iterations	Fragmentation and higher staffing needs
Hybrid	Mid-size to enterprise organizations	Balanced autonomy and standards	Requires strong governance and coordination

***Table 11.1**: Summary of SRE team models*

SRE culture in small organizations

In smaller organizations like startups, the SRE function is rarely a formal title. It is a mindset and a collection of responsibilities shared across a small, nimble engineering team. The SRE culture in such organizations is shaped by speed, limited resources, and the need for rapid growth. Reliability is critical, yet the discipline is often informal, evolving, and deeply tied to the mindset of the engineering team. Let us look at the key characteristics, practices, and challenges of SRE culture in smaller organizations.

The key characteristics of SRE culture in smaller organizations are as follows:

- **Engineers wear multiple hats**: There is rarely a notion of a dedicated SRE. Everyone is a software engineer, and developers are expected to handle SRE, DevOps, QA, and security tasks. Roles are fluid and shift based on product needs.
- **Velocity and pragmatism**: The primary driver is often speed-to-market. Reliability is important, but it is balanced against the immediate need to ship features and find product-market fit. Error budgets are understood intuitively rather than calculated formally. The team might accept more risk to achieve a strategic goal.
- **High ownership culture**: Engineers own the feature end-to-end as they design, build, deploy, and operate it. The person who wrote the feature is the same person who gets woken up at 3 a.m. when it fails, which enforces the high ownership culture. Production noise must be addressed quickly, as speed to market is crucial.
- **Simplified infrastructure**: Systems are less complex. There may be only one or two core services, a single database, and a straightforward deployment pipeline. This reduces the unknowns and makes the system more comprehensible to a single individual.

- **Fast decision-making**: Small teams communicate quickly and directly. In a small team, every line of code, every on-call shift, and every postmortem has a massive visible impact on the company's trajectory. There are fewer layers of abstraction between an engineer's work and the user's experience.
- **Cost-conscious tooling choices**: There is a heavy use of open-source tools and managed cloud services. Smaller teams prefer simpler, easier-to-maintain solutions.

The following SRE practices are commonly effective in smaller organizations:

- **Collective ownership**: The entire team takes responsibility for reliability. Postmortems are blameless and involve everyone.
- **Lightweight toil automation**: Engineers automatically script repetitive tasks like server provisioning, certificate renewal, or log rotation as the focus is on quick wins that save precious time.
- **Implement appropriate SLOs**: The team focuses on meaningful SLIs to track availability, latency, and error rates of only critical paths. Alerts are simple and immediately actionable. Error budgets are used for decision-making; however, the process is simple.
- **Lightweight incident response**: Smaller teams benefit from a simple `#incident` channel and a short and structured incident message template. They have clear ownership and lightweight postmortems with a high focus on the learnings. The goal is learning rather than documentation.
- **Self-service deployment and debugging**: Smaller organizations expect developers to deploy safely, access logs safely, and query metrics without needing experts. They also expect rollbacks to be instantaneous and independent. This autonomy reduces bottlenecks and accelerates recovery.
- **Setup basic observability**: It is essential even for small teams to have logs, metrics, and traces along with unified dashboards where alerts are tied to user experience. A minimal observability setup is essential.

The following are the challenges usually encountered in smaller organizations:

- **Pressure to ship features over reliability**: Since for smaller organizations, speed to market is essential, they often focus on innovation, and reliability becomes an important but not urgent need. This leads to the silent growth of the backlog of reliability tickets as performance issues get deferred in favor of customer requests. This is the most common SRE pitfall in smaller organizations.
- **Tool sprawling**: In the rush to build, teams often adopt a patchwork of point solutions for monitoring, logging, and deployment without a long-term strategy. This creates technical debt due to issues like partial automation, manual deploys, ad hoc alerts, fragmented dashboards, and incomplete runbooks. This also leads to operational risks.

- **Burnout**: Only a few senior engineers end up knowing the entire architecture, owning deployments, handling incidents, maintaining CI/CD, and managing infrastructure. These engineers become the single point of failure and are always engaged, making burnout a real danger. The lack of formal processes makes it hard to manage workload fairly.
- **Growing complexity outruns team size**: As the product grows with more features, microservices multiply, data pipelines expand, deployment frequency increases, and operational responsibilities increase drastically. In such situations, without planned SRE investments, teams struggle to keep systems stable as complexity grows faster than the organization.

The small organization's SRE culture is lean, intense, and deeply integrated as it is built on ownership, agility, lightweight processes, and autonomy. While small teams benefit from speed and closeness to the product, they face challenges in capacity, specialization, tooling, and burnout. Agility, which is the greatest strength of smaller teams, becomes their vulnerability as the company grows. The key is to recognize when the informal model is starting to crack and to proactively introduce more structure.

SRE culture in large organizations

In a large enterprise, the challenge is not a lack of resources but an overabundance of complexity. As organizations scale, both in product complexity and team size, the culture and practice of SRE evolve dramatically. Large enterprises deal with sprawling architectures, global customer bases, regulatory pressure, and deeply interdependent systems. Hence, the SRE culture is defined by standardization, specialization, and structured collaboration to manage this complexity.

This section breaks down the key characteristics of SRE in large organizations, focusing on what can make it successful and the operational challenges that arise with scale.

Key characteristics

The key characteristics are as follows:

- **Standardization, processes, and governance**: To coordinate across hundreds of engineers, processes are essential. Hence, large organizations rely on formal SLO frameworks, standard incident management workflows, global reliability policies, unified observability platforms, consistent production readiness checklists, and common CI/CD pipelines. Standardization ensures consistency and reduces variance across many teams. This also includes formal error budget policies, **change advisory boards (CABs)** for risky deployments, and standardized incident command systems.
- **Formal SRE roles and organizational structure**: Larger companies maintain dedicated SRE teams, clear ownership boundaries, well-defined service boundaries, escalation,

and on-call rotation schedules. SRE is a formal discipline with dedicated job families, clear career progression, and specialized roles.

- **Platform mindset**: A central SRE or platform engineering team focuses on providing tooling, guidelines, and oversight to other teams. They build and maintain self-service platforms for monitoring, deployment, and capacity management, reducing the cognitive load on product teams and ensuring consistency. Product teams own the reliability of their services. This allows the organization to scale without losing alignment.
- **Data-driven reliability decision-making**: Large organizations rely heavily on SLO dashboards, Error budget burndown charts, reliability scorecards, predictive capacity models, and trend-based decision frameworks for making reliability decisions.
- **Cross-functional collaboration and inter-team dependencies**: SREs in large organizations partner with product engineering, infrastructure, security, compliance, data engineering, and architecture groups to connect them through shared reliability goals. Additionally, a significant portion of an SRE's work in a large organization involves understanding and managing the reliability of interactions between services. The failure of one team's service can cascade, making cross-team communication and SLI/SLA alignment critical.

Effective practices

The following practices are adopted by large organizations to support reliability at scale:

- **Unified SLOs and formal error budgets**: Large organizations must adopt a standardized SLO definition model, error budget policies governing feature launches, standardized SLO tooling that integrates into dashboards, and regular SLO reviews with leadership. Error budgets are not just a concept but an explicit agreement between a product team and the business. Exceeding the budget results in a mandatory focus on reliability work, enforced through automation that can freeze feature releases.
- **Production readiness reviews (PRRs)**: Before a new service can be launched or a major feature released, it must pass a review by an SRE team. This ensures it meets baseline standards for observability, fault tolerance, and operational procedures.
- **Standardized incident management**: This includes tiered severity levels, trained incident commanders, automated paging and escalation, blameless postmortems, and organized follow-ups and ownership. A clear, practiced incident command system is used across the organization. Roles like incident commander, communications lead, and scribe are well-defined, ensuring efficient and effective response during outages. Large organizations emphasize consistent, repeatable incident response practices.
- **Culture of continuous reliability learning**: Large organizations build a reliability culture by sharing learnings across teams, maintaining internal knowledge bases,

creating monthly reliability reviews, and conducting resilience workshops. The goal is to institutionalize knowledge and prevent silos.

- **Tooling that reduces operational load**: Large organizations invest in tools that reduce operational load, such as auto-remediation systems, intelligent alerting, predictive scaling, advanced RBAC, dependency mapping tools, and production readiness scoring algorithms. Automation is essential as human-driven operations are difficult to scale.

Challenges

Large organizations bring maturity and resources, but also complexity and friction, which leads to the following challenges:

- **Bureaucracy and slow down**: The very processes designed to ensure reliability can sometimes slow down development to a crawl. A high number of teams means long decision cycles, conflicting priorities, delays in alignment, and complex cross-service incident scenarios. Finding the right balance between guardrails and autonomy is a constant struggle.
- **Siloed knowledge**: Large organizations struggle with differences between infrastructure, platform, and product teams, slow communication channels, missing context between groups, and duplication of tools and solutions. In a decentralized model, SREs can become isolated within their product teams, losing connection to the broader SRE community and leading to inconsistent practices. Breaking these silos requires intentional cultural work.
- **Resistance to change**: Mature organizations have legacy systems, long-standing workflows, culturally embedded habits, and compliance constraints. Additionally, integrating SRE practices into old, monolithic systems that were not designed for observability or automation can be a monumental effort. So introducing SLOs, new deployment methods, or production readiness standards may face friction.
- **Reliability chain reactions**: Large organizations operate vastly interconnected systems. This leads to failures that often propagate in unpredictable ways. e.g., a small API latency spike can cascade across multiple services or rollouts, breaking downstream consumers. Managing such complexity requires specialized reliability strategies.
- **Cost management**: At scale, every percentage point of reliability has a cost. SREs must constantly make trade-offs between reliability, feature velocity, and infrastructure spend, and should be able to communicate the business rationale for these decisions to the stakeholders.
- **Scaling on-call without burnout**: Large organizations need to manage complex rotation structures, handovers across time zones, maintain the quality of alerts, ensure on-call fairness, and balance deep specialists with general responders. If the on-call is not designed keeping these points in mind, it can lead to widespread burnout.

The large organization's SRE culture is one of engineering rigor and scalable processes. While they benefit from resources, structure, and deep expertise, they face challenges like coordination complexity, siloed work, tool sprawl, and cultural inertia. Successful SRE culture in large-scale organizations can be built by marrying rigorous reliability practices with flexibility and human-centric collaboration and ensuring that reliability remains a shared responsibility across the entire engineering ecosystem.

SRE culture in small vs. large organizations

Let us look at the key attributes of SRE culture in large and small organizations in a table to visualize the contrast:

Attribute	Small organization SRE	Large organization SRE
Team structure	Generalists, multi-hat roles	Specialized SRE teams
Processes	Lightweight	Standardized, formal, and repeatable
Tooling	Open-source	Enterprise-grade and automated
Ownership	Shared and fluid	Clear service owners
Incident response	Informal	Structured and multi-layered
Decision-making	Fast, based on immediate context	Deliberate, based on data and cross-team impact
On-call	Minimal and shared by the entire engineering team	Well-defined rotations per service or team
Primary focus	Feature velocity and product-market fit	System stability, scalability, and cost efficiency
Communication	Informal, direct, and rapid	Formal, documented, and structured
Key challenge	Avoiding burnout and preparing for scale	Avoiding bureaucracy and managing complexity

Table 11.2: *SRE culture in small vs. large organizations*

This table represents a spectrum, and most organizations will find themselves somewhere between these two poles. The key takeaway is to recognize an organization's position on the spectrum and adopt context-appropriate practices.

Embedding SRE in engineering teams

As organizations grow from small to medium size, the fully centralized or fully decentralized SRE models start showing their flaws. Centralized SRE teams provide governance and consistency, while distributed teams offer proximity to product engineering. Therefore, most mature organizations adopt a hybrid approach where the SREs are directly embedded within the engineering teams and are supported by a central SRE team that provides common tooling, standards, and guidance. This hybrid model emerges as a powerful compromise, and a key tactic within this model is the practice of embedding SREs.

Definition of embedded SRE

An embedded SRE is a dedicated SRE who is temporarily or permanently assigned to a specific product engineering team while still aligning with a central SRE organization's principles, tools, and best practices. These embedded SREs sit with the engineering teams, join their ceremonies, build or review reliability features, and share responsibility for uptime, performance, and operational excellence.

Characteristics of embedded SRE

The embedded SRE becomes the team's reliability expert, enabling faster iteration without compromising on stability. The following are the key characteristics of an embedded SRE:

- They work with a specific product engineering team.
- Deeply understand the team's architecture, constraints, and release cycles.
- They serve as the team's reliability champion.
- Follows central SRE guidelines and tooling standards.
- Helps translate the organizational reliability goals into team-specific goals.

Purpose of the embedded SRE model

The embedded SRE approach is designed to unite speed with reliability. The purpose is to teach and enable the development teams to own reliability as a service. They act as a catalyst for cultural change. The following are the highlights of the purpose that the embedded SRE model serves:

- **Coach and mentor**: They teach developers about SRE fundamentals like SLOs, alerting based on symptoms, reducing toil, and writing production-ready code.
- **Hands-on partner**: They pair with developers to instrument code with meaningful metrics, build automated runbooks, and design fault-tolerant architectures.
- **Scaling reliability across multiple teams**: Embedded SRE allows for distributed scaling of reliability expertise, consistency across multiple teams, and higher adoption of SLO, observability patterns, and incident response practices. Each embedded SRE becomes a multiplier who can spread the reliability knowledge organically.
- **Align reliability with product priorities**: Embedded SRE helps teams balance new features with technical debt and operational risk by translating error budget signals into roadmap decisions, highlighting customer impact of technical debt, and ensuring features are built with reliability-by-design principles.

- **Improving incident response and operational maturity**: Embedded SRE helps build team-specific runbooks, standardize dashboards and alerts, mentor engineers in debugging practices, and improve on-call quality. Thus, over time, operational maturity rises across the company.

Embedded SRE in practice

The embedded SRE is the human link between high-level SRE principles and the practical challenges of a specific team's codebase and challenges. They translate theory into practice. The embedded SRE operates on a dual alignment model where the primary alignment is with the product team, where they work with product managers, backend and frontend engineers, QA, DevOps, and user experience engineers. The secondary alignment of the embedded SRE is with the central SRE team, where they receive training and mentorship, tools and templates, observability infrastructure, incident response guidelines, and architectural standards, which they then proceed to implement within their own product engineering teams.

Best practices

Embedded SRE works well only when both the product team and the central SRE team deliberate on practices designed for alignment, clarity, and growth. Let us look at some of the best practices for successful embedding of SRE engineers within the product team:

- **Define clear priorities**: The SRE and the product team manager should agree on specific, measurable goals for the embedding period. (e.g., establish SLOs for all core user journeys). Explicit responsibilities and non-responsibilities must be well-defined.
- **Set duration**: Embeddings can be rotational (e.g., 6-month rotations) or permanent for critical services. Rotations will help spread SRE knowledge across many teams.
- **Maintain community**: Embedded SREs must regularly meet with the central SRE chapter to share learnings, standardize tools, and prevent siloing. They should join SRE guild meetings, participate in reliability councils, and attend training programs.
- **Empower the team**: The SRE's role is to coach, advise, and enable, whereas the product team must retain ownership of its service. The SRE team must empower the product team to architect reliable designs, build foundational tooling, and improve operations.
- **Standardize tooling**: To avoid tool fragmentation, embedded SRE must ensure that all teams use the same observability stack and reliability libraries are standardized. Additionally, CI/CD pipelines should come from the central source, and logs, alerts, and dashboards should follow organization-wide templates.
- **Reliability as a shared responsibility**: Embedded SRE works well when on-call rotations include both SREs and developers, and SLOs are co-created. Incident reviews should involve the entire team, and operational tasks are shared fairly across the team.

- **Maturity model guides progress**: Embedded SREs could measure improvement through matrices like the reliability score cards, incident response quality, automation coverage, error budget discipline, and production readiness adoption. Tracing progress through these maturity models will guide the team from ad hoc to world-class practices.
- **Start small and expand**: Embedded SRE should start small from one or two high-impact teams with clear outcomes and structured learning. This helps the teams avoid chaos and refine the model before organization-wide rollout.

The hybrid embedding model is arguably the most effective way to scale an SRE culture beyond a small, centralized group, as it builds reliability capability directly into the engineering organization. When implemented with clear charters, strong organizational alignment, and mature tooling, embedded SREs can significantly elevate an organization's reliability culture, accelerate product velocity, and ensure long-term scalability.

Managing complexity in distributed systems

As organizations evolve from monolithic architectures to distributed systems and microservices, complexity becomes one of the biggest challenges to achieving reliability at scale. Distributed systems create new failure modes, hidden interdependencies, uneven performance characteristics, and cascading risks that do not exist in simpler architectures. While these systems offer agility, scalability, and development speed, they also demand stronger reliability engineering practices. So, the SRE's role evolves from managing the reliability of a single machine to managing the reliability of a vast, dynamic graph of interdependent services.

Nature of complexity in distributed systems

In distributed systems, individual components must cooperate across networks, environments, and boundaries, which increases the complexity of these systems. Distributed systems mean that each service must be independently deployable, but none operates in isolation. The following are some of the points that highlight the complexity in distributed systems:

- **Microservices multiply failure points**: A system composed of many microservices can fail in many unpredictable ways while interacting among these microservices. Common failure points include network timeouts, latency spikes, dependency failures, inconsistent data states, partial data replication, and cross-service race conditions. Additionally, each new microservice increases the complexity exponentially rather than linearly.
- **Hidden and implicit dependencies**: Most of the services depend on databases, message queues, authentication services, logging pipelines, and external APIs, which are often poorly documented. Such hidden dependencies often lead to failures that seem to be unrelated to the service experiencing symptoms.

- **Distributed failure can cascade**: A failure in one service can propagate through API calls, message queues, database locks, shared caches, and load balancers and lead to cascading failures. Such failures are often difficult to trace in distributed systems and can lead to data inconsistencies like conflicting updates, stale caches, partial writes, and out-of-order event processing. Such inconsistencies in data can make debugging extremely difficult.

SRE strategies for managing complexity

For SREs, managing complexity is about containing it, understanding it, and making the system resilient to it. The following are some of the core strategies that can be used to ensure reliability in distributed systems:

- **Define and track dependencies**: The first step is to know the system well. We can use service meshes (like Istio) and **application performance monitoring** (**APM**) tools (like Dynatrace) to automatically map the dependency graph and create real-time topology maps. This also creates tracing across all critical interactions. SREs need to understand which services are critical upstream dependencies for our user journeys. This makes it easier to diagnose failures and predict impact before making changes.
- **Implement SLOs for dependencies**: It is difficult to manage what we are not measuring. Hence, teams must define SLOs not only for their own services but also for the services that they depend upon. The reliability of a service is a function of its own reliability and the reliability of its dependencies. SLOs help simplify distributed systems by focusing on the outcomes instead of the internal complexities.
- **Build in resilience patterns**: Ensure strong architectural governance and standards by implementing standard service design patterns, defining clear API versioning rules, standardizing communication protocols, and enforcing common reliability libraries. These reliability libraries can include common resilience engineering architectural patterns like circuit breakers, bulkheads, rate limiting, timeouts, retries, and graceful degradation. These resilience patterns help prevent localized failures from escalating into global outages.
- **Capacity planning and load modeling**: Distributed systems have unpredictable performance under load. Hence, SRE engineers use load tests, stress tests, capacity forecasts, autoscaling policies, and bottleneck identification to ensure that systems are not overwhelmed during real-world usage spikes.
- **Standardize observability**: In a complex system, debugging is a cross-team effort. Standardizing on a common set of tools for metrics, logging, and tracing ensures that every service emits metrics in the same format and that traces can flow seamlessly across service boundaries. This is a primary responsibility of a central SRE team. Observability must reveal not just failures, but trends and anomalies before they impact users.

- **Chaos engineering and failure simulation**: Chaos engineering is essential for distributed systems as it helps in failure simulation by injecting failures, simulating latency, shutting down nodes, breaking network paths, and testing failovers. This helps identify unknown failure characteristics.
- **Automated rollbacks and standardized deployments**: A single, secure, and reliable deployment pipeline used by all teams reduces variability and prevents *works on my machine* scenarios. The central SRE team provides the paved road while the product teams focus on their business logic. Additionally, distributed systems need automated canary analysis, blue-green or rolling deployments, and auto rollbacks on failure to ensure that failures do not become outages.

Distributed systems offer immense power along with significant complexity. This makes managing complexity one of the core responsibilities of the SRE. By combining a deep understanding of system dependencies with robust resilience patterns and pervasive automation, SREs can bring order to the inherent chaos of distributed systems.

Communicating reliability to stakeholders and leaders

Communicating reliability is one of the most underestimated responsibilities of an SRE organization. The most technically brilliant SLOs and the most elegant automation are worthless if the business does not understand their value. A critical, and often overlooked, function of an SRE is to act as a translator between the technical world and the business world, where the SRE translates deeply technical concepts into clear, concise, business-aligned narratives that help influence decisions and shape organizations. This ensures that the leaders know the trade-offs required, the risks involved, and the long-term consequences of the operational decisions taken. Since this is not straightforward, SRE teams generally struggle with this.

Reliability communication is not only about sending status reports. It is about:

- Ensuring leadership understands why reliability needs investment.
- Aligning feature delivery with operational risk.
- Building a culture where reliability becomes a business enabler.
- Helping business stakeholders make informed trade-off decisions.
- Reducing friction between product, engineering, and SRE teams.
- Maintaining trust during incidents or while there is pushback on unrealistic deadlines.

Good communication builds credibility and ensures that reliability efforts get the budget, time, and organizational support that we need.

Challenges with reliability communications

Reliability communication often involves technical jargon (like P99 latency), which is meaningless to non-technical leaders. Reliability is often seen as an abstract quality until it fails, as it is hard to prioritize work that prevents something that has not happened yet. Leadership may also see reliability as an additional cost, which slows down feature delivery without a clear return on investment. The following are some examples that will help in understanding the challenges:

- **Technical complexity vs. business simplicity**: Reliability metrics like P99 latency, SLO violations, or request saturation are difficult for non-technical stakeholders to understand.

  Example:

  - **SRE reports**: Hitting 5% error budget burn rate due to internal timeouts.
  - **Business interprets**: It is fine, so we can move ahead with the product launch.
  - Which results in underestimating the risk of error budget exhaustion.

- **Misaligned priorities**: Engineering and product teams focus on delivery velocity, whereas SRE focuses on risk and stability.

  Example scenario: Product wants to ship a new checkout flow for the festive season sale:

  - **SRE warns**: Service is operating at 80% capacity and risks degradation.
  - **Leadership**: pushes for new checkout flow deployment, leading to a high-impact incident.

- **Reactive instead of proactive communication**: Often, stakeholders hear about reliability only during or after outages and not during the planning phases.

  Example: SRE raises concerns about scaling requirements late in the quarter when the product roadmap is already locked.

- **Information overload**: SREs sometimes overwhelm leaders with dashboards, alerts, SLO spreadsheets, and postmortem details. Whereas stakeholders need the bottom-line impact, not a data dump.

Communication framework for reliability

The following are some frameworks that can be leveraged for communicating reliability to business leaders and stakeholders.

IRA framework

This is a 3-part structure highlighting the **impact, risk, and action** (**IRA**) that works well with executives:

- **Impact**: Highlighting what is happening or likely to happen.
- **Risk**: Highlighting what is at stake from the customer, revenue, or compliance point of view.
- **Action**: Highlighting what decision or investment is needed to mitigate the risk.

For example:

- **Impact**: Checkout latency increased 18% during load testing.
- **Risk**: High-probability of checkout failures during peak sales, which can lead to potential revenue loss of an estimated amount.
- **Action**: Require investment to expand the database read replicas and improve the cache layer.

This is a short, crisp, and business-aligned communication framework that works well with non-technical executives.

SLO communication pyramid

The SLO communication pyramid talks in terms of the user journey in simple terms and aligns them to the business goals. The pyramid structure can be as follows:

1. **User journey and business goals**:
    a. **Example**: seamless checkout experience leads to revenue growth by 10%.
2. **Customer-facing reliability metric**:
    a. **Example**: success rate and latency of the current checkout process.
3. **Technical reliability metric**:
    a. **Example**: SLO and error budget of the checkout service.
4. System behaviors and root causes.
5. Recommended actions.

This is easy to understand, as the business context is the starting point of the pyramid.

THR status model

The **traffic health risk** (**THR**) model is a concise yet powerful framework for communicating the holistic state of a service as it includes the highlights about the THR associated with the system. The reporting under this framework is structured under three pillars, shown as follows:

- **Traffic**: This quantifies the demand on the system, which includes current load, traffic patterns, growth trends, and projected future demand.
- **Health**: This measures the system's reliability and stability against its promises like SLI/SLO adherence, non-technical summaries of recent incidents, error rates and latency.
- **Risk**: This proactively identifies challenges that could impact service reliability or business continuity. It includes upcoming deadlines, technical debt, capacity limitations, and external dependencies.

This model is especially effective in leadership reviews and quarterly planning meetings.

One-page SRE update framework

This is a single-page report that is used for sharing monthly or quarterly reports with business leaders or stakeholders. It contains the following information:

- Reliability summary
- SLO compliance
- Recent incidents non-technical summaries
- High-risk areas with business impacts
- Resilience improvement roadmap
- Decision points including budget, staff, time, or prioritization changes

Effective communication strategies

The following are some of the reliable and repeatable communication strategies that can help SREs communicate clearly and persuasively with stakeholders and business leaders:

- **Translate technical metrics into business impact**: Stakeholders think in terms of customer trust and revenue. Hence, it makes more sense to translate technical terms like *we hit 1200ms P99 latency* to customer-impacting language like *5% of customers are facing slow checkout, leading to checkout abandonment*.
- **Focus on trade-offs**: SREs need to frame reliability investments as trade-offs to help leaders make rational decisions with clarity. Example:
  - Higher velocity will lead to higher operational risk.
  - Lower reliability will lead to higher churn.
  - Reduced observability will lead to slower incident resolution.

- **Use visual aids**: Simple visuals depicting patterns instead of raw metrics make a bigger impact on business leaders and stakeholders. Examples of some visuals are:
    - Reliability heat maps.
    - Error budget burn-down charts.
    - Dependency risk graphs.
    - Before and after performance comparisons.
- **Communicate reliability early in the planning cycle**: Effective SRE teams get involved in roadmap planning, go-to-market timeline decisions, architectural decisions meetings, and capacity planning and budgeting sessions. It is important to communicate reliability challenges during these discussions to prevent conflicts later.
- **Normalize transparency and blamelessness**: SREs should be open about risks to build trust, as clear, transparent communication builds trust.
    - **Example**: SREs can communicate that the current authentication service is nearing its capacity and needs to be scaled before the launch next quarter.
- **Incident stories to drive learnings**: Incident stories that link technical metrics with customer impact and recommended actions help connect to business leaders and stakeholders. Storytelling makes reliability real and relatable:
    - **Example**: During last month's sale, database contention increased retries by 40%, slowing orders for 12,000 customers. This incident highlights the need for connection pooling and query optimization.
- **Present actionable choices**: Instead of presenting problems, SREs should present the actionable choices with their trade-offs to the leadership team to help them make rational decisions.
    - **Example**: Instead of saying *we have a reliability problem*, SREs can say we have three options: scale infra, optimize code, or reduce traffic. Here are the costs and benefits of these three options.

Effective communication is one of the most strategic functions of SRE. By translating metrics into business impact, adopting structured communication frameworks, and engaging proactively with leadership, SRE teams can create alignment, secure support for reliability investments, and build a culture that values resilience as a strategic asset to the business.

Conclusion

This chapter explored how SRE implementation varies across organizations of different sizes, from nimble startups to complex global organizations. Small teams thrive with a generalist SRE culture with a focus on velocity, whereas large enterprises require structured and specialized SRE teams to manage the distributed complexity. We also compared SRE culture in small and large organizations, highlighting distinct characteristics, operating styles, and maturity patterns. We examined centralized, decentralized, and hybrid team models, highlighting the effectiveness of embedding SREs within product teams to spread reliability culture. We also discussed methods to manage complexity in distributed systems through observability, standardization, automation, and dependency governance. Finally, SREs must master the art of communicating reliability effectively to stakeholders and business leaders through business-aligned framing, structured communication frameworks, and proactive engagement. Together, these insights will help any organization adopt the SRE principles in a way that fits its scale, culture, and goals.

In the next chapter, we will look at the future of SRE. We will look at the emerging trends of AIOps and self-healing systems. The discussion will focus on how the SRE role is evolving beyond manual intervention to designing systems that are autonomously reliable, and what skills will be needed to thrive in this new era.

CHAPTER 12
Future of SRE

Introduction

Over the past two decades, SRE has evolved from a niche set of operational practices created at *Google* to a global discipline that is shaping how modern systems are built, scaled, and maintained. Its core tenets, such as systematically managing toil, embracing risk through error budgets, and conducting blameless postmortems, have successfully enabled organizations to scale systems. However, in modern distributed systems, microservices, cloud-native architectures, polyglot data layers, and dynamic multi-cloud environments are creating a high-level of dynamic, high-dimensional chaos, leading to increasing demands on reliability engineering.

The contemporary SRE practice, while highly disciplined, still remains largely reactive, whereby an engineer is largely expected to triage, diagnose, and manually remediate an issue. The very observability tools designed to provide clarity now generate a deluge of metrics, logs, and traces that can obscure signals with noise, becoming a liability without the means to synthesize them into actionable intelligence.

This chapter introduces a transformation that is currently reshaping reliability engineering. This transformation is led by **artificial intelligence** (**AI**), **machine learning** (**ML**), autonomous systems, and AIOps platforms. What began as a discipline built on automation, SLIs, SLOs, and incident response is now transitioning into a world where machines not only assist humans but will increasingly predict, prevent, and remediate failures autonomously. The future of SRE will transform the nature of reliability engineering itself. This evolution marks a decisive journey from a reactive model to a proactive, predictive, and autonomous model of intelligent system governance. Instead of replacing SREs, AI will empower them, automating the mundane tasks while amplifying human strategic efforts. This evolution is essential for managing the increasing scale and complexity of modern distributed systems.

Structure

The chapter covers the following topics:

- Improving reliability using AI
- Future of reliability and self-healing systems
- Skills and team structures needed for the future of SRE
- Building future-ready SRE skills
- AI tools for SRE
- WisdomAI as a featured tool

Objectives

This chapter dives into the evolving landscape of SRE in an AI-driven world. We will examine how AI is transforming reliability, from predictive incident detection to automated remediation using AIOps and observability tools. We will gain insight into how ML can augment human decision-making, reduce toil, and enhance system observability. We will discuss how technologies related to AI can be used to augment **root cause analysis** (**RCA**) and reshape how SREs manage complexity at scale. We will also look ahead into the future of reliability, which will shift from reactive practices to proactive intelligent systems. We will showcase some of the upcoming AI tools tailored for SRE workflows, which will provide a forward-looking perspective on how reliability engineering will continue to evolve, empowering teams to engineer and maintain increasingly complex and resilient systems at scale.

Improving reliability using AI

The integration of AI into SRE marks a fundamental shift in how we understand and manage systems. It introduces a layer of intelligence that has been woven throughout the entire reliability workflow. AI brings capabilities that go far beyond the reach of traditional rule-based monitoring or manual analysis. This augmentation transforms each stage from a manual, reactive task into a streamlined, proactive, and intelligent process.

AI-augmented SRE workflow

With AI, the classic incident response lifecycle is being re-engineered. AI creates a continuous, closed-loop system where each step is enhanced, like detection becomes preemptive, diagnosis becomes causal, and remediation becomes automated. The human SRE is elevated from a first responder to a conductor, overseeing the symphony of automated processes and intervening only for truly novel, edge-case scenarios that require human intuition and creativity.

Leveraging AI across the reliability lifecycle shifts the way detection, triage, diagnosis, remediation, and learning happen, as explained in the following subsections.

Intelligent observability

The traditional observability tools are excellent at collecting telemetry like metrics, logs, traces, and events; however, they are limited in their ability to analyze the data automatically. So, humans are left with the burden to interpret the patterns hidden within millions of signal combinations. When observability is powered by AI, it can apply advanced algorithms to make sense of the massive, high-dimensional data that is generated by modern systems. AI-powered observability can perform the following:

- **Log clustering and pattern recognition**: AI can process millions of log lines in seconds, using techniques like clustering to group similar messages and identify the unique fingerprint of an incident. This reduces **mean time to detect** (**MTTD**) from hours to seconds by immediately highlighting the most relevant entries for the engineer.
- **Topology-aware correlation**: By integrating with service mesh and dependency graphs, AI can understand the service topology, so when a service (say service *A*) fails, it can instantly identify and prioritize the impact on critical downstream services (like services *B*, *C*, and *D*) and provide a holistic view of the incident's blast radius.

An AI-powered observability engine would be able to output statements like:

The error rate of service *A* increased by 200% following a configuration update to service *B*, which introduced incompatible API behavior.

This level of automated correlation dramatically improves detection speed, reduces false positives, and helps SREs surface critical issues earlier.

Predictive incident detection

Most traditional monitoring relies on static thresholds to identify incidents. These static thresholds are prone to false positives during legitimate traffic spikes and often lead to missing the gradual degradations that signal impending failure. Whereas, AI-powered predictive incident detection uses historical behavior, ML, and pattern recognition to forecast potential failures.

AI predictions can include forecasting when CPU or memory saturation will breach SLOs, predicting latency degradation based on traffic patterns, identifying signals that usually precede cascading failures, detecting early signs of resource exhaustion, and risk-scoring deployments that resemble problematic past changes.

The following are ways in which AI-powered prediction can work:

- **Anomaly detection and ML**: Unsupervised learning models are trained on historical metric data to learn the daily, weekly, and seasonal patterns of a service. They can then flag deviations from this baseline with high precision, detecting issues like memory leaks, creeping latency, or unusual backend error rates long before they breach a static threshold and impact users.

- **Multi-stage correlation**: Where a human sees four different alerts like CPU increase, minor jump in error rate, small dip in cache hit ratio, and a new code deployment, AI will analyze these signals simultaneously, identifying the correlation and presenting a unified hypothesis. E.g., the v1.5.1 deployment of user-profile-service is causing increased CPU utilization and a 3% error rate due to an inefficient new database query.

AI-augmented root cause analysis

RCA is one of the most time-consuming SRE responsibilities, as it is crucial for learning; however, it is often a manual process. AI can transform RCA by building causal graphs from telemetry, linking anomalies across multiple layers, identifying points of deviation from the trend, matching current incidents with historical patterns, highlighting suspicious changes in configuration or deployments, reconstructing timelines automatically, and even suggesting probable root causes.

AI can act as an expert assistant by accelerating and enriching the RCA by performing the following:

- **Automated timeline generation**: By ingesting data from version control, CI/CD pipelines, configuration management, and monitoring tools, the AI can automatically construct a precise, second-by-second timeline of the events leading to the incident.
- **Causal inference**: In addition to simple correlation, advanced AI models can use techniques like causal inference on the service topology to suggest the most probable root cause.

Some examples of AI-augmented RCA are as follows:

- The incident originated from a spike in database lock contention due to a newly deployed query pattern rolling out at 15:05 UTC.
- There is a 96% probability that the configuration change to the load balancer pool at 12:14 UTC caused the connectivity errors in the payment service.

Automated remediation

The most transformative application of AI in SRE is moving from diagnosis to action without any human intervention. This acts as a foundation for self-healing systems. AI-driven remediation can happen in four stages, given as follows:

1. **Assisted remediation**: The first step is to codify human knowledge into automated runbooks for common, well-understood failures. AI can learn failure patterns and suggest the playbook to execute. Human intervention would be required for approval, upon which AI can execute the playbook.

Example:

- Restart the cache worker pool.
- Quarantine the nodes showing memory corruption.

2. **Supervised automation**: In this stage, AI acts as the intelligent trigger and executes the playbooks when a specific recognized failure pattern is identified. However, AI will ask for approvals when deviations occur in the failure pattern.

3. **Autonomous remediation**: This is the stage where AI-driven decision-making happens, where AI itself selects the optimal remediation path. In such situations, AI might evaluate multiple potential actions (like scale resources, restart a service, block a malicious IP, or rollback a deployment) and predict the likely outcome of each action. It then executes the action with the highest probability of success within a safety guardrail policy defined by humans.

   Examples of auto-remediation:

   a. Autoscaling clusters based on predicted load.
   b. Restarting failed pods or replicating degraded nodes.
   c. Automatically rebalancing traffic across regions.

4. **Fully intelligent systems**: At this stage, AI systems have learned continuously from their past actions and refined future actions. AI would remediate the incident and can be configured to notify the same to SRE.

   Figure 12.1 shows the AI-augmented incident response loop consisting of the following:

   a. **Observability**: A constant stream of telemetry data (metrics, logs, traces) flowing in.
   b. **Detection and analysis**: AI/ML engines do anomaly detection, topology correlation, log clustering, pattern recognition, and causal inference
   c. **Decision**: The AI system generates a hypothesis with a confidence score and acts on it or escalates the action to a human for approval based on how high the score is.
   d. **Action**: The automated remediation engine executes the playbook or AI-orchestrated actions
   e. **Learn**: The outcome of the loop is fed back into the AI/ML engine, creating a continuous learning loop that will improve future detection and decision-making.

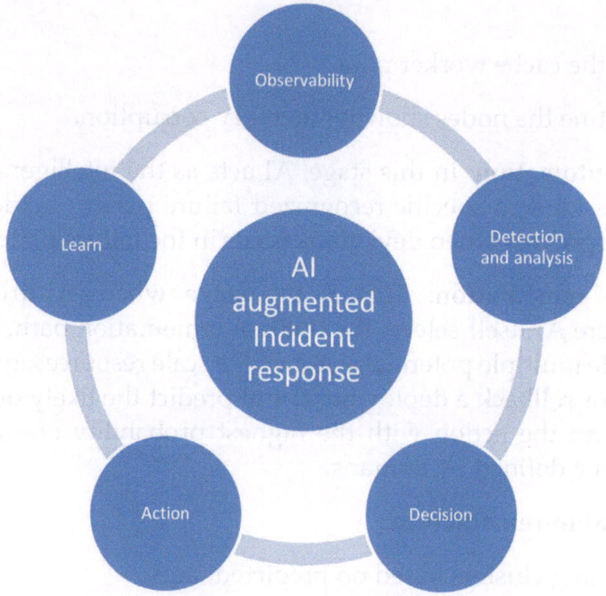

Figure 12.1: AI-augmented incident response loop

This is the true future of reliability, where systems can identify, respond, and prevent issues in real-time. This enables SRE teams to concentrate on high-value engineering tasks rather than operational firefighting.

The following table summarizes the AI-augmented approach and key AI technologies that are used for the different stages of the SRE workflow:

SRE stage	AI-augmented approach	Key AI technologies
Monitoring and detection	Proactive anomaly detection and forecasting of SLO burn rates	Unsupervised learning, time-series forecasting (e.g., Prophet)
Triage and diagnosis	Automated log clustering, topology-aware correlation, and causal analysis	**Natural language processing** (**NLP**), clustering algorithms, causal interface graphs
Remediation	Automated execution of playbooks. AI selected remediation actions	Reinforcement learning, automated runbooks (using tools like Ansible or Kubernetes operators)
Postmortem and learning	Automated timeline generation and linking to past incidents	Knowledge graph analysis. **Generative AI** (**GenAI**) for summarization

Table 12.1: AI approach and applications across the SRE workflow

Future of reliability and self-healing systems

As systems grow more complex, distributed, and dynamic, the traditional approaches to reliability may not scale. The need then is for a self-healing system, which is an infrastructure that can autonomously maintain its own health and performance, anticipating problems, diagnosing root causes, and implementing repairs in real-time. These self-healing systems are the ultimate expression of AI-driven SRE, especially when powered by advancements in AI, ML, and real-time observability.

Defining a self-healing system

A self-healing system is a closed-loop control system designed to maintain a desired state of reliability, as defined by its **service level objectives** (**SLOs**). It does this by automatically detecting deviations from that state (like predicting failures) and executing corrective actions (like restoring service health) to return to it. The goal is not faster remediation but continuous and adaptive resilience.

The key characteristics of a self-healing system are as follows:

- **Awareness**: The system uses deep, real-time observability of its own state and behavior to identify patterns or anomalies using rules, ML models, or statistical baselines.
- **Diagnosis**: The system analyzes dependencies, error patterns, or performance regression to determine the fundamental root cause of the deviation.
- **Action**: Upon diagnosis, the system executes predefined or learned actions to safely effect change within the system to restore health. Examples of such actions are restarting failed services, shifting traffic, rolling back deployments, updating configurations, killing runaway processes, or rebalancing load across clusters.
- **Learning**: ML models adapt based on historical incidents, feedback loops, or reinforcement learning with the aim of improving their diagnosis and corrective strategies over time.

Even though remediation is automated, SREs maintain governance, guardrails, validation rules, and escalation paths for oversight. The aim of self-healing systems is to replace manual toil, allowing SREs to focus on reliability strategy, architecture, and business-impacting improvements.

Core components of self-healing systems

A self-healing system is not a single tool, but an architectural pattern composed of multiple layers that work together. The following are the building blocks of self-healing systems:

- **Predictive analytics layer**: Self-healing begins with strong observability (using Metrics, logs, traces, and events) to measure the system state. This layer then uses time-series forecasting to predict future SLO violations before they occur. E.g., it may forecast that the database connection pools will be exhausted in 30 minutes based on the current traffic growth.

- **RCA and diagnostic layer**: Once the anomaly is detected, the system determines why it happened. This uses a real-time, dynamic map of the entire software architecture, including service dependencies, infrastructure links, and configuration relationships. This is essential for an accurate, topology-aware RCA using techniques like configuration drift detection, deployment and release event correlation, distributed trace failure path analysis, and AI-driven root cause summarization.
- **Policy and governance layer**: This is a set of human-defined rules that govern the AI's actions. It specifies whether the automated remediation should be executed immediately, escalated to humans, request approval, do nothing, or generate a learning signal. SRE teams can also define guardrails. Examples of guard rails are rollback only if error rate > X%, restart container only twice per minute, or move traffic only when downstream dependencies are healthy. The purpose is to maintain control and prevent automation from creating further incidents.
- **Automated remediation engine**: This is a secure execution environment that runs the automated playbooks and orchestrates complex remediation workflows, all sanctioned by the policy framework. Common automated actions can include restarting or recycling pods, containers, or **virtual machines (VMs)**, autoscaling horizontally or vertically, executing system healing scripts to refresh cache or clean up the database connection pool, or rolling back faulty deployments or scaling back unstable canary deployments.
- **Learning and feedback loop**: A robust feedback loop is needed to update the model and policies with the learnings from incident postmortems, human overrides, false positive/negative detections, and historical remediation performance. This transforms a static automation system into a continuously improving autonomous reliability engine.

Architecture of self-healing systems

The architecture of self-healing systems consists of the following layers:

- **Data layer**: This layer consists of sources of telemetry from applications, infrastructure, network, and business events.
- **AI/ML layer**: This layer consists of stream processing, an acausal inference engine, and a forecasting engine.
- **Policy and governance layer**: This layer consists of the action registry (catalog of all approved and automated actions) and policy engine (which evaluates and approves actions against safety, cost, and security rules).

- **Execution layer**: This layer consists of the orchestrator (which executes and monitors automated runbooks), IaC (Terraform or CloudFormation), and Kubernetes operators (for containerized workloads).
- **Presentation and oversight layer**: This layer provides a dashboard for human operators, which consists of the system health, log of autonomous actions, and requests for human input on some issues.

The following figure depicts the architecture of self-healing systems:

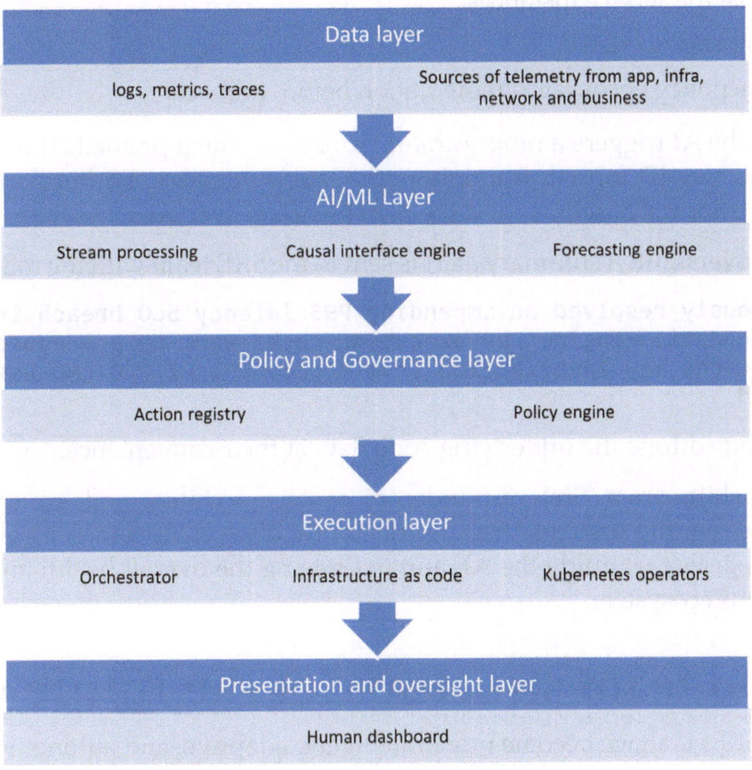

***Figure 12.2**: Architecture of self-healing systems*

Case study of self-healing microservice

Let us look at the case study of a self-healing microservice to understand the internals of how self-healing works. The microservice that we are looking at is a recommendation engine microservice in an e-commerce platform. The following steps illustrate how self-healing works for this microservice:

1. **Pre-failure or predictive**: The predictive model notices the P95 latency is steadily increasing and is on a trajectory to breach its 100ms SLO in 45 minutes. It correlates this with a rising rate of cache misses.

2. **Diagnosis**: This is where the autonomous workflow initiates. The AI consults the causal graph. It identifies that the latency increase is tied to the cache-miss rate and traces the issue to a recent deployment that changed the product ID format, invalidating the current cache keys. Root cause: *Inefficient cache warming logic after deployment v2.1.0.*
3. **Decision**: The AI evaluates actions against the policy framework. Allowed actions include the following alternatives:
    a. Warm the cache with new keys.
    b. Scale the service instances.
    c. Roll back to v2.0.0.
    d. The policy encourages remediation before rollback.
4. **Action**: The AI triggers a *cache warm-up* runbook, which preloads the cache with data using the new ID format. It monitors the latency metrics. Within 5 minutes, latency returns to normal baselines, and the SLO breach is averted.
5. **Human oversight**: A summary alert is sent to the SRE team with the following content:

```
Autonomously resolved an impending P95 latency SLO breach in
'recommendation-engine' by executing cache warm-up procedure. Root
cause: cache key invalidation from deployment v2.1.0. No user impact
occurred
```

The team can then address the underlying code flaw at their convenience.

The SRE's role shifts from first responder to system architect and governor. SREs are responsible for designing systems that are inherently observable and controllable, defining the intelligent policies that guide the AI, and overseeing the overall health and effectiveness of the autonomous ecosystem.

Skills and team structure for the future of SRE

As the systems SREs manage become more intelligent, adaptive, and autonomous, SRE teams themselves must undergo a fundamental transformation. The role of SRE, which has been centered on manual troubleshooting and reactive incident response, must evolve to adapt to embrace new skills, tools and ways of working. Future SREs will be expected to collaborate closely with data scientists, platform engineers, and product teams while developing fluency in AI, ML concepts, and automation frameworks. Organizational structures will shift toward cross-functional, outcome-driven teams, where human judgment is augmented by AI-driven insights. This evolution enables SRE teams to perform their SRE role while adapting to the rapidly changing AI landscape.

Evolution of SRE role

The classic SRE role, which is often visualized as an expert operator and firefighter, will evolve into a strategic orchestrator and engineer. Future SREs will become system designers, automation architects, AI-augmented engineers, intelligent workflow creators, and human-AI orchestrators. They would spend less time responding to alerts and more time building intelligent systems that respond on their behalf. The following points highlight how the SRE role will evolve:

- **Automation builder**: SREs will spend less time fixing issues and more time engineering the sophisticated automation systems and AI policies that prevent issues altogether.
- **Resilient system designer**: SREs' focus will shift left as they will work closely with the development teams to architect systems that are inherently AI-friendly, that are highly observable, failure-isolated, and built with a clean API for control and automation.
- **AI model trainer and validator**: SREs will be responsible for ML lifecycles as they pertain to reliability by curating training datasets, validating model accuracy, and monitoring for model drift to ensure that the AI's decision remains sound as the system evolves.

Key competencies for future SRE teams

Keeping the evolution of the SRE role in mind, let us look at the key technical, analytical, and soft skills that the future AI-powered SRE teams will need.

Technical skills should include ML literacy, advanced automation, observability engineering, data analytics and interpretation, distributed system expertise, infrastructure as code expertise, event-driven workflows, and resilience engineering.

Analytical skills for SREs should include understanding statistical signals, differentiating noise from patterns, correlation vs causation, and ML model evaluation.

Soft skills needed for SREs should include decision-making under uncertainty, communication across teams, risk assessment, human-machine collaboration, and system-level thinking.

New roles in AI-ready SRE teams

As the SRE team evolves to incorporate AI into reliability engineering, new specializations will emerge within the SRE discipline. The following are some examples of such roles:

- **AI-SRE hybrid**: This role possesses deep software engineering skills coupled with a strong practical understanding of ML. They can implement custom anomaly detection models and integrate AI capabilities directly into the reliability platform.
- **Reliability model trainer**: A specialized role focused on MLOps for SRE. They manage the training, deployment, and continuous evaluation of the ML models used for prediction and diagnosis, ensuring they remain accurate and relevant.
- **SRE platform engineer**: This role builds and maintains the internal developer platform that product teams use to access SRE capabilities, abstracting away the complexity of the underlying AI and automation tools.

Cross-functional pods

The future of AI-powered high-performance reliability lies in dissolving the organizational boundaries between development and SRE. The most effective structure will be small, cross-functional pods, which can be called the product reliability pod. Its structure can be summarized as follows:

- The pod includes application developers, a product manager, a designer, and an AI-SRE hybrid.
- This pod is jointly accountable for everything about their service, ranging from feature development and user experience to its reliability, performance, and cost in production.
- The embedded SRE ensures that reliability is a high-priority concern from the design phase and that the service is instrumented to be managed by the central AIOps platform.

This model fosters a culture of shared ownership, accelerates the feedback loop from production to development, and ensures that the entire team understands and contributes to the system's reliability.

Building future-ready SRE skills

Navigating the transition to AI-augmented reliability engineering requires a deliberate and strategic approach to skill development for both individuals and organizations. As AI becomes embedded in reliability workflows, SREs must expand beyond traditional systems knowledge to include data literacy, ML fundamentals, and automation-driven operations. Whereas organizations must invest in structured learning, hands-on experimentation, and cross-functional collaboration to build these capabilities sustainably. Similarly, skill development should focus not only on tooling but also on critical thinking, model interpretation, and human oversight of automated decisions. Let us look at the different aspects of skill development for AI-empowered SRE roles.

Software engineering and data fluency

With AI, the distinction between a software engineer and SRE will continue to blur and mastery of software engineering becomes non-negotiable for SRE:

- **Software engineering**: Proficiency in languages like Go or Python becomes essential. This includes skills in designing APIs, writing tests, and understanding software design patterns to build robust, maintainable automation and services.
- **Data fluency**: SREs must become adept at working with data, which encompasses the following:

- **Data analysis**: Using SQL and data manipulation libraries to query and analyze telemetry data.
- **Statistics**: A solid grasp of concepts like percentiles, distribution, and regression is crucial for interpreting AI outputs and avoiding analytical pitfalls.
- **Basic ML concepts**: Understanding the difference between supervised and unsupervised learning, model training/evaluation, and key metrics like precision/recall is necessary for effective collaboration with data scientists.

Core competencies

SREs will also need to upskill themselves for core competencies like ML literacy, systems thinking, and AI tool proficiency. The following points explain this:

- **ML literacy**: While not all SREs need to be data scientists, they must be literate in ML concepts. They should be able to frame a reliability problem in ML terms and work effectively with data specialists.
- **Systems thinking**: The ability to understand and reason about complex, interconnected systems is more critical than ever. SREs must anticipate the second and third-order effects of changes, especially when those changes are made autonomously by an AI.
- **AI tool proficiency**: Hands-on experience with the AIOps and MLOps tools discussed in the next section is becoming a core requirement of the job.

Unchanging core

While AI handles most of the technical toil, the intrinsically human skills like critical thinking, communication, and ethics become even more important. This can be understood from the following points:

- **Critical thinking and judgment**: SREs need the ability to question the AI's hypothesis, to recognize when a model is likely flawed, and to make the final, high-stakes judgment call.
- **Communication and diplomacy**: SREs will serve as the bridge between the technical AI systems and business stakeholders. They must be able to explain complex, AI-driven incidents in clear, simple terms and advocate for the necessary investments in reliability.
- **Ethical reasoning**: SREs will need to define the policy frameworks that govern AI. Hence, they must grapple with ethical questions (like is it fair for AI to throttle traffic from one region to save another, or who is accountable if an autonomous action causes an outage?) to ensure the ethical and transparent use of AI.

As an organization, it is recommended to invest in continuous, targeted learning and support certifications in cloud platforms, data engineering, and ML. Organizational upskilling strategies will include training SREs on ML basics, data interpretation, and AI toolchains. Workshops on AIOps and intelligent observability must be held along with collaborative programs with data science teams. Internal communities must be created where SREs can share knowledge about AI and automation. The goal should be to build a culture of continuous learning and adaptation.

AI tools for SRE

As AI is being embedded into reliability engineering, the AI tools ecosystem has rapidly evolved to embrace the two foundational pillars of AI-driven operations, namely AIOps and MLOps.

AIOps empowers SREs by reducing noise, predicting failures, automating runbooks, and augmenting diagnosis. MLOps, on the other hand, ensures the reliability of ML systems themselves, which is now mission-critical for businesses across fintech, e-commerce, healthcare, and cloud services. AIOps platforms add intelligence to existing monitoring, and MLOps tooling is used for building custom reliability models. A third emerging category of tools, called AI-native SRE platforms, is designed from the ground up for autonomous operations.

Together, they form the intelligent reliability stack, which enables SRE teams to transition from reactive firefighting to proactive autonomous operations. Understanding the distinctions and appropriate applications of each is crucial for teams navigating this transformation.

AIOps platforms

AIOps platforms are traditional monitoring and observability tools enhanced with AI and ML capabilities. They represent an evolutionary approach by applying ML, pattern recognition, NLP, and graph-based analytics that add intelligence layers to the existing operational workflows and reimagine them.

Characteristics of AIOps platforms

The general characteristics of AIOps platforms are as follows:

- AIOps platforms are primarily designed to reduce alert noise and accelerate incident response.
- AIOps platforms are built to work with existing toolchains through extensive connectors and APIs.
- With AIOps, AI provides recommendations and insights; however, humans make the decisions and execute actions.
- AIOps support incremental adoption, as teams can enable AI features gradually without changing the core workflows.

AIOps help resolve issues like alert fatigue due to noisy signals, delayed detection due to manual correlation, human-unfriendly log volumes, slow and inconsistent incident triage, and fragmented observability across toolsets by bringing intelligence, speed, and automation to these issues.

AIOps conceptual architecture

The following figure shows the high-level conceptual architecture of AIOps platforms:

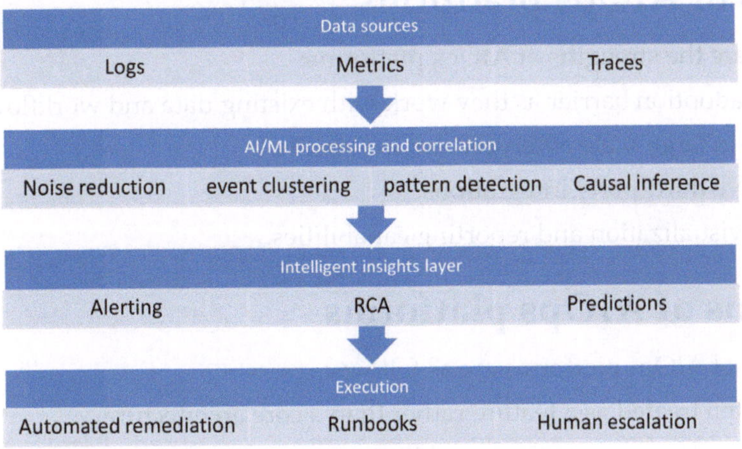

***Figure 12.3:** AIOps conceptual architecture*

Examples and applications

The following are some examples of applications that use AI and the problems they address using AIOps:

- **Moogsoft**: It uses AI-powered event clustering to reduce noise dramatically. The ML correlation engine automatically groups alerts and suppresses false positives, giving the SREs a clean and high-quality signal.
- **Dynatrace Davis AI**: It uses automatic dependency mapping and causal AI for precise problem detection. It is best for enterprises needing out-of-the-box AI capabilities with minimal configuration.
- **Splunk ITSI**: It leverages ML for anomaly detection and event correlation within the Splunk ecosystem. It is ideal for organizations deeply invested in Splunk's data platform.
- **Datadog ML**: It provides ML-based alerting and Watchdog features for RCA suggestions across its unified platform. It is suited for teams wanting integrated AI across metrics, logs, and APM.

- **New Relic AI**: It offers predictive analytics and anomaly detection with a focus on developer experience and application performance. It also uses baselines and ML to detect unexpected deviations.
- **StackStorm**: It is an event-driven automation platform. Here, AIOps can be used to trigger runbooks or workflows automatically based on learned patterns. Opsgenie, combined with automation, can also be used for such use cases.

Strengths of AIOps platforms

The following are the strengths of AIOps platforms:

- Lower adoption barrier as they work with existing data and workflows.
- Proven in large-scale enterprise environments.
- Extensive third-party integrations.
- Strong visualization and reporting capabilities.

Limitations of AIOps platforms

The limitations of AIOps platforms are as follows:

- AI is often treated as a feature rather than a core architecture.
- Limited autonomous action capabilities.
- Historical data analysis is often stronger than predictive capabilities.
- Can perpetuate existing workflow inefficiencies.

MLOps platforms

MLOps tooling provides the infrastructure and frameworks for building, deploying, and managing custom ML models tailored to specific reliability challenges. MLOps tools are about making intelligence operational with a build-your-own approach for organizations with unique requirements or advanced data science capabilities.

ML systems have unique reliability challenges like data drift, bias, degraded accuracy, slow inference, and inconsistent deployments, which directly affect the business outcomes. Hence, SRE teams increasingly help ensure the uptime, performance, and correctness of ML pipelines.

Characteristics of MLOps platforms

The following are the key characteristics of MLOps platforms:

- MLOps platforms focus on the complete ML lifecycle from data preparation to model serving.
- MLOps enables teams to create customized solutions for specific reliability problems.

- MLOps is engineering-intensive as it needs significant ML engineering expertise and resources.
- MLOps platforms are both flexible and complex as they offer maximum flexibility at the cost of implementation complexity.

MLOps introduces the concept of continuous training and deployment for reliability. In addition, it also brings additional capabilities like model versioning, lineage tracking, reproducibility, automated monitoring of model performance, drift detection, lifecycle governance, and safe rollout strategies.

MLOps conceptual architecture

The following figure shows the high-level conceptual architecture of MLOps platforms:

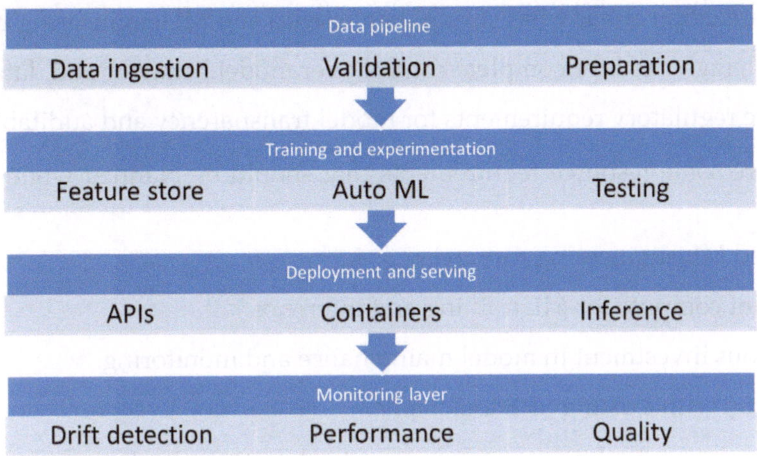

***Figure 12.4**: MLOps conceptual architecture*

Examples and applications

The following are some MLOps tools and the solutions they provide:

- Kubeflow is an end-to-end ML platform for pipeline orchestration for Kubernetes. It is ideal for building custom anomaly detection models that run close to production workloads.
- MLflow is another platform for managing the ML lifecycle, which includes model tracking, packaging, and registry. It is useful for tracking experiments and deploying reliability models across different environments.
- Seldon Core is an ML model deployment on Kubernetes, which is excellent for serving custom prediction models for capacity forecasting and failure prediction.
- Feast is a feature store for managing and serving ML features. It is valuable for creating consistent feature sets across multiple reliability models.

- Why labs is another tool used for high-volume ML pipeline monitoring and anomaly detection. It is used for tracking changes in input feature distribution, target shifts, and prediction degradation.
- Arize AI is a tool used for debugging and continuous ML observability. It extends classical observability into the ML domain, including feature quality, inference latency, fairness, and model stability.

Implementation considerations

It is essential to understand when to use MLOps and the resource requirements needed to implement MLOps. The following are the scenarios that advocate the usage of MLOps:

- There are unique reliability challenges that are not addressed by commercial tools.
- The organization already has strong data science and ML engineering capabilities.
- There is a high need for complete control over model behavior and data.
- There are regulatory requirements for model transparency and auditability.

The following are some resource requirements that should be planned while implementing MLOps:

- Dedicated ML engineering resources.
- Significant compute for ML training and inference.
- Continuous investment in model maintenance and monitoring.
- Integration with existing SRE toolchains.

MLOps can be used for building custom anomaly detection, predictive capacity planning, failure prediction, and cost optimization. However, the resource requirements must be kept in mind while planning for MLOps investments.

AI-native SRE platforms

AI-native SRE platforms are purpose-built systems that are designed from the ground up with AI as the core architectural foundation rather than an added capability. Unlike traditional tools that retrofit AI features onto existing workflows, these platforms reimagine reliability engineering around autonomous decision-making, predictive analysis, and continuous learning. They leverage ML models, large language models, and intelligent correlation engines to interpret telemetry, understand system behavior, and anticipate failures before they occur. Such proactive management, automated remediation and context-aware insights provided by AI-native SRE platforms greatly reduce operational toil while empowering teams to manage complex and distributed systems with greater speed, accuracy and confidence.

Characteristics of AI-native SRE platforms

The following are some of the key characteristics of AI-native SRE platforms:

- They are designed with an autonomy-first approach for autonomous detection, diagnosis, and remediation.
- They are proactive with a high focus on prevention and prediction rather than reaction.
- They are closed-loop systems that have built-in feedback mechanisms for continuous improvements.
- They have policy-driven operations where human oversight is provided through governance frameworks rather than direct control.

Some example tools:

- Grafana ML is used for intelligent observability, where it provides forecasting, baselines, and anomaly detection.
- Event-driven Ansible is used for autonomous runbooks, where it can execute policies automatically.
- Gremlin is used for reliability testing using AI, where it executes controlled chaos experiments.

WisdomAI as a featured tool

WisdomAI is an emerging AI-native SRE platform, which is a fundamental rethinking of SRE tooling that is designed specifically for DevOps, SRE, and platform engineering teams. Built with a modern foundation of LLMs, real-time telemetry ingestion, and autonomous workflows, WisdomAI demonstrates what a next-generation AI-native SRE tool looks like.

Foundational design principles

WisdomAI is an AI-native operational intelligence assistant that integrates with logs, metrics, traces, events, and configuration sources to deliver real-time insights, RCA support, autonomous diagnostics, and smart workflows. It acts as a cognitive companion for SRE teams, reducing noise, accelerating root cause detection, and enhancing observability. It follows the design philosophy, less time hunting issues, more time engineering reliability.

The foundational design principles used for building WisdomAI are as follows:

- **Autonomy by default**: Systems should heal themselves for known failure patterns.
- **Continuous learning**: Every incident and learning improves future performance.
- **Causal intelligence**: Understanding why failures occur and not just that they occurred.
- **Human governance**: Humans define policies and boundaries, and AI operates within them.

AI-powered capabilities

The WisdomAI suite is powered by three engines, namely Wisdom Cortex, which is the autonomous observability engine, Wisdom Autopilot, which is the self-healing system, and the Wisdom Copilot, which is the human-AI collaboration interface. Let us look at these engines in detail:

- **Wisdom Cortex**: This is the autonomous observability engine, which has continuous learning intelligence and predictive analytics.

  The continuous learning intelligence does behavioral baselining by creating dynamic, context-aware baselines that adapt to daily, weekly, and seasonal patterns without the need for manual configuration. Additionally, it does topology discovery by automatically mapping service dependencies and understanding failure propagation paths. It also does signal relevance analysis, which identifies the metrics that actually matter for reliability, thus reducing noise by 90%.

  The predictive analytics is able to predict incidents 15-60 minutes before they impact users by using advanced time-series models. It also predicts SLO burn rate and warns teams when current trends will breach reliability targets. It also does capacity forecasting by anticipating resource needs based on business growth and usage patterns.

- **Wisdom autopilot**: Wisdom autopilot is the self-healing system of WisdomAI. It does intelligent diagnosis and autonomous remediation using self-healing workflows.

  Intelligent diagnosis consists of a causal inference engine that uses Bayesian networks to identify root causes with >90% accuracy. It evaluates multiple potential causes with confidence scoring and is context aware as it considers recent changes, dependencies, and environmental factors during diagnosis.

  Autonomous remediation executes automated responses within human-defined guardrails. It includes gradual escalation, which starts with the least invasive actions before progressing to more significant interventions. This engine learns from each outcome as every action and its results are fed back into the AI model for continuous improvement.

  Self-healing workflows include common issue resolution, whereby it automatically handles memory leaks, stuck processes, or dependency failures. It also does intelligent rollbacks by safely reverting deployments when error thresholds are exceeded. Additionally, it does resource optimization by dynamically scaling infrastructure based on predictive load analysis.

- **Wisdom Copilot**: Wisdom Copilot is the human-AI collaborative interface, which consists of intelligent alert management and knowledge management. The human-AI collaborative workflows suggest but do not enforce fixes, thus keeping SREs in control.

Intelligent alert management provides context-rich notifications that include RCA, impact assessment, and recommended actions. It also does priority-based routing, where the incidents are automatically directed to the appropriate teams based on service ownership. It also provides a collaborative workspace, which is a real-time interface for team collaboration during complex incidents.

Knowledge management includes automated playbook generation, where playbooks are created and refined based on successful resolutions. Current issues are linked to similar past incidents and relevant documentation, creating incident knowledge graphs. It also provides AI-assisted onboarding that accelerates the training of new team members through intelligent guidance.

The following are some of the AI-powered capabilities that are available in Wisdom AI:

- **Natural language querying of operational data**:

  SREs can ask the following questions:

  - Why did latency spike yesterday?
  - Show the top contributors to CPU exhaustion in the last hour.

  WisdomAI fetches insights, correlates signals, and provides explanations.

- **Automated incident contextualization**: It stitches together metrics, traces, logs, and deployment events to generate incident summaries that include impacted services, probable root cause, timeline reconstruction, and blast radius estimation.
- **Predictive insights and patterns**: WisdomAI identifies patterns across historical telemetry and predicts emerging hotspots, capacity risks, config drifts, dependency failures, and cascading failure risks.
- **LLM-augmented RCA**: For complex distributed failures, the system uses graph reasoning and telemetry embeddings to highlight suspect components with human-readable explanations.
- **Smart runbook documentation**: When an issue is detected, WisdomAI suggests runbook steps or troubleshooting commands relevant to the incident profile.

Unique features of WisdomAI

The following are some of the unique features of WisdomAI:

- **True causal understanding**: While most tools excel at correlation, WisdomAI's causal inference engine establishes actual cause-and-effect relationships. This enables more accurate RCA and prevents scenarios where symptoms are treated rather than underlying causes.
- **Autonomous action framework**: Unlike AIOps platforms that stop at recommendations, WisdomAI includes a secure execution environment for autonomous remediation.

This is governed by a sophisticated policy engine that ensures AI actions remain within safe boundaries defined by human operators.

- **Continuous adaptation system**: The platform employs online learning techniques that allow models to adapt continuously without requiring full retraining. This means the system improves with every incident and resolution, becoming more effective over time.
- **Unified architecture**: Rather than integrating multiple point solutions, WisdomAI provides a unified platform for observability, analysis, and action. This eliminates integration complexity and ensures consistent data flow from detection to resolution.
- **Cross-tool correlation engine**: WisdomAI can connect and correlate data from tools like Prometheus, Grafana, Kibana, Datadog, New Relic, Kubernetes, and cloud platforms.
- **Conversational private LLM tuned for SRE**: The LLM has been designed specifically for SRE so it can interpret operational concepts, system architectures, and debugging workflows.

Integration into SRE workflow

Let us look at how WisdomAI integrates into the SRE workflow at different aspects of SRE activities:

- **Enhanced observability**: WisdomAI provides intelligent baselining and anomaly detection, so humans are expected to review AI-generated insights and validate the findings.
- **Incident detection**: WisdomAI uses anomaly detection to surface early warnings and correlates alerts from multiple sources. Humans are expected to validate the warnings and take proactive actions.
- **Incident response**: WisdomAI provides real-time incident briefings, suggests troubleshooting steps, generates Slack or Teams-ready incident summaries, highlights failing components, and predicts the blast radius expansion, helping humans to act proactively and reduce the MTTR.
- **RCA**: The causal inference engine of WisdomAI synthesizes logs, traces, and config changes and identifies root causes automatically, so humans are expected to review the AI diagnosis and provide context where needed. It also generates a structured RCA documentation automatically.
- **Remediation**: WisdomAI suggests and can execute approved remediation actions, whereas humans are expected to approve the actions or handle novel scenarios.
- **Post-incident reviews**: WisdomAI rewrites timelines into human-readable summaries and identifies recurring patterns, thus recommending process improvements.

- **Day-to-day reliability engineering**: WisdomAI can answer architectural questions, troubleshoot performance issues on demand, explain dashboards and anomalies, and suggest optimizations for resilience, cost, and performance.

WisdomAI can integrate with existing monitoring tools, using them as data sources while providing superior analytics and automation. However, teams can proceed with progressive replacement of their existing tools, whereby they can gradually shift responsibilities from their traditional tools to WisdomAI as their confidence in AI capabilities grows. Eventually, teams can move into a hybrid operation mode whereby they maintain critical manual processes while automating routine operations and using AI for complex analysis.

WisdomAI claims that its usage can result in a 70-90% reduction in alert noise, 50-80% faster MTTR, 40% reduction in cloud infrastructure costs, 90%+ autonomous resolution rate, and a shift in SRE focus from 70% operational tasks to 70% strategic work.

The AI tooling landscape for SRE continues to evolve rapidly with AIOps, MLOps, and AI-native SRE platforms, but the clear trend is toward greater autonomy and intelligence. Whether through enhanced existing tools, custom-built solutions, or next-generation platforms like WisdomAI, AI is becoming an indispensable partner in managing the reliability of complex modern systems.

Conclusion

The integration of AI into SRE marks the beginning of a new era of intelligent resilience. This chapter has charted the path from human-operated monitoring to AI-orchestrated autonomy, where self-healing systems and predictive analytics become foundational. AIOps and MLOps enable SRE teams to move from firefighting to foresight by automating detection, accelerating diagnosis, and enabling autonomous remediation. AI-powered tools are becoming essential collaborators, augmenting human judgment and reducing operational toil. The future SRE team will function as strategic architects and policy stewards, leveraging AI to manage scale and complexity while focusing on higher-order engineering challenges. The ultimate goal here is a symbiotic partnership where AI handles operational predictability, empowering humans to focus on innovation, design, and the governance of increasingly autonomous systems.

Appendix A
Tools and Templates

Introduction

This appendix provides a practical collection of tools, templates and checklists to facilitate the implementation of SRE principles within any organization. While the main chapters focus on principles and frameworks, this section serves as a practical toolkit for adopting SRE practices at any stage of maturity. These resources are intended as a starting point and would need to be customized to fit the specific use case, technology stack, processes and organization culture during adoption.

We will go over curated tools for SRE, followed by tools that are available for chaos engineering implementation, along with scenario-based guidance on when and where each tool is most effective. In addition to this, we will also see templates for **service level objective** (**SLO**), **service level agreement** (**SLA**), runbooks, incident checklists, and **root cause analysis** (**RCA**) templates, all of which may need to be customized for your organization.

Structure

This appendix covers the following topics:

- SRE tools
- Sample on-call runbook template
- Sample incident response checklist
- Customizing template for your organization
- Chaos engineering tools
- Sample SLO template
- Sample RCA template

Objectives

The objective of this appendix is to provide SRE practitioners with a practical and actionable toolkit of curated technologies and ready-to-use templates that can help accelerate reliability engineering initiatives. We will learn to evaluate and select appropriate monitoring, **continuous integration/continuous deployment** (**CI/CD**) and chaos engineering tools based on specific organizational context and maturity levels. This appendix delivers applicable artifacts like on-call runbooks, incident response checklists and RCA templates that can be further customized for real-world implementations. This bridges the gap between SRE theory and practice and empowers teams to operationalize reliability principles, standardize incident response and build systemic resilience without starting from scratch.

SRE tools

This section provides an overview of widely used SRE tools that support monitoring, alerting, observability, service management, automation and reliability insights. For each category of tools, we will briefly look at the purpose, followed by popular tools in that category and then the considerations that need to be taken into account for selecting a particular tool. These categories and tools are listed in the following subsections.

Monitoring and observability

Let us look at the purpose of monitoring and observability tools and go over the popular tools and the considerations for selecting a particular tool:

- **Purpose**: The purpose of these tools is collection, visualization and alerting based on system metrics (SLIs and SLOs).
- **Popular tools**: The following are the popular tools in this category:
    - **Prometheus**: It is an opensource tool with a **powerful query language** (**PromQL**) and pull-based model, ideal for cloud-native environments and most suited for microservices with high metric cardinality.
    - **Grafana:** It is the leading opensource dashboard and visualization layer that integrates with virtually every data source. It is ideal for cross-team observability views.
    - **Datadog:** It is a unified **software as a service** (**SaaS**) platform providing metrics, traces and logs in a single pane of glass with excellent out-of-the-box integrations. It is suitable for startups to enterprises.
    - **New Relic**: It is a developer centric **application performance monitoring** (**APM**) and observability platform with deep code level insights and synthetic monitoring.
- **Selection consideration**: Choose the tool based on the need for open-source vs. managed SaaS platforms. Also, keep existing cloud provider integrations, team expertise, and total cost of ownership, including operational overhead in mind while selecting the tool.

Distributed tracing

Let us look at the purpose of distributed tracing tools and go over the popular tools and the considerations for selecting a particular tool:

- **Purpose**: The purpose of these tools is to map the request lifecycle across service boundaries to identify latency bottlenecks and errors.
- **Popular tools**: The following are the popular tools in this category:
  - **Jaeger**: It is an open-source, **Cloud-native Computing Foundation** (**CNCF**)-graduated tracing system built for microservices, offering robust data collection and querying.
  - **Zipkin**: It is a simpler and veteran open-source distributed tracing system that is easy to deploy and get started with.
  - **AWS X-Ray**: It is the native AWS service that provides automatic instrumentation and tracing for applications running on AWS infrastructure.
  - **Honeycomb**: It is an event-centric observability platform that uses high-cardinality traces as its primary data model for powerful debugging.
- **Selection consideration**: Distributed tracing tools are essential in the microservices architecture. Organizations should prioritize tools that integrate with their service mesh (if any) and application frameworks while considering the verbosity of data collection and associated storage costs. Most enterprise APMs like New Relic or Dynatrace have the ability to perform distributed tracing, so if the organization has selected an enterprise observability tool, they may not need a separate tool for distributed tracing.

Log management and aggregation

Let us look at the purpose of log management and aggregation tools and go over the popular tools and the considerations for selecting a particular tool:

- **Purpose**: These tools are used for centralized collection, indexing, storage, and analysis of system and application log events.
- **Popular tools**: The following are the popular tools in this category:
  - **Elastic stack (ELK)**: This is a very popular open-source suite consisting of **Elasticsearch, Logstash and Kibana** (**ELK**) used for searching and analyzing large volumes of data in real-time.
  - **Grafana Loki**: It is a log aggregation system designed for efficiency that indexes only metadata while storing compressed log lines. It is tightly integrated with Prometheus and Grafana.
  - **Splunk**: It is an enterprise-grade platform for searching, monitoring, and analyzing machine-generated big data, with a powerful SPL query language.
  - **Sumo Logic**: It is a cloud-native, SaaS machine data analytics platform that focuses on security and operational intelligence.

- **Selection consideration**: Choose the tool based on log volume, required retention period, real-time search needs, and the team's ability to manage scaling and indexing complexity. Again, most APMs provide log management as a feature that can be enabled if needed. However, the cost of log management via an APM vs. open-source should be taken into consideration in addition to the team's skill set and the tool should be selected accordingly.

Incident management and on-call

Let us look at the purpose of incident management and on-call scheduling tools and go over the popular tools and the considerations for selecting a particular tool:

- **Purpose**: These tools are used for alert routing, on-call scheduling, configuration and execution of escalation policies and collaborative incident response.
- **Popular tools**: Following are the popular tools in this category:
    - **PagerDuty**: This is the industry-standard tool for incident response automation, with robust scheduling, escalation, and post-incident analytics.
    - **Opsgenie (Atlassian)**: Flexible incident management tool with strong Jira integration, suitable for multi team (DevOps teams) environments.
    - **VictorOps (Splunk on-call)**: This tool focuses on reducing alert noise and improving collaboration during incidents with timeline-based war rooms.
- **Selection consideration**: Tools should be evaluated based on ease of scheduling, experience on mobile, integration depth with the organization's monitoring and chat tools and features for Post-incident review.

Error and exception tracking

Let us look at the purpose of error and exception tracking tools and go over the popular tools and the considerations for selecting a particular tool:

- **Purpose**: These tools are used for aggregation, deduplication, and triage of application-level errors and exceptions.
- **Popular tools**: The following are the popular tools in this category:
    - **Sentry**: This tool provides full-stack error monitoring with rich context, showing the exact line of code that broke and the user journey that led to it.
    - **Rollbar**: It provides real-time error monitoring with intelligent grouping and workflows that integrate directly into the development lifecycle.
    - **Datadog error tracking**: It automatically aggregates errors from traces, providing a unified view of performance and stability issues.

- **Selection consideration**: These tools are crucial for development teams to prioritize stability while working. It is recommended to look for tight integration with the organization's version control and issue tracking systems to streamline fixes.

Infrastructure as code

Let us look at the purpose of **infrastructure as code** (**IaC**) tools and go over the popular tools and the considerations for selecting a particular tool:

- **Purpose**: IaC tools are used for declarative, version-controlled provisioning and management of cloud and infrastructure resources.
- **Popular tools**: The following are the popular tools in this category:
  - **Terraform**: It is the default standard tool for multi-cloud provisioning using a **human-readable configuration language** (**HCL**).
  - **AWS CloudFormation**: This is an AWS native service for modeling and provisioning AWS resources using JSON or YAML templates.
  - **Pulumi**: This tool enables defining infrastructure using general-purpose programming languages (Python, Go, TypeScript) which is appealing to developers.
- **Selection consideration**: Terraform is cloud agnostic. AWS CloudFormation offers deepest AWS integration, and Pulumi offers developer familiarity. The tool should be selected based on cloud strategy (single or multi-cloud environment) and team skills. Terraform is a highly recommended tool in this category as it is cloud agnostic and the skillset is widely available in the industry.

Configuration management

Let us look at the purpose of configuration management tools and go over the popular tools and the considerations for selecting a particular tool:

- **Purpose**: Configuration management tools are used for automated management of system configuration and application deployment across a fleet of servers.
- **Popular tools**: The following are the popular tools in this category:
  - **Ansible**: It is an agentless, **YAML Ain't Markup Language** (**YAML**)-based automation tool focused on simplicity and ease of getting started that uses **Secure Shell** (**SSH**).
  - **Chef**: This tool uses a powerful Ruby-based **Domain Specific Language** (**DSL**) for defining recipes that ensure systems converge to a desired state. It has a client-server model.

- o **Puppet**: This is a declarative model-driven automation tool with a mature ecosystem for managing complex and heterogeneous infrastructure at scale.
- **Selection consideration**: It is recommended to prefer Ansible for simplicity and agentless operation. Whereas Chef or Puppet can be used for complex, ongoing state enforcement across large, static fleets.

Synthetic monitoring

Let us look at the purpose of synthetic monitoring tools and go over the popular tools and the considerations for selecting a particular tool:

- **Purpose:** Synthetic monitoring tools are used to proactively test system availability and performance by simulating user transactions from external points.
- **Popular tools**: Popular tools in this category include:
  - o **Grafana synthetic monitoring**: This is an open-source performance testing tool and cloud service that allows us to write tests as code in JavaScript.
  - o **Pingdom**: This is a simple, reliable uptime and transaction monitoring from multiple global nodes with clear status pages.
  - o **Checkly**: This tool monitors **application programming interface** (**API**) endpoints and browser-based flows and is built for modern development teams with a focus on developer experience.
- **Selection consideration**: Synthetic monitoring tools are essential for measuring true user experience based on our SLOs. For tool selection, consider the need for scripting complex user journeys vs. simple uptime checks, and integration with the organization's alerting system.

Secret management

Let us look at the purpose of secret management tools and go over the popular tools and the considerations for selecting a particular tool:

- **Purpose**: Secret management tools are used for secure storage, access control, and auditing of sensitive data like passwords, API keys, and certificates.
- **Popular tools**: The following are the popular tools in this category:
  - o **HashiCorp Vault**: This is a widely used, comprehensive secrets management, data encryption, and identity-based access control system.
  - o **AWS Secrets Manager**: It is a native AWS service for managing secrets with automatic rotation for **Relational Database Service** (**RDS**), Redshift, and DocumentDB.

- Azure Key Vault: This tool is native to Microsoft Azure and is a managed service for safeguarding cryptographic keys, certificates, and secrets.

- **Selection consideration**: Secret management tools are critical for security and compliance. The tool should be chosen based on cloud provider lock-in preference, need for advanced features like dynamic secrets, and complexity of integration.

CI/CD and deployment automation

Let us look at the purpose of CI/CD and deployment automation tools and go over the popular tools and the considerations for selecting a particular tool:

- **Purpose**: These tools are used for automating build, test, and deployment pipelines to enable reliable, frequent software releases.
- **Popular tools**: The following are the popular tools in this category:
  - **Jenkins**: This is a widely used and de facto tool for CI/CD and deployment automation. It is a venerable, highly extensible open-source automation server with a massive plugin ecosystem and pipeline as code capabilities.
  - **GitLab CI/CD**: This tool is a native and tightly integrated CI/CD platform within GitLab that provides a seamless DevOps experience from planning to deployment.
  - **GitHub Actions**: This is an event-driven workflow automation directly within GitHub that enables CI/CD, project management, and repository operations.
  - **CircleCI**: This is a cloud-native CI/CD platform focused on fast execution, intelligent parallelism, and developer experience with a robust orbs ecosystem.
  - **Argo CD**: This is a declarative, GitOps continuous delivery tool for Kubernetes that automatically syncs and deploys applications based on Git repository state.
- **Selection consideration**: For selecting a CI/CD and automation tool, it is essential to evaluate these tools based on integration with our version control, support for containerized workloads, cloud vs. self-hosted preference, team familiarity, and compliance/audit requirements. However, GitOps tools like Argo CD are essential for Kubernetes environments.

Sample implementation scenarios

Let us look at some sample scenarios and the considerations that should be taken into account while choosing an appropriate monitoring stack:

- **Startup and cloud-native**: This is a scenario where the company is a startup with a small team running applications on Kubernetes with a strong open-source preference.

   - **Recommendation**: The recommendation for such an environment is to use Prometheus for metrics collection as it integrates seamlessly with Kubernetes. This can be paired with Grafana for generating dashboards. Loki can be used for logs. This is called the **Grafana, Loki, and Prometheus** (**GLP**) stack, which is cohesive and cost-effective.

- **Large enterprise with mixed environment**: This scenario is of a large organization with legacy data centers, multiple clouds, and a need for strong support.
   - **Recommendation**: In such a scenario where there is a large enterprise with mixed environment a commercial SaaS observability platform or APM like Datadog, Dynatrace or New Relic is recommended. Such platforms provide a unified agent, reduced operational overhead, and vendor support that can justify the cost for complex, business-critical environments.

- **Heavy AWS investment**: This is a scenario where the organization is heavily invested in the AWS platform with services like Lambda, Fargate and DynamoDB.
   - **Recommendation**: Since the organization is already heavily invested in AWS, they should leverage AWS native services (like CloudWatch, X-Ray) extensively. These tools provide deep, out-of-the-box integration with AWS resources, though may lack strong multi-cloud or advanced analytics features.

Chaos engineering tools

Chaos engineering tools are used to validate resilience by deliberately injecting failure into the system. Let us look at popular chaos engineering tools along with their key features and the best use cases for them:

- **Chaos Monkey**: This is the original chaos tool from *Netflix*, which randomly terminates production instances to ensure that resilience is designed in and not an afterthought. This tool is primarily focused on AWS infrastructure and hence it is best for teams with mature AWS environments who are seeking to validate that their services can withstand individual instance failures without manual intervention.

- **Chaos Mesh**: This tool provides rich failure types (like Pod kill, network latency, AWS Fault simulation) directly in Kubernetes with a declarative workflow design and an intuitive dashboard. This tool is primarily used for Kubernetes environments where teams are running complex, stateful workloads that need fine-grained scheduled experiments and a centralized management UI.

- **Litmus Chaos**: This is a developer centric platform with a focus on CI/CD integration and a large hub of predefined experiments for cloud-native components.

  This tool primarily focuses on cloud-native and Kubernetes environments and is used for integrating chaos experiments into the DevOps pipeline to validate new deployments and test specific cloud-native failure modes.

- **Gremlin**: This is a SaaS platform with a simple UI and API for running safe and controlled chaos experiments. It also includes security chaos engineering capabilities. Gremlin is a full-stack tool that focuses on Host, Network, Kubernetes and cloud. It is generally used when organizations want a managed, enterprise-grade platform to run coordinated chaos across hosts, containers and cloud services without the operational overhead.
- **AWS Fault Injection Service (FIS):** This is a fully managed AWS service to safely perform fault injection experiments on live AWS workloads without installing agents and with pre-built templates. FIS is generally used by teams that are heavily invested in AWS and want a native, low-overhead way to test AWS specific failures like availability zone outages or instance stop/reboot.

Tool selection guide

Let us look at a scenario-based tool selection and implementation guide that talks about different scenarios, the tool that suits the scenario and a brief guide on implementing chaos engineering using that tool in that scenario:

- **Scenario 1: Starting out**: If the organization is just starting out with chaos engineering, Chaos Monkey should be preferred. It can be configured to randomly terminate non-critical instances in production during business hours to increase the priority of chaos experiments. This forces teams to build automatic recovery and redundancy from day one, validating that our system truly tolerates individual host failures.
- **Scenario 2: Building practice**: As the team matures, they can introduce validation in staging as well by introducing more targeted experiments using Chaos mesh or Litmus Chaos in a non-production Kubernetes environment. Teams can run controlled experiments like pod kill or network latency on specific services to validate defined failure modes and runbook procedures.
- **Scenario 3: Testing cloud dependencies**: If the application depends heavily on AWS services, the team can use AWS FIS to simulate an availability zone failure or instance reboot. This helps in testing the application's failover logic and dependency resilience within the AWS ecosystem.
- **Scenario 4: Advanced and continuous resilience testing**: Once teams mature the SRE practice and chaos engineering, they can use a platform like Gremlin to schedule regular, automated chaos tests in production. Such platforms can be used to coordinate complex scenarios (like simulating a regional cache failure while degrading network bandwidth) to test system wide resilience and team response procedures.

To summarize, the chaos engineering maturity path starts from using simple tools like Chaos Monkey to automate the termination of individual resources and is followed by using tools like Chaos mesh or Litmus Chaos for defining experiments and moving from random to hypothesis-driven testing. Teams also embed chaos tests in deployment pipelines (CI/CD) using tools like Litmus or custom scripts to validate resilience before production deployment. The most mature stage is when teams use platforms like Gremlin or FIS to run coordinated multi-service experiments across our entire stack to discover unexpected cascading failures and validate cross team incident response.

Sample on-call runbook template

An on-call runbook provides a pre-defined set of steps for handling alerts and guides on when to escalate it to an incident and the steps to be followed for the same. The following is a sample runbook template:

- **Alert title**: Service name and alert type
- **Service**: Service name
- **Severity**: Sev-2/Sev-3 can be auto tagged and modified later
- **Ownership**: Team owning the service
- **Primary contacts**: Contact details of service owner

Summary:

Brief summary of type of alert.

E.g., checkout API is experiencing a spike in 5xx errors (>5% for last 5 minutes)

Immediate actions:

This is the list of actions to be performed in the first 5 minutes:

- Acknowledge the alert in incident management tool.
- Check dashboard [link to specific dashboard].
- Identify pattern [generic list of known patterns identified till date].
- Check dependencies [list of dependencies that need to be checked with link to their dashboards].
- Communicate by posting to `#incident` channel.

Diagnostic steps: A generic set of diagnostic steps that should be followed for this type of alert is listed as follows:

1. Review logs by searching for the relevant error in the affected service.
2. Check recent deployments to see if the start time of the error correlates with the deployment time [link to deployment history].
3. Trace a failed request or error: [link to Tracing UI].

Mitigation and escalation steps:

1. If bad deployment is identified, initiate rollback via [link to CI/CD pipeline].

2. If a dependent service is down, failover [link to failover script or UI].
3. If the root cause is unknown after 15 minutes, escalate by paging the primary contact and update the **`#incidents`** channel regarding the same.

Resolution and handoff steps:

1. Once stable, confirm the error rate is back to baseline.
2. Post resolution update on **`#incidents`** channel.
3. Create an incident ticket to track RCA.

Escalation matrix:

- Sev3 protocol and contact details.
- Sev2 protocol and contact details.
- Sev1 protocol and contact details.

Sample SLO template

This template can be used to define the SLO of an API or a service. This template is filled with sample data for ease of understanding, as shown in the following table:

Service: *Authentication service*

SLI	Target	Measurement method	Notes
Availability	99.9% monthly	Uptime from monitoring tools	Critical service applies to `/api/v1/auth` endpoint
Latency	< 200ms P95	APM metrics	Applies to `/api/v1/`... endpoint

***Table Appendix A.1**: Sample SLO template*

- **Error budget**: 0.1% (43 min 12 Sec downtime allowed per month)
- **Warning alert rule**: Burn rate of 2x for 1 hour
- **Critical alert rule**: Burn rate of 10x for 5 minutes

Sample incident response checklist

This is a chronological sample incident response checklist to guide the incident commander, as follows:

- **Pre-incident (preparation)**:
  - o Ensure on-call rotation is up-to-date and contact details are correct
  - o Dashboards are reviewed
  - o Alerts are tested
  - o Know how to declare a major incident

- **During the incident**:
  - **Identification (0-5 minutes)**:
    - Acknowledge the alert.
    - Open an incident bridge or video call.
    - Designate roles like incident commander, scribe and communications lead.
  - **Assessment and mobilization (5-15 minutes)**:
    - Incident commander gathers facts like what is broken, user impact and starting time to assess the severity of the incident.
    - Communications lead posts the initial update to the `#incidents` channel and status page.
    - Inform stakeholders.
    - Mobilize relevant technical responders (e.g., backend, database, infrastructure).
  - **Resolution (15+ minutes)**:
    - Focus on mitigation instead of identifying the root cause.
    - Document all major actions and decisions.
    - Communications lead provides regular updates to the stakeholders and on the `#incidents` channel.
    - If there is no progress after the escalation timeframe (e.g., 30 minutes), escalate to the next level or to management.
  - **Recovery and handover**:
    - Once mitigated, capture metrics from monitoring and confirm recovery.
    - Communication lead posts final resolution update.
    - Incident commander schedules a debrief meeting in the next 24 hours to hand over the incident to the designated person for RCA.
    - Incident ticket is created with all timelines and logs.
- **After the incident**:
  - RCA conducted.
  - Follow up actions assigned.
  - Update runbook and dashboards.
  - Review SLO impact.

Sample RCA template

Following is an RCA template that can be used to document the RCA for future reference:

Incident details:

- Incident title
- Start date and time
- End date and time
- Reported by
- Incident commander
- Severity
- Services impacted
- Customer impact

Incident timeline:

Time	Event	Actions taken
12:05	Monitoring alert—high latency on payment service	PagerDuty notifies the on-call engineer
12:07	On-call engineer joins the bridge and declares Sev2 incident	The incident commander's role assigned
...	...	...

***Table Appendix A.2**: Sample incident timeline template*

Let us look at the details:

Incident summary:

A brief factual summary of the incident that can be easily interpreted by the leadership.

Root cause:

- The primary underlying cause identified by using the 5 whys technique or any other technique.
- Contributing factors that led to the primary cause.

Incident trigger:

- The immediate trigger that caused the failure or incident.

Detailed impact analysis including:

- User impact
- Business impact
- System impact

Detection gaps:

- List of missed alerts or gaps in monitoring that can help detect or predict such incidents.

Corrective and preventive actions:

Action item	Owner	ETA	Category
Add integration test for connection pool behavior under load	Developer	1 week	Preventive

Rollback configuration changes to version 4.1	Team	Completed	Corrective
...	...	...	...

Table Appendix A.3: Sample template for corrective and preventive actions

Lessons learned are as follows:

- What went well?
- What could be improved?

Sign off:

- RCA lead
- Engineering manager

Customizing template for your organization

The following are some tips that will help in the adoption and customization of these templates as per your organization's needs and SRE maturity:

- It is recommended to begin with the incident response checklist and a single critical runbook. These can be used for the next few incidents and refined based on the feedback.
- The links of actual dashboards, log queries and deployment pipelines should be directly embedded into the runbooks for ease of access.
- An imperfect but used template is better than a perfect template that is not being used. The imperfect template will improve over time as more and more feedback is integrated into it.
- These templates should be reviewed quarterly in reliability retrospectives and updated as needed.
- SLOs should be aligned with user experience and not engineering convenience.
- Runbooks should be treated as living documents and should be updated after each major incident.
- Incident checklist should be tailored based on organizational escalations and tooling.
- Chaos engineering tools should be used in a controlled and incremental manner with proper approvals.

Conclusion

This appendix serves as an operational foundation for implementing SRE effectively within our organizations. By adapting these tools and templates to our environment, we can accelerate our reliability journey while maintaining consistency and clarity across teams. Also, the true value of these tools and templates is realized when they are adopted, socialized and consistently used by our teams to build a more reliable and resilient system.

Appendix B
Case Studies

Introduction

This appendix will contain real-world applications of SRE across diverse industries. We will discuss the implementation of SRE in the fintech industry, where there is a need to balance feature delivery with strong regulatory and security requirements. Next, we will discuss the case of implementation of SRE in the e-commerce industry, where it can be used to handle significant traffic spikes during sales while optimizing infrastructure cost during off-peak hours. We will then dive into organization specific use cases and discuss the implementation of SRE in a few organizations like Spotify, LinkedIn and DBS Bank, showcasing how global teams manage reliability at scale through automation, culture and robust tooling. These case studies provide practical insights on how SRE principles are adopted to meet organization specific business needs.

Structure

This appendix covers the following topics:

- SRE in fintech
- SRE in e-commerce
- LinkedIn case study
- Spotify case study
- DBS Bank case study

Objectives

In this appendix, we will understand how SRE principles are successfully implemented across diverse industries through real-world case studies. By examining the transformation journeys of fintech, e-commerce, *Spotify*, *LinkedIn*, and *DBS Bank*, we will learn to identify common challenges, recognize effective implementation strategies, and understand the measurable benefits of SRE adoption. This appendix will equip technology leaders, engineers and decision makers with practical insights to navigate their own SRE journeys, adapt proven practices to their organizational context, and build resilient, scalable systems that drive business growth and customer trust.

SRE in fintech

A fintech organization operated a digital payment and lending platform serving millions of customers. Its systems processed real-time transactions, handled sensitive financial data and were subjected to strict regulatory and compliance requirements. The fintech system faced frequent system outages and performance degradation, especially during peak transaction periods. These disruptions led to customer dissatisfaction, financial losses and increased regulatory scrutiny. The company's existing traditional IT operations model, which relied on manual interventions and reactive firefighting, was no longer sustainable.

Challenges before SRE

Before SRE implementation, the company faced several reliability and operational challenges, which are listed as follows:

- Frequent production incidents during peak transaction hours.
- High **mean time to recover** (**MTTR**) due to manual incident handling.
- Lack of clearly defined reliability targets for critical services.
- Friction between product teams pushing for faster releases and operations teams focused on stability.
- Stringent regulatory requirements and the need to comply with financial regulations while implementing automation.
- Development and operations teams worked independently, leading to slow incident response and a culture of blame.
- Legacy systems intertwined with modern microservices created monitoring and scalability challenges.
- A requirement of near 100% uptime to maintain customer trust and avoid financial penalties.

These issues resulted in increased customer complaints, increased operational costs and growing risk exposure.

SRE implementation approach

To handle the previously mentioned challenges, the fintech decided to adopt SRE in a phased manner, as mentioned in the steps as follows:

1. **Cultural alignment and training**:
    a. Leadership championed the SRE initiative.
    b. SRE was embedded alongside the development teams, promoting a shift towards shared ownership between development and operations teams.

c. Cross-functional SRE teams were formed, including members from development, security and compliance.

d. Shared ownership of reliability was encouraged through blameless postmortems and regular reliability reviews.

2. **Defining service reliability targets**:

a. Critical customer-facing services were identified and SLIs and SLOs were defined for those services.

b. Error budgets were introduced to balance innovation with reliability, allowing teams to quantify risk.

3. **Automation, observability and monitoring**:

a. End-to-end monitoring was implemented across transaction flows, focusing on latency, error rates and availability. Dashboards were aligned with **service level objectives (SLOs)** rather than infrastructure metrics alone.

b. Manual operational tasks were automated, including alerting, failover and basic remediation.

c. Automated incident detection and response pipelines were built using tools like Prometheus and PagerDuty.

d. Standardized incident response framework was introduced with clear roles, escalation paths and Post-incident reviews.

e. Continuous testing and chaos engineering were introduced to proactively identify vulnerabilities.

4. **Compliance integrated SRE**:

a. Automated compliance checks were embedded into the deployment pipelines.

b. Audit trails and logging were automated to meet regulatory requirements without extensive manual overhead.

Benefits of SRE implementation

After implementing the previously mentioned steps to adopt the SRE practices, the organization experienced the following benefits:

- 50% reduction in MTTR as automated incident response slashed recovery time from hours to minutes.
- 99.99% uptime achieved for critical services like payments and transactions, exceeding regulatory requirements.

- Improved deployment frequency from 3 to 15 per week with an increase in stability and implementation of automated deployments.
- Better collaboration between development, operations and compliance teams.
- Fewer outages led to improved customer trust and reduced transaction failures, resulting in higher customer satisfaction and retention.
- Reduced manual operational costs by 30% through automation.

In summary, SRE adoption helped the fintech organization move from reactive firefighting to proactive reliability management while meeting regulatory expectations. SRE in fintech requires balancing automation with compliance and the success hinges on integrating regulatory requirements into the SRE framework.

SRE in e-commerce

An e-commerce organization operated a large online marketplace with seasonal traffic spikes during sales events and holidays. The e-commerce platform struggled with site performance during high traffic events like Black Fridays and holiday sales. Slow page loads, cart failures and occasional full-site outages resulted in lost revenue and damaged brand reputation. The existing infrastructure struggled to dynamically scale to handle traffic spikes. This results in poor customer experiences, degraded site performance and availability that directly influenced conversion rates and revenue.

Challenges before SRE

The e-commerce platform struggled with the following challenges before SRE adoption:

- Site slowdowns and outages during high traffic sales events, as unpredictable surges during such sales events overwhelmed the servers.
- Limited visibility into system bottlenecks and failure points.
- Reactive incident handling that heavily depended on on-call engineers.
- Operations team manually provisioned resources, leading to delays and errors. Additionally, it was difficult to predict infrastructure scalability during sudden demand.
- Multiple tools provided inconsistent alerts, causing delayed incident responses.
- Inconsistent deployment practices across multiple teams.
- Downtime directly impacted sales and customer loyalty.

SRE implementation approach

The e-commerce company embedded SRE practices into its core operations with a strong focus on scalability and resilience with the following steps:

1. **Unified observability stack**:
   a. A centralized monitoring dashboard was implemented using Grafana and Datadog, which provided real-time insights into system health.
   b. SLIs were defined around page load time, checkout success rate and availability.
   c. SLOs were defined for user-facing metrics like page load times and checkout success rate that helped prioritize engineering efforts based on customer impact.
2. **Proactive capacity planning**:
   a. Load testing and traffic simulation were automated to forecast demand before peak sales events.
   b. Autoscaling policies were implemented in the cloud to handle traffic spikes seamlessly.
   c. Capacity planning became a continuous activity rather than a one-time exercise.
3. **Proactive monitoring and alerting**:
   a. Monitoring shifted from static thresholds to symptom-based alerts tied to customer experience, which reduced alert fatigue and improved response times.
4. **Continuous deployment and rollback**:
   a. Canary releases and feature flags were introduced to enable stable, frequent deployments without downtime.
   b. Automated rollback mechanisms were adopted to ensure quick recovery from faulty releases.
   c. Error budgets were used to govern release velocity during unstable periods.
5. **Resilience engineering**:
   a. The platform adopted practices such as redundancy, graceful degradation, and chaos testing to ensure the system could tolerate failures.
6. **Incident management automation**:
   a. ChatOps integration using Slack and OpsGenie was done, which enabled real-time incident collaboration.
   b. Runbooks were automated to handle common failure scenarios like database failover or cache warming.

Benefits after SRE implementation

After the adoption of SRE via the previously mentioned steps, the e-commerce organization achieved the following benefits:

- 95% reduction in downtime and peak event outages dropped from 15% to 0.5%.
- Faster MTTR as incident resolution time improved from 8 hours to 2 hours.
- Higher deployment frequency without compromising on stability. Weekly deployments rose from 3 to 10, enabling faster delivery.
- Stable performance during peak sales generated millions in revenue (estimated), which was earlier lost.
- Improved customer experience and faster site performance led to higher conversion rates.

For e-commerce, SRE is essential to manage scalability and ensure reliability during high-stakes events. Automation and proactive monitoring are critical to maintaining a seamless customer experience. In summary, SRE enabled the e-commerce organization to scale confidently during high-demand periods while maintaining system stability.

SRE in fintech vs. e-commerce

Let us look at the key takeaways from the case studies of the implementation of SRE in the fintech industry vs that in the e-commerce industry and identify the similarities and differences in both industries. These case studies highlight that SRE is not a one-size-fits-all solution and hence implementations must be tailored to industry needs.

The fintech case study emphasizes reliability, compliance, and transaction integrity, whereas the e-commerce case study focuses on scalability and customer experience. However, for both case studies, defining SLOs, automating operations and fostering a reliability-focused culture are common success factors.

These case studies demonstrate how SRE acts as a practical framework for managing complexity and reliability across diverse industries, and the long-term benefits of implementing SRE extend beyond technical improvements to measurable business outcomes.

LinkedIn case study

LinkedIn is the world's largest professional networking platform, serving over 1.5 billion unique visitors per month with more than 850 million members as of 2022. By the early 2010s, the company faced severe operational challenges due to rapid growth, leading to unreliable services and daily outages. To address this, LinkedIn adopted SRE as a fundamental transformation in how reliability is engineered into systems.

Let us discuss in depth the challenges LinkedIn faced before the implementation of SRE, followed by the details on SRE implementation, and eventually look at the benefits they derived after the implementation of SRE practices.

Challenges before SRE implementation

As LinkedIn's member base and product offerings grew rapidly, the platform started facing increased operational strain. LinkedIn's operational model was fragmented and reactive. The primary challenges in their model included the following:

- **Daily outages and high MTTR**:
  - Systems experienced outages almost daily.
  - Outages in one service cascaded to feeds, messaging, and search, affecting millions of users.
  - MTTR was 1500 minutes (25 hours), which meant that issues often remained unresolved for more than a day.
- **Siloed teams and manual processes**:
  - Operations teams were divided into vertical silos, namely systems, network, applications and database teams.
  - Communication between these teams happened via ticket systems, leading to delays and a blame culture.
  - Developers had no access to production while the operations teams manually deployed code with limited visibility.
- **Pager fatigue and alert overload**:
  - Operations staff received an average of 3 alerts every 5 minutes, leading to burnout.
  - On-call engineers had trained family members to monitor alerts while they slept.
  - Increasing alert volumes and repetitive tasks had drained engineering morale.
- **Lack of observability and scalability**:
  - They lacked instrumentation to monitor demand or system performance.
  - Microservices multiplied faster than the operations teams could handle, leading to further scalability challenges.
  - Monolithic architecture and hardware-based load balancers created a single point of failure.
- **Cultural anti-patterns**:

- Teams had a firefighting mentality where they were reacting to incidents rather than preventing them.
- Operations were following the gatekeeper culture where they were controlling releases and slowing down innovation while also creating friction with developers.

SRE implementation details

LinkedIn's transformation was bold and systematic, requiring a complete overhaul of people, processes, and technology. They adopted SRE as a disciplined evolution of DevOps with a heavy focus on proactivity, automation and shared accountability for uptime. The following are the SRE implementation details:

- **Organizational commitment and cultural shift**:
    - There was leadership buy in as all affected VPs supported the transition, signaling top-down commitment.
    - LinkedIn halted product development for 3 months to focus entirely on operational transformation.
    - In 2013, the AppOps team was rebranded to SRE and the role was refined from operations to engineering.
- **Embedding SREs and empowering developers**:
    - They adopted the embedded SRE model where SREs were distributed across product engineering teams, ensuring close collaboration and shared ownership.
    - Developers were empowered by giving production access and were encouraged to join on-call rotations.
    - Deployment pipelines were built to allow developers to deploy their own code using canary releases to a single instance, followed by automated metrics validation and finally gradual rollout to the full production environment.
- **Architectural modernization**:
    - They shifted from monolithic services to microservices, thus reducing dependencies and improving scalability.
    - Replaced hardware load balancers with software solutions to provide flexibility and resilience.
    - Single points of failure were eliminated by moving away from monolithic databases.
    - Implemented systems to degrade gracefully rather than failing entirely when under load.

- **Automation and tooling**:
    - o Automated incident response was implemented to auto-remediate systems and replace the manual NOC process.
    - o Self-service portals were created for developers to monitor service metrics, benchmark performance and optimize resource usage.
    - o Observability stack was setup to provide real-time visibility into performance and failures.
- **Cultural and hiring principles**: LinkedIn's SRE culture is built on 3 core principles as follows:
    - o **Site-up**: Its aim is to make every engineer and system think of reliability as much as possible.
    - o **Empower developer ownership**: This asserts that developers own their work end-to-end from code to production and not just in the development phase.
    - o **Operations is an engineering problem**: This emphasizes solving operational challenges through engineering and not manual intervention.

  The hiring philosophy at LinkedIn focuses on hiring SREs who can tackle ambiguous systemic problems, who not only have the required technical skills but also have a problem-solving mindset.

SRE setup at LinkedIn

LinkedIn's SRE practice is now a mature, globally distributed function that operates at a massive scale with engineering excellence at its core. As of 2017, there are over 300 SREs across four major offices. They follow the hybrid SRE model where SREs are embedded within product engineering squads, as well as there is a centralized SRE team that focuses on platforms, tooling and cross-cutting concerns. Engineers are motivated to choose their team type based on their interests. They can choose system focused or software development focused roles.

LinkedIn is spread over 20,000+ production machines with 1500+ microservices. There are 100+ Kafka clusters handling 7 trillion messages daily. Their storage spans across 600+ TB of data. Each SRE is responsible for approximately 500 machines, which fluctuates based on system needs.

They have setup a comprehensive monitoring and metric pipelines which inform all reliability decisions. Developers use internal tools to deploy, monitor, and optimize their services without SRE intervention. The SREs apply computer science principles, statistical analysis and machine learning to build scalable automation and diagnostic tools. They have a well-defined incident management system with 24x7 coverage supported by automated alerts and runbooks.

Over time their SRE practice has evolved the organization culturally. They have regular blameless postmortems and hack weeks. Engineers are encouraged to take risks and learn from failures without fear of punishment. SREs have a problem-solving mindset and they proactively hunt for systemic problems that traditional operations might avoid. Additionally, LinkedIn is investing in global talent development like building a strong SRE hub in Bangalore, where they are investing in junior engineers and rebranding SRE as an engineering discipline rather than operations.

Benefits after SRE implementation

The SRE transformation led to drastic improvements in reliability, efficiency and scalability, given as follows:

- They saw a drastic reduction in MTTR from 1500 minutes in many cases to same day incident resolution.
- Daily outages were eliminated as system reliability improved significantly, with outages becoming rare events.
- They scaled up the development frequency by enabling 15000 commits and 600+ feature ramp-ups per day through self-service deployment pipelines.
- SREs are encouraged to proactively hunt for systemic problems. For instance, they solved a Python compiler bug, which once fixed saved 233 hours of engineering time every day.
- Their culture shifted from reactive firefighting to a culture of prevention, automation and shared responsibility.
- SRE enables LinkedIn's mission to create economic opportunity for every member of the global workforce by ensuring platform reliability at a global scale.

Key takeaways

LinkedIn's SRE journey demonstrates that reliability is an engineering discipline and not an operational afterthought. The following are the key takeaways that led to their success:

- Leadership encouraged to pause feature development and invest in foundational change.
- Structural integration of SRE within product teams.
- Empowering developers through tools, access and ownership.
- A cultural shift from gatekeeping and firefighting to collaboration and engineering rigor.

LinkedIn's SRE practice is a strategic engineering discipline that enables innovation at scale while ensuring the reliability of one of the world's most trafficked platforms. The company's transformation stands as a testament to how SRE can turn a crisis-prone organization into a model of scalability, resilience, and continuous innovation.

Spotify case study

Spotify operates one of the largest audio streaming platforms in the world, serving hundreds of millions of users across geographies, devices and network conditions. Users expect instant playback, uninterrupted listening, and highly personalized recommendations. This means that reliability is not just an engineering goal but a core product requirement.

From its early days, Spotify prioritized speed and reliability, targeting sub-200ms song load times to ensure that music felt instantaneous. However, as Spotify entered a phase of hypergrowth during the 2010s with monthly active users more than doubling from 3 million to 7.4 million in one year, its infrastructure struggled to keep pace. This rapid growth exposed significant reliability and scalability challenges, prompting Spotify to formally adopt SRE in 2011, inspired by Google's pioneering model.

Challenges before SRE implementation

During the hypergrowth phase, Spotify added supporting infrastructure to handle the sudden increase in users. This, in turn, increased the complexity of the underlying infrastructure. This growing complexity challenged the reliability and scalability of the system. Let us look at the critical operational and cultural hurdles faced by Spotify before SRE implementation as follows:

- The peer-to-peer hybrid fetch model implemented at Spotify was not designed to handle exponential user growth and the resulting microservice sprawl.
- Maintaining sub 200ms load times for music became increasingly difficult as systems scaled, directly impacting user experience.
- Engineering teams operated in autonomous squads, which led to inconsistent deployment, monitoring and incident response practices.
- There was significant developer toil as they spent significant time on repetitive operational tasks, which distracted them from feature development and innovation.
- Infrastructure spends began outpacing revenue growth with lack of ownership and visibility into the cost drivers at the team level.

SRE implementation details

Spotify's SRE journey was not only about adopting the Google SRE model. They focused on embedding reliability into their unique organizational fabric through culture, structure and tooling as shown in the details as follows:

- **Organizational and cultural integration**:
    - SRE is setup as a guild within the Spotify SRE model. In this model, SREs are embedded within cross-functional product squads, ensuring tight collaboration with developers while they also belong to the SRE guild. This guild is a community of practice that promotes knowledge sharing and consistency across the company.
    - Spotify has shared ownership model whereby reliability is treated as everyone's responsibility. Developers actively participate in on-call rotations, incident response, and blameless postmortems, fostering a culture of collective accountability.
    - Spotify promotes psychological safety and learning from failure. This is depicted by a notable example that happened in 2018 when an engineer accidentally deleted a production Kubernetes cluster. Instead of blame, Spotify treated it as a learning opportunity, leading to improved guardrails and disaster recovery processes. This culture encourages risk-taking and continuous improvement.
- **Platform engineering and developer enablement**:
    - Backstage is Spotify's flagship SRE-led initiative. It is an open-source internal developer platform that centralizes service management, documentation and tooling. The key features of this platform are as listed as follows:
        - It contains predefined self-service templates for creating services, deployments and monitoring, thus reducing variability and manual toil.
        - It integrates real-time cloud cost visibility into the developer workflow, thus making cost optimization an engineering concern rather than a financial afterthought.
    - SREs focus on automating repetitive tasks such as deployment, scaling and incident response thus freeing developers to concentrate on feature development.
- **Collaborative incident management**:
    - SREs act as first responders leading incident response as they have specialized tools, training and system knowledge, thus ensuring 24x7 coverage and rapid mitigation.
    - Developers are also involved and contribute deep codebase knowledge during incidents while working alongside SREs to diagnose root cause and implement fixes.
    - Post-incident, both groups participate in a blameless retrospective and drive systemic improvements.
- **Cost engineering as SRE discipline**:

  - Cost ownership is done at the squad level. Through the cost insights plugin in Backstage, squads are empowered to monitor and optimize their own cloud spend, turning cost control into a shared engineering challenge.
  - Additionally, engineers are motivated to reduce costs through peer recognition and the understanding that savings contribute to company profitability and personal shareholdings.

SRE setup at Spotify

The SRE setup at Spotify is now a mature and deeply integrated function that blends engineering rigor with cultural empathy.

The organizational structure at Spotify has embedded SREs, SRE guild and platform teams. SREs are embedded within product squads and across tribes where they work to ensure that reliability is built into the services from inception. The SRE guild serves as a cross-company hub to standardize practices, sharing tools and advanced SRE discipline. The platform teams maintain and evolve backstage and other internal platforms that enable developer autonomy and operational consistency.

Hack weeks are held, which are regular innovation sprints where teams prototype new tools and features. Backstage, their internal developer platform itself originated from a hack week project. Regular game days and disaster drills are held to ensure proactive testing of failure scenarios and recovery procedures to ensure resilience. Additionally, SREs are encouraged to experiment with new technologies, share knowledge and stay current with industry trends.

Spotify has now expanded and the SRE setup now supports hundreds of millions of users and a vast microservice ecosystem. The engineer-led cost optimization has reduced annual cloud spends by millions of dollars. Additionally, Spotify is now an open-source leader as their platform Backstage and its plugins are now widely adopted beyond Spotify, thus contributing to the broader DevOps and platform engineering community.

Benefits after SRE implementation

The strategic adoption of SRE has yielded significant technical, cultural and business benefits, given as follows:

- Proactive monitoring, automation, and standardized practices have increased service uptime and resilience, even during hypergrowth.
- Automation and self-service platforms like backstage reduce operational toil, allowing engineers to focus on innovation and code quality, thus improving developer productivity.
- Squad-level cost ownership and visibility have led to substantial reductions in cloud expenditure, thus optimizing costs drastically.

- Spotify has had a cultural transformation, which has promoted a blameless and learning oriented culture, which has in turn increased the psychological safety, collaboration and shared ownership of reliability.
- Standardized golden paths and automated deployment pipelines now enable faster, safer releases, supporting Spotify's rapid iteration and competitive edge.
- Spotify's SRE model, particularly its organizational structure and open-source platforms, has influenced many companies across sectors, from tech to finance, thus increasing their industry influence.

Key takeaways

Spotify's SRE journey showcases that reliability is not just a technical goal but a cultural and organizational one. The key takeaways are listed as follows:

- SRE can be embedded in decentralized organizations.
- Alignment and shared principles can replace central control.
- Developers must be empowered via platforms and autonomy so they can own reliability and costs.
- Psychological safety promotes continuous learning through blameless postmortems, experimentation, and failure injection.
- Reliability must be measured in user-impact terms and not just infrastructure metrics.
- Operations should be treated as an engineering discipline so that it enables scale, innovation and sustainable growth.

Today, SRE at Spotify is a cornerstone of its engineering excellence, enabling the company to deliver reliable, low-latency audio streaming at a global scale while maintaining a culture of innovation, collaboration, and continuous learning.

DBS Bank case study

DBS Bank, headquartered in Singapore, is one of Asia's largest financial services groups. In the early 2010s, facing disruption from fintech startups and changing customer expectations, DBS embarked on a radical digital transformation journey to become a technology company that does banking. With this vision, DBS repositioned itself to become a technology company that delivers banking services. As a part of this transformation, DBS recognized that scale and resilience must go hand in hand for online banking, mobile apps, payment systems and digital channels that serve millions of customers daily. Hence, the adoption of SRE and DevOps practices to improve system resilience, accelerate delivery, and enhance customer experience was a critical part of this transformation.

Challenges before SRE implementation

Before embedding SRE practices, DBS faced several reliability and operational challenges, which are typical of highly digital and regulated financial organizations, which are listed as follows:

- DBS was heavily reliant on monolithic systems and mainframes, which were legacy infrastructure.
- Development and operations teams worked in silos, which led to slow releases and inefficient incident response.
- They followed the traditional waterfall development cycles, which meant that new releases took months to reach customers.
- The banking was experiencing major digital outages, leading to significant customer impact and regulatory scrutiny.
- They were facing cultural resistance as they had a risk-averse, traditional banking culture resistant to agile and DevOps way of working.
- As a major regulated institution, DBS had to demonstrate strong operational risk management and resilience in compliance with the **Monetary Authority of Singapore** (**MAS**) while increasing deployment frequency.

SRE implementation details

DBS embedded SRE principles into its engineering governance, tooling and organizational practices, so that they could scale their digital platforms. This journey evolved in well-defined stages as follows:

1. **Early adoption and organizational alignment**: DBS started implementing SRE around 2019 by establishing an SRE task force of leaders across technology units. A hub and spoke model was adopted, where the central SRE function set standards and provided tools, whereas smaller SRE groups supported specific technology units. Some of the key steps during this phase were:
    a. Defining SRE principles that were tailored for the banking environments.
    b. Integrating reliability into architecture, development, testing, observability, incident response, training and education.
    c. Shifting from reactive operations to structured reliability governance.
2. **SRE transformation program**: To accelerate the adoption and scale of SRE practice across multiple teams and ensure consistency across teams operating at different maturity levels, DBS launched the SRE transformation program, which was based on the following three pillars:

   a. Technology transformation that focused on modernizing applications to meet SRE standards.

   b. SRE enablers where tools and services were built to support reliability.

   c. People transformation, which focused on training and accrediting engineers in SRE skills and mindset.

3. SRE-centric tools and automation: DBS developed a bunch of in-house tools and platforms to operationalize SRE at scale. These tools aligned with the strict regulatory requirements of a banking domain while reducing manual toil, automating responses and increasing resilience. Some of these tools are listed as follows:

   a. **DBS Auto Remediation Engine (DARE)**: It is a tool that automates recovery when known failure conditions are detected.

   b. Error budgeting and observability tooling was developed that supported the ability to track system performance metrics.

   c. Chaos and resilience testing tools (named Wreckoon) was developed to proactively uncover weakness.

   d. Additionally, machine learning models were used to provide predictive capacity planning.

4. **People and cultural change**: DBS invested in SRE training and upskilling, whereby over 4000 technical staff participated in SRE programs, which helped foster an engineering mindset oriented around reliability, automation and operational excellence.

5. **Regulatory alignment and governance**: In response to service disruptions and regulator expectations, DBS strengthened governance practices, clarifying incident ownership and improving proactive problem management across internal teams and third-party providers.

SRE setup at DBS Bank

Today DBS is recognized as a global leader in digital banking and SRE adoption. Their team structure consists of over 1000 engineers who practice DevOps/SRE with the Tribe-Squad model. They have a dedicated cloud and SRE center of excellence.

Their deployment velocity has increased from quarterly releases to over 10000 deployments per year. They are using canary releases and feature flags for safe and incremental rollouts.

Their mature internal SRE ecosystem supports uptime, observability and automated recovery, improving the reliability metrics to 99.995% availability for digital banking services.

Automation and tooling have helped reduce manual intervention while freeing teams for strategic work. Operational risk and technology governance structures reinforce accountability and monitoring. This has helped reduce MTTR by over 70%.

DBS was awarded the world's best digital bank by Euromoney (2016-2022). MAS also awarded DBS for the best risk-adjusted returns for technical resilience.

Benefits after SRE implementation

The adoption of SRE principles and tooling at DBS bank has produced measurable and strategic benefits as follows:

- Increased resilience and stability as the systems are now more robust through automated remediation and proactive capacity planning.
- Unified engineering processes balanced with reliability guardrails have resulted in faster and safer innovation.
- Automation tools such as DARE and chaos testing tools like Wreckoon have greatly reduced manual toil while increasing operational efficiency.
- Predictive tools and improved observability have drastically reduced the MTTR.
- Widespread SRE training built internal capability whereby reliability thinking has become a shared responsibility across product and SRE teams.
- Enhanced customer experience has led to the mobile banking app being ranked as #1 in Asia for usability and reliability.
- Operational resilience resulted in zero major outages since 2020.
- Cost efficiency led to 30% reduction in infrastructure costs through cloud optimization.
- Innovation acceleration resulted in the launch of new digital products (E.g., *Digibank India*) in months instead of years.
- Recognized as a top employer for tech talent in Singapore.

Key takeaways

DBS's SRE journey highlights several broader insights that are highly relevant to other digital-first or regulated organizations. These takeaways are listed as follows:

- SRE must be adapted. DBS found value in defining SRE principles relevant to banking, not just copying tech industry models.
- Tooling and automation are foundational to scaling reliability across hundreds of systems. Automated testing, deployment, and incident response are essential for reliability at scale.
- SRE is a cultural journey where success requires a top-down vision, psychological safety and relentless focus on customer outcomes.

- Regulatory requirements can be integrated into DevOps pipelines without slowing innovation.
- SLOs, error budgets, and resilience metrics drive continuous improvement.

Conclusion

The case studies presented in this appendix, namely regarding fintech and e-commerce with detailed SRE implementation insights for LinkedIn, Spotify and DBS bank, collectively affirm that SRE is a strategic enabler of business, resilience, innovation and growth. SRE began as a discipline pioneered by Google to manage hyperscale systems, but it has evolved into a versatile framework that can be adapted across industries, regulatory environments, and organizational structures.

At its core, SRE redefines the relationship between development and operations by embedding engineering thinking into the fabric of reliability. This transformation is as much cultural as it is technical.

Each organization faced distinct challenges. Fintech navigated compliance and security. E-commerce battled unpredictable traffic spikes. Spotify scaled with a squad-based model, whereas LinkedIn overhauled a legacy operational culture and DBS bank struggled with strict regulatory requirements. Yet, all of them converged on a common outcome which includes measurable gains in system reliability, operational efficiency, developer productivity and customer trust.

SRE is not a destination but a journey of continuous refinement. As infrastructure grows in complexity and user expectations rise, the principles of SRE provide a durable foundation for scaling with confidence. Whether an organization is a regulated financial institution, a global retail platform, a streaming giant, a social network, or any other business case, SRE offers a path to operational excellence that aligns reliability with business agility. In this era of digital dependence, SRE enables reliability, innovation, and growth, which offers a competitive edge to any business.

References

1. **https://www.srepath.com/rundown-of-linkedins-sre-practices/**
2. **https://www.srepath.com/inside-spotifys-site-reliability-engineering-sre-practice/**
3. **https://medium.com/dbs-tech-blog/site-reliability-engineering-at-dbs-bank-32c02228ccf4**

Index

A

E

J

K

L

M

S

T

V

W